DONNA SUMMER

The Thrill Goes On

A Tribute

DONNA SUMMER

The Thrill Goes On

A Tribute

Nik A Ramli

www.nikaramli.com
www.facebook.com/donnasummerthethrillgoeson

Book Guild Publishing
Sussex, England

First published in Great Britain in 2012 by
The Book Guild Ltd
19 New Road
Brighton, BN1 1UF

Typeset in Garamond by Ellipsis Digital Limited, Glasgow

Printed in Great Britain by
CPI Group (UK) Ltd, Croydon, CR0 4YY

A catalogue record for this book is available from The British Library.

ISBN 978 1 84624 740 8

From one music lover to another... welcome to a voyage of discovery that I hope you will share with me.

Nik A Ramli

Contents

A Note From The Author

Having spent the best part of the last ten years thinking about writing this book, gathering information and ideas, and then putting it all together over the last eighteen months, I could never have imagined that I would be publishing it in such sad circumstances.

As we finalised the details and prepared it for publication I heard the unbelievable news that Donna Summer had died. It was such a shock to all of us who hadn't realised that she had been fighting cancer. How were we to guess? She looked better than ever and had appeared to be enjoying life and we were all waiting for her next album of music. Alas this was not to be and her passing has left so many people with a huge sense of loss.

This book was written as a tribute to the music of one of our greatest artists and that is how it remains. I have not edited or changed anything, so the book reads as if Donna is still with us. We might not be privileged to hear Donna Summer sing live again but we have the music that she left behind and so many happy memories.

It will take a long time for the fact that she is no longer with us to sink in. However, ultimately, through her music, the memories she left behind and the countless ways that she touched people's lives, Donna Summer will live on for a long time to come.

Our thoughts and prayers are with her family. We will never forget you, Donna.

Nik A Ramli
20th May 2012

Foreword

by Bruce Roberts

It was the late 1970s. I was a young songwriter and she was Donna Summer. The specifics of our first meeting are hazy, but when people have known each other as long as we have, the details of how it all began seem fairly inconsequential. I don't remember what I said or what she wore or who was there. What I do remember is the immediacy and intensity of our friendship, a connection that has not dimmed in all the years we've known each other.

I've been fortunate to know a lot of celebrities in my life and as such, I have learned how so often those stars are unable to live up to the fantasy of their goodness, with their deceptive reality. But not Donna. She has not only lived up to my dreams of her, but, like a true star, soared far above them.

There is an undeniable magic to her. In everything she does she radiates elegance and charm, beauty and brilliance. As clichéd as it may sound, she is an old soul, full of wisdom and courage. Some of the best memories I have of her involve the two of us, a piano and her spectacular voice.

It is that voice that connects us all. Like Donna herself, it finds the light within the darkness, empowering and embracing each one of us. In the time we have spent writing songs together, I have been given a front row experience to her exceptional talent and effortless grace. I remember a night spent in Paris, in a dark bar at the Ritz Hotel. With my fingers on the piano keys and her voice in the air, the time sped away from us, lost forever to the music.

There is a beautiful honesty to Donna, a person completely devoid of pretence. She is what she is. Grateful and gracious, playful and joyous. She's the kind of friend who would dress you up as one of her "Bad Girls" (wig and all) to perform alongside her in Vegas. Someone who would bring you into her home and into her family, welcomed as if you were long-lost siblings.

In all the years our lives have been entwined, she has revealed herself to be an embodiment of everything that is good. There is a wonderful brilliance to her, evident in how she paints, how she writes, how she sings and most extraordinarily, how she lives.

Bruce Roberts, Los Angeles, 2011

Preface

Donna Summer ...

Is a singing sensation who brings joy to all music lovers, a gifted individual
and major figure in the entertainment world whose colourful melodies and
tales stay eternally in every fan's heart.

The 16th June 2004 was the date of the first conversation I had with
Donna Summer. A very brief encounter, I introduced myself and told her
how wonderful she is. She looked at me, smiled and said 'Thank you'. I
remember asking whether her new album would be in store any time soon.
She looked at me and, with a charming expression on her face, said:

'Hmm ... maybe in ten to twenty years' time?'

Rightly or wrongly, I had a little laugh and smiled. After she signed a
CD and her book, I took the opportunity to say more:

'You know, I've written an article about you ... well, your music. I've
been compiling it since 1999. I don't know what I'm going to do with it
yet. Maybe I will release it someday ... I don't know how, but we'll see.'

Summer, her eyes slightly wider, looked at me and said:

'Oh ... hmmm!'

She turned to her husband and they both looked at me and smiled
(perhaps in their minds saying 'Get out of here, you stalker!'). I said goodbye
(thinking 'Oh God, now she's going to sue me!' and 'Don't you dare!') and
thanked both of them. Did I say 'I Love You'? I can't remember!

But now here we are, my tribute book is finally released. Readers, before
we begin I would love to share the story of how I came to love Donna
Summer.

It was on Malaysian TV in 1979 that I was first introduced to 'Love To
Love You Baby'. I loved the song instantly and it was the way Summer
played a role – sexy and otherworldly – that drew me to the American star.
Everything about the song and the whole image produced a 'WOW' factor.
A couple of years later, in 1981, 'Love To Love You Baby' again appeared
in my life when one of my sisters borrowed the LP from her boyfriend
(now husband). She explained the concept of the song and I adored it

immediately. I was also fascinated by the delightfully designed album sleeve and was impressed with the non-stop mix and the voice that came out of the hi-fi. The rest is history.

My parents often comment on 'Love To Love You Baby':

'Here we go again ... it's the kinky song!'

My parents only hear the steamy melody when I'm at home (once or twice a year) during my vacation. When I was still living at home, the song taken from 'On The Radio: Greatest Hits Volumes I & II' was extended for my own amateur 'home-made 1990 mix'. My parents were forced to listen to the 'uuhhhs' and 'aarrrhhhhs' of 'Love To Love You Baby' for over twenty minutes!

On the last day of the school term at the end of November 1983, I bought my first Donna Summer cassette, 'She Works Hard For The Money'. Although I bought all her releases, it wasn't until I was in the UK that I became a serious collector of her work. 'Mistaken Identity' was my first UK Donna Summer cassette, purchased on 24th March 1992, and at 11.50 a.m. on 21st January 1994, I bought my very first Summer CD, 'The Donna Summer Anthology', as a birthday gift to myself. I didn't actually own a CD player at that time! I had to visit a friend's place to hear 'Spring Affair', 'The Wanderer', 'Cold Love' and yes, of course, the anticipated 'I'm A Rainbow', 'Don't Cry For Me Argentina' and 'Carry On'. These songs opened up a whole new musical landscape for me. There were many Summer tracks that I hadn't heard as I didn't own her earlier albums. Besides copying the tape recordings (rightly or wrongly) of other fans, it was only after a friend gave me 'Endless Summer: Donna Summer's Greatest Hits' as a birthday present that I started compiling her complete catalogue, including rarities.

The 1996 concert at the Royal Albert Hall, London, was my first experience of her performing live and I also saw the *Discomania* show hosted by her on 11th June 2004. It was magical and remains a fond memory. Prior to this the only 'live' shows I had seen were, on TV, the *A Hot Summer Night* concert video, which I finally obtained on 5th January 1998 and *VH1 Presents Donna Summer: Live & More Encore!* when it was released in 1999.

The purchase of a 1996 concert book from her official website led to an email correspondence with Summer's son in-law, thanking me and telling me that he was looking after the site. Unfortunately, I didn't keep any record of the exchanges. I received the order on 22nd May 2000.

Over the years, as a hardcore fan, I'm pretty sure I've annoyed and irritated many individuals and companions as a result of my love for Summer's music! May I take this opportunity to apologise and ... well, get over it.

A DJ who I regularly pestered to play Summer's songs in the club he worked in, ran up to me one night and showed me Patrick Cowley's twelve inch remix of 'I Feel Love '82'. I had never seen it before and I remember him saying:

'I saw this in my house and thought of you! I'll play it to you later.'

To make it clear, this is not intended to be a vanity project. As well as being my tribute to a great artist, it is also a way of sharing the knowledge that I have gained since I started enjoying Donna Summer's work and began researching. It also gives me a sense of personal satisfaction that I was able to complete a work that has been off and on for quite some time.

I accept, and expect, that the book will be subject to some criticism. If certain information is missing or incorrect then I will be more than happy to be corrected. People are also entitled to disagree with my opinions on various matters. Donna Summer is not endorsing this work but neither am I aware that she disapproves of it. It would have been the icing on the cake if she had offered to contribute directly but, then again, this is a tribute project after all.

A telephone call to New York, followed by an email the same day, (18th January 2010) led to this email reply from Donna Summer's associates:

'. . . Donna's business manager will be contacting you direct. Thank you for your interest.'

Following that I received an e-mail from Summer's manager on 21st January 2010 at 9.24 p.m.:

'Nik, would it be possible for Donna to see a manuscript . . .? She would keep it confidential. Please let me know.'

I was thrilled! Still, the manuscript had not even had a first edit yet. Personally, I didn't feel entirely comfortable with the idea of delivering a working draft to Donna Summer so early in the writing process. However, I guess it's a matter of politeness to Donna Summer and her manager to let them know what the aims and objectives of the project are. On the 1st February 2010 the project summary and selected working chapter titles were e-mailed and followed by the complete chapters' summaries including one complete chapter e-mailed/posted on the 19th April 2011 to Summer's management. To me, the most significant element is that Donna Summer is aware of the work.

There have been many enthusiastic individuals, music writers, fans and music lovers, national and international, in and out of the music industry who have contributed to the book. They share many sweet memories and a great deal of knowledge about her songs and work. I have received help and support from so many individuals and I can't thank them enough. They are mentioned in the acknowledgements.

Donna Summer: The Thrill Goes On celebrates Summer's recording and artistic achievements and traces her creative journey in the world of entertainment. I have compiled and analysed research findings and fresh interviews and put it all down on paper in chronological order. The book looks at Summer's musical career – from a brief introduction to her early success in Germany to the present day – and discusses her albums, singles, special project releases and chart positions. However, these are not all happy stories. There have been points in Summer's career that were testing, times of ups and downs for her in the charts. But Summer is a magnetic name, her influence and inspiration continues to gather tributes from fans and media around the world. By continually evolving as an artist, she remains relevant to the world of popular music that she inhabits.

Obviously, the book cannot be entirely objective because I'm a huge fan of the subject. I try my best to be rational and fair, although a little positive bias is inevitable at some level. Although Donna Summer's output in the music charts has slowed down, she remains busy touring and working in the studio, exploring different styles of music. Donna Summer is still highly respected and credited by the music industry and the music-loving public worldwide.

This book is a tribute to Donna Summer, a thank you for her beautiful melodies that will always thrill and entertain music fans. Devotees will know most of what is contained in these pages but I hope there are a few nuggets of new information there. For newcomers, I hope this project will introduce her to a whole new generation of music lovers and help them understand what an incredible recording act Donna Summer is.

I present the book with selected photographs related to Donna Summer's musical journey, not her personal life. The photos (within budget and copyright) are my personal choices. Nevertheless, I did take other people's views about some of the pictures, just to get some different opinions about which images people liked the most and their reactions to them. After careful consideration, five photographs were selected out of eighty-eight surveyed for this first edition. I had originally selected over 367 images. Those shown in this book are the ones that I love; there are some of my own photographs and also some given to me by Summer's fans.

Writing this book has been a lot of work but worth it. I hope you will all enjoy it.

Mission accomplished!

2012

Acknowledgements

My loving parents Mohamad Said Alias Ramli Othman and Wan Nik Aminah Wan Sulaiman for everything – moral support, endless love, prayers, believing, understanding and also for spoiling me and being very strict with me when they needed to be! Without them I would have not been here on this, God's beautiful green earth. Abah, your strength of character and always helping others will always inspire me. Mak, you have shared your interest in music with me since I was four years old, I still listen to those records – I will cherish this forever.

To my sisters and brother and my in-laws, nieces, nephews including their partners, grandnieces and grandnephews, aunties, uncles and cousins: thank you for your moral support.

To my late grandparents, Othman Omar and Jaharah Jano, Wan Sulaiman Wan Yusof and Aishah Hassan – I miss you.

I would like to thank the following gifted individuals for their contributions to this project:

The Fame, Lights And Music ...

To Bruce Roberts, sincere thanks for your contribution for the foreword. Your time, knowledge and experiences with Summer's music made a vital input to this venture. From 'No More Tears (Enough Is Enough)', 'Sometimes Like Butterflies' to 'To Paris With Love' all thrill me and many music fans endlessly. Thanks to Pete Waterman, the power behind Summer's smash hit album *Another Place And Time* and Gloria Gaynor, the first 'Disco Diva', for giving their precious time and valuable information. Thank you Chaka Khan, I cherished your time and the sincere help you gave for the project. To Martyn Norris, thank you for your contribution. Louis Walsh, I'm grateful to you and glad you share the same musical interests as me. For Tim Letteer, Francissca Peter, Hypnogaja with Mark Nubar Donikian and Jason 'ShyBoy' Arnold, Peter Stengaard: it was great to have your points of view. As for Uji Rashid, Dagmar, Darrell Russ, Inanna, Roslan Aziz, Mark Tara, and Salamiah Hassan thank you for your input, it will always be greatly appreciated. O'Mega Red, I thank you for your time and sharing the information on the single 'Angel' even before it was released. I thank you Bob Esty for your time and willingness to share your information at short notice. To Jody Watley, thank you so much for sharing your thoughts with me, I will always treasure them.

To the Professional Writers and Broadcasters ...
To Paul Gambaccini and Joel Whitburn, it was a great opportunity to have interviewed you. Reading and researching your publications was a fantastic experience and I thank you for the facts and opinions shared. As for Christian John Wikane and Ian Shirley, I would like to thank you for your time and your knowledge on the subject matter.

Summer Time ...
Eddie Sorell, I can't thank you enough for sharing some of your exceptional collections with me for the project. Cathy Hawkins, for all these years your insight has made the research possible. Bryan Cooper and Tricia Walsh Smith, thank you for the interview and sharing your experiences. For Brad Adams, Jeff Chaykowski, Stor Dubine, Vicken Couligian, Joseph Solis, Raphael K. Pfau, Moreno Manfredini, Kimberly Honnick and Wes Miller, many thanks for your time, the photos and other information provided for the venture.

The Other Side Of The Arena ...
The three individuals that have seen the evolution of this endeavour: Rashidah, one of my loving siblings, I thank you for your sincere analysis and believing in me; Dr. Wendy Henderson, for listening, for moral support, endless encouragement and thank you for reading a few pages of the manuscript; most importantly, Dr. J. Williams for helping with the editing, reading the complete manuscript and for his great input. I appreciated your help more than you know.

Sue Kerridge at BBC Radio, thank you for the information provided and Naomi Smith from Mercury Music Group UK, I am very grateful for your correspondence. To Jonathan Tattersall at the Official British Chart department, BPI (The British Phonographic Industry) Research Department, I thank you for the prompt reply and Jennifer DeChamplain from the CRIA (Canadian Recording Industry Association) I'm indebted for the data so quickly received. Thank you Simon Ngo from Absolute Radio for your help with the complete Donna Summer track listing for UK radio play. My appeciation to James Curran for your time analysing Summer's play time using an airplay monitoring company called 'Radio Monitor'. Also, thank you to Gennaro Castaldo, the Head of Press and PR (HMV and Fopp) for your time and sincere help. Thank you to Radio Monitor, comparemyradio.com and chartsinfrance.net.

Also, thank you to the individuals from the record labels for answering my enquiries – Pete Waterman Entertainment, Chaka Khan Enterprises, Almighty Records, Universal/Mercury Music UK, Sony Music UK, Sony Music USA and Warner Bros. Records UK. Everybody I have spoken to and emailed, I am obliged.

A number of individuals helped with the survey to choose some of the best photographs for the book; for this I wish to thank Dr. Earl Williams, Pushpinder Padam, Dr. J. Williams, Dr. Wendy Henderson, David Alan Weale, Fadzil Ismail, Adam Johan, Wendy Liu, Clara Oh, Mark Miller, Dino Abrams, Gaya Giacometti, Kate Nicholson, Suraya Adnan-Ariffin, Lindsey Bradley, Nash Nor, Dr. Jacqueline Gowland, Dr. Stephen Gowland, Satya Sagu, Nabila Nagi, Ricardo Do Prado, Analiza Ching and Minakumari Periasamy.

And I Would Love To Say . . .
Thank you to friends that have shown great interest and encouragement in the progress of the project. BooBoo 'A' Bey – what can I say? It's finished and thank you, love eternally, Yosrie Yunos fabulous friend, you have done so much and I can't thank you enough. To Kapka George, the lady who approached me and her friend loved my hat so much you took a picture in Soho and in return provided me with vital information for the mission! I thank you Simon Wilson, Norman Musa, Mohd Khairul Mohd Salleh, Lyanna Dee, Bibiana Peter, Daryl Rita Osekreh, Muhammad Jeffery Lee, Nor Azli Mohd Nor Azian and the kind person I spoke with from the University of Massachusetts, Boston. Not forgetting Jeff Smith, Lee Tyler, Mukhlis Nor, Judy Cooper, Tammy McCrary, Adrien Chabal and Lynn Cleckner for their sincere help. I thank you Barbara Hawes at The British Library and Leicester Central Library. And to all those individuals who share my passion, I'm obliged.

I also would like to thank Donna Summer's management for all the telephone conversations and emails.

I would also like to thank The Book Guild and their team.

To all my Donna Summer tribute facebook group members, I thank you for being such active members on the wall posting! If the group ever takes a bow, just move to the official tribute book page.

Finally thank you for reading my book. I hope you enjoy it!

Donna Summer Lovers Say ...

'Donna Summer is a great talent. She has one of the most powerful voices and her longevity is a testament to that. Love her!'
Chaka Khan, 19th July 2011, US.

'The music of Donna Summer is a class unto itself. As both a songwriter and a vocalist, she successfully explores different musical styles and, in the process, records groundbreaking music. With each new release, she unveils yet another facet of her boundless creativity. From number one hits to Grammy Award-winning performances to innovative album concepts, Donna Summer's impact on popular music is indelible, and will continue to influence and inspire future generations of artists.'
Christian John Wikane, 20th August 2011, US.

'We were offered the chance to remix and release "Carry On" from the States, which we were very excited about; it was a great opportunity for us to release such an iconic artist on Almighty. Later, in 2004, we were given the opportunity to remix two further Donna Summer tracks for Universal to be released on Casablanca, including the iconic "I Feel Love". Donna Summer was the most inspiring diva in the disco era.'
Martyn Norris, MD of Almighty Records, 8th September 2011, UK.

'I'm a massive Donna Summer fan myself! She's one of a kind ... an incredible diva ... There are many female acts come and go but Donna Summer is everlasting. Born with the voice that is strong, vibrant and full of emotion she has defined the pop music to another level. I love the diva Donna Summer!!!!!'
Louis Walsh, 24th October 2011, UK.

'Donna recorded and performed some classic era-defining songs that are timeless and will always find an audience...Get her performing at Glastonbury as the Sunday icon, I say!'
Gennaro Costaldo the Head of Press and PR
(HMV and Fopp), 24th March 2012, UK

'Donna Summer's music transcends through all genres of music and stands the test of time…her music is still being played decade after decade and still is relevant to this day.'
O'Mega Red, 15th April 2012, US.

'Donna Summer had the most glorious voice. Great range and depth, but more importantly, a singular singing style that had no bounds. Her music was a unique expression of her life experiences in her own words, and her melodies went from simple to complex. And she could sing everything in one or two takes!!! She often said, "I'd rather go shopping!!" What an absolute joy for me and an honour to have worked with Donna Summer!!!'
Bob Esty, 20th May 2012, US.

Excerpts from the Interview; Entertainment.
'Very few people have really distinctive and brilliant voices and she does. Having a great voice is difficult and she has got one of the really great voices, and it's lasted.'
Pete Waterman, 10th May 2010, UK.

'The uniqueness of Donna Summer is her voice quality. She has a very different voice … unique and very recognisable … rich and strong voice.'
Gloria Gaynor, 12th May 2010, US.

'Donna Summer has always been an original – as well as an innovator … She's an artist who's always had a unique point of view and one that's been able to transcend genres and has stood the test of time – a true inspiration for all of us who endeavour to have a career in music.'
Hypnogaja, 11th June 2010, US.

Excerpts from the Interview; A Broadcaster
'Donna was the flagship star of a global movement … Donna Summer was big news everywhere.'
Paul Gambaccini, 26th May 2010, UK.

Excerpts from the Interview … Across The Atlantic
'Donna Summer has been blessed because dance music will always be … needed in the market… her music is still very much alive …'
Francissca Peter, 26th January 2010, Malaysia.

1

Introduction

Boston-born Donna Summer was introduced to music by her loving parents, Andrew and Mary Ellen Davis Gaines. This home environment led her to fall in love with the music of Mahalia Jackson and other great gospel singers and made her determined to realise her dreams of becoming a singer and an actor.

Her earliest performances singing in church led Summer's parents to realise that their daughter had talents that could take her to better places and they decided to support her ambition. To fulfil her dream, Summer left school three weeks before her high school graduation. This was disappointing for her parents, but seeing their daughter's determination they reluctantly gave their consent. Summer held a variety of low-paid, unskilled jobs; she had no qualifications but singing was still her passion. Donna Summer first started singing with a rock group called Crow. It was while singing with them that she started thinking of pursuing another ambition of hers – acting.

In Summer's autobiography *Ordinary Girl: The Journey* (written with Marc Eliot, 2004) she says:

'I wanted to use my singing as a springboard to what had secretly become my new career goal: becoming a movie actor.'

She eventually managed to combine her dreams of being a singer and actor in Germany and Austria in musical theatre. It was in Europe that Summer was given the opportunity to sing as a background vocalist and later recorded her demo tapes.

Her first recording was in the late 1960s in Europe. 'The Hostage' was Donna Summer's first European hit single, and her first international break came in 1975 with the seductive, sexy hit single 'Love To Love You Baby', a song which created so much controversy that it 'made' Donna Summer. Known as the Queen Of Disco, Summer was the most well known and popular act of that genre in the 1970s.

Donna Summer's success was celebrated with her family. Summer's late mother, Mary Ellen Davis Gaines told the *A & E Biography* show that her daughter bought her parents a new home before she purchased one for herself.

Back in 1978, Summer was given her first movie role in *Thank God It's*

Friday. Disco was a massive trend and having one of the biggest disco stars of the time in the film was ideal. Her acting received mixed reviews by fans and the media. Her award-winning song in the film, 'Last Dance', became a big hit and remains one of Summer's personal favourites. Summer's creativity is also expressed in her painting. Her artwork has been described as 'music for the eyes', delivering the same pleasure as listening to her music. In the 1990s, Donna Summer exhibited her paintings in galleries in New York, Los Angeles, Chicago and Miami.

However her career has not been all about happy stories. There were testing times during the 1980s and 1990s, times of mixed success in the charts. But Summer continued with her creative work and came through with flying colours! Several special recording projects maintain their popularity in the tough world of the music business.

In March 1998 Donna Summer was awarded the Golden Key, an honorary doctorate in fine arts from the University of Massachusetts, Boston, for her achievements and contribution to the community.

Most of Donna Summer's major hits have been updated by DJs and her songs have been recorded and sampled by many major recording acts and have also appeared in movies, TV dramas, series and commercials.

Her composition, 'Down, Deep Inside' with the late John Barry for the movie *The Deep* was a UK Top 10 hit in 1977. 'Hot Stuff' appeared in the blockbuster 1998 movie *The Full Monty*. Hit TV shows such as *Sex And The City* have featured her songs, including a new studio track, 'I Got Your Love', before it was available in stores! The car manufacturer Mercedes-Benz featured one of her songs as the soundtrack to their advert, followed by Gucci for a perfume commercial.

She is an icon and an inspiration who has influenced so many people; entertainment acts, fans and the media around the world. Her songs have been covered and sampled by major acts from Madonna and Beyonce to The Red Hot Chili Peppers.

Many Summer tributes are to be found on the net. Summer's music not only gives endless pleasure to her fans but also helps in other ways; bringing lovers closer together, accompanying couples walking up the aisle and providing healing to those who have lost loved ones.

Although the recordings have slowed down in the twenty-first century, Summer remains busy touring and experimenting in the studio.

Her 2008 production, 'Crayons', was a Top 20 hit in the *Billboard* album chart and most of the singles released from the album have become no.1 *Billboard* dance hits! Donna Summer is still highly respected and credited by the music industry and still able to produce albums that sell in huge numbers.

2

The Beginning Of The Dream

The Donna Summer tale begins around 9.30 p.m. on New Year's Eve in 1948. She was brought up at the 16 Parker Hill Avenue in the Mission Hill section of Roxbury. Summer, real name LaDonna Adrian Gaines, was the third child in a family that grew to include six girls and one boy.

Summer's parents told Weller/Grossman Productions for *A & E Biography* that it took them a while to decide on a name for their newborn girl. Her father suggested the name 'LaDonna' but Mrs. Gaines was unsure. They later discovered that 'LaDonna' is translated as 'a lady that sings' and soon both her parents agreed that LaDonna was the right name for their beautiful daughter. Summer said in the 2004 article 'Donna Summer: The Empress Of Herself' that she did not use 'La' very much, preferring Donna. However, sometimes her sisters would call her LaDonna to be 'grand' and simply to tease the young 'diva'.

Growing up in a family that was hardworking and churchgoing, Summer was introduced to gospel legend Mahalia Jackson's songs by her parents. Later she became Miss Mahalia's follower and at a very early age, Summer started performing with church choirs. Mahalia Jackson was a giant within the gospel arena, winning a Grammy Award in 1961 for the song 'Everytime I Feel The Spirit'. She even had a weekly CBS radio show. Mahalia Jackson passed away in 1972.

In *A Change Is Gonna Come: Music, Race And The Soul Of America*, Craig Werner says that Mahalia Jackson introduced gospel music and then propelled the genre to another level. Jackson brought her love for gospel 'into the homes of white Americans'. The author said that at the time, white Americans in New Orleans and Chicago would have not been seen anywhere 'near the black churches.'

Mahalia Jackson, who had a powerful voice, remains a favourite of the black churchgoing community. One of Jackson's biggest fans was, and still is, the young Summer. Donna Summer finally had a chance to sing to the congregation when one Sunday, by luck, a choir member who was supposed to sing a solo fell ill. She sang a Mahalia Jackson tune 'I

Found The Answer, I Learned To Pray' at Boston's Grant African Methodist Episcopal Church. Summer told the *People Weekly* publication that she was 'singing, not whispering or screeching', and as she sang she saw many people, including her parents, start to cry. The young Summer had touched the congregation. This was the very first time the public had a taste of the talent of Donna Summer. From that day on, Summer continued to sing in the church with the blessing and support of her parents.

'It was then I knew I had been given a very special gift from God … It was just a matter of how to best use it' (taken from a 1999 Epic Records press release about Summer).

Donna Summer also sang in other churches, solo or as part of the choir. Summer's love for entertaining people not only manifested itself at home and in the Grant A.M.E church but also at her former high school, Jeremiah E. Burke High. Her former history teacher recalled Summer as dynamic and vibrant, always participating in the school play. Joseph Day told the *A & E Biography* show in 1995 that his student was not as passionate in his history lessons as she was when entertaining, but she was always well behaved and enthusiastic in the classroom.

In her autobiography *Ordinary Girl: The Journey*, Summer tells how she joined a group called Young Adults, a 'dancing-and-singing' group which performed around Boston. Jim Haskins and J.M. Stifle said in *Donna Summer: An Unauthorized Biography* (1983) that Summer used to spend hours in local record shops, sitting in the soundproof booths and listening to the latest releases, or discussing with the sales clerks the newest trends in the music scene. This was only natural for someone who loved music and singing so much.

In *Off The Record: An Oral History Of Popular Music* by Joe Smith and Mitchell Fink, it was noted that everybody in Summer's home enjoyed singing. The book said that many famous singers would be imitated; Summers and her sisters pretended to be The Supremes or Dionne Warwick, or even Barbra Streisand and Aretha Franklin.

In search of her dream, Donna Summer became a vocalist for a rock group called Crow, named in honour of herself, the only black member of the group. It was certainly an attention-grabbing name. Haskins and Stifle wrote that Summer's mother wasn't too keen on the name but Summer thought it was cute and had no objection to the band's decision to name itself after her.

Jim Haskins says that Crow's first show was at Boston's Psychedelic Garden. That was a long time ago and many fans might be eager to know what Crow sounded like. Summer, in an interview with Craig Rosen for *Billboard* magazine, said that they were influenced by Janis Joplin. The group wrote their own material with very 'hippy' and 'psychedelic' lyrics. Crow not only wrote songs in the style of Joplin, but they also performed at the same place – the Psychedelic Supermarket, the place that Janis Joplin started performing.

Unfortunately, after the debut show at the Psychedelic Garden there were no invitations to perform and no recording contracts forthcoming. However, the group did secure a few gigs a month at college fraternity parties and Summer states in *Ordinary Girl: The Journey* that Crow played in most of the clubs in Boston. They even performed in New York City at the Purple Onion. The young Summer surely caught attention and received promising offers but these did not include the rest of the band. Dispirited by their initial lack of success, the group developed internal disputes over their creative direction. These disagreements resulted in the break up of the group, the band members going their separate ways.

Donna Summer continued to pursue her dream and recorded demos from time to time. As well as her dream of becoming a singer, she still wanted to act. According to *Donna Summer: An Unauthorized Biography,* Summer loved Bette Davis and Katharine Hepburn and dreamt of being like them. She was especially fond of their comic roles. However, Summer realised that there were few roles for black actors in the movies or television at that time.

At that time it was still difficult for black actors to succeed in film. Historically, most famous black artists had to 'humble' themselves to feature in a film. For example, in 1947 jazz legend Billie Holiday was given a part playing 'Endie' in the musical drama *New Orleans*. Even though she was very popular, her part was only as a 'singing maid'. Another black sensation, Louis Armstrong, played himself and sang with Holiday in the movie. Jim Haskins notes in *Donna Summer: An Unauthorized Biography* that only Sidney Poitier had the opportunity to act in good Hollywood roles at that time. In Sidney Poitier's 'Acting Career' section in 'Wikipedia' it states:

'Poitier was the first male black actor to be nominated for a competitive Academy Award (for *The Defiant Ones*, 1958). He was also the first black actor to win the Academy Award for Best Actor (for *Lilies Of The Field* in 1963).'

Summer, according to her autobiography, planned to become like Judy Garland and 'sing her way' to achieve her desire, but she knew her appearance was not like Dorothy Dandridge or even Lena Horne. Perhaps Summer kept her dream of becoming an actor a deeply veiled secret, even from her family and friends. Eventually, to combine both her dreams of being a singer and an actor, Summer looked towards musical theatre.

3

Journey To Her Heart; The Virgin Tracks

During her late teens, Donna Summer moved to New York and at this time auditioned for a part in the Broadway production of *Hair*.

The audition session was actually to replace Melba Moore. It was said as many as three hundred people applied. Self-motivated, Summer went for the audition with her two sisters. It was written in *Off The Record: An Oral History Of Popular Music*, that the three sisters and shall I say 'Gaines's Angels' were the last ones in the line.

Some of Summer's die-hard fans may have already read her own words in *Ordinary Girl: The Journey*. She came to the audition dressed as a 'hippie/ street-cutie' with 'a short mini dress with ancient Rome-Style sandals that laced up' to her knees.

Despite this, she missed out on the part, but landed a role in a German production of the show in 1968. A young Donna Summer flew to Germany on 28th August 1968, starting her journey as an independent, young and beautiful American woman in the European entertainment world – to play Dionne in the musical *Hair*.

Donna Summer, in an interview for *A & E Biography* produced by Ruben Norte, explained that she knew that her greatest asset was a good singing voice – not her looks. Summer's mother, Mary Ellen Davis Gaines, said in the same show that she knew from the minute her daughter was born that she was blessed and would live to sing. Mary Ellen recalled that her daughter would sing during breakfast, lunch through to supper. Summer wrote in *Ordinary Girl: The Journey* that her mother encouraged her to sing various melodies. The little Summer would also sing her father's favourite songs by the jazz superstar Dinah Washington, and the rock 'n' roll, rhythm and blues act Brook Benton. Dinah Washington was famous for 'Mad About The Boy' and 'What A Difference A Day Makes' and Brook Benton was popular for 'It's Just A Matter Of Time' and his 1970 sentimental come-back hit 'Rainy Night In Georgia'. Whenever the household had guests, Summer and her sisters would sing to them. Their regular tune was 'We've Come This Far By Faith'. This faith from 'the above power' has been an important part of her life as a theatre performer until the present day.

The idea of travelling is thrilling for many people, but like anyone moving to another country, whether to study, work or just starting over, not knowing where the journey and life may lead will bring both nervousness and excitement in equal measure. As Summer said herself, she was scared! Only God would have known her true feelings at that time. A young, gifted American girl with little experience of the world was to be away from her native land, and soon fitted in just fine with the system, language and life!

Donna Summer in 'The Queen And Her Crayons: An Interview With Donna Summer' (popmatters.com, Christian John Wikane, 20th May 2008) explained that she only moved overseas after she 'could leave home, and became an adult to look after herself legally'. She had her own ideas for her life and was ready for new challenges.

Donna Summer chose Germany because her parents spoke the language and her father used to live there. Summer talking to *Billboard* in an interview in 1994 for her twentieth anniversary celebration, said she thought this would be a good chance to learn how to speak another language. Young, full of creativity and anticipation, Summer had lots of ideas about how to move forward in her career. She also made new friends and had new experiences and adventures in her personal life.

In Germany, Summer met a lady named Dagmar, a photographer for *Hair*. Dagmar recalls the time she met Summer:

'I called her my "little sister". I took her under the wings a bit, when she was new to it all, in Munich. She met my mother too and immediately there was a connection.'

Dagmar recalled that it was a great moment. Summer was not yet fluent in German, so it was fantastic that Dagmar's mother spoke good English and the meeting between the young American girl and her mother was friendly; they were soon 'giggling' together. Watching Summer settling down and making friends, Dagmar was amazed at how quickly her friend picked up German words, even the local dialect. *Hair* was the beginning for both of the friends – Summer's first real stage appearance, Dagmar's first real job as a photographer. They will always have this special bond and have remained close companions.

Donna Summer balanced her social and work life very well. Her part in the musical as Dionne was actually rather small, only featuring a few numbers to showcase her powerful vocal talent. She did have a moment of becoming The Supremes when she took the lead role and performed 'White Boys'. Summer's singing and performances with the other two cast members received a good response from audiences. It was such a privilege to hear from

Dagmar, who recalls how everyone loved Donna Summer herself and her wonderful voice. She said:

'I watch, I'm there, but I like to "disappear", so my subjects are not really aware of my presence. Then I snap my selection of defining seconds of expression or behaviour. I like to catch the special moments, the fleeting expressions ...'

Dagmar explained that she would wait for the 'important' look or move from the cast. The photographs are candid – a split second shot capturing a moment in time, pictures that tell a story. For the many fans curious to know, Dagmar said that she didn't think that the young Summer had any enemies or jealous cast members in either *Hair* or any other productions.

In Russell Sanjek's *American Popular Music And Its Business: The First Four Hundred Years 1900–1984 Vol. III,* he notes that Summer became a star in Germany with the success of *Hair.* It brought modest fame, German style. Summer performed 'Let The Sun Shine In' and 'Aquarius' in the show.

After working hard on this production for some time, Summer switched to the Viennese cast of the show. She subsequently had parts in different musicals and gained more experience with the Vienna Folk Opera – with *Showboat* and *Porgy And Bess.* She eventually moved on to other musicals and returned to Germany to extend her musical journey within the theatre, including *Godspell* and *The Me Nobody Knows.*

Donna Summer had a great time in *Hair.* Writing in her autobiography, she said that the production presented a lifestyle dramatised by all the cast members in the play, but which was being lived and practiced in real everyday life by them all, off stage. Hitting it off on stage and off, the *Hair* production team and actors were surely thrilled that the play was a success. Success demands hard work, but there was also time for having fun. It was one of the happiest times for Summer and all those close to her.

Dagmar has said that during the making of *Hair,* Summer would pull faces and cross her eyes – usually behind the back of some very serious 'important' person! 'Bad' Donna Summer! Dagmar went on to say that her friend would relax everybody and put the nervous cast members at ease. When Summer sang, she was totally involved and seemed in a world of her own; serious and deep in concentration. Then she would snap out of it and make a joke! She had a quick wit and good sense of humour, making the *Hair* cast laugh even in complicated situations. Generally, Summer liked to be the 'clown' of the company. Dagmar says sometimes though she would sit quietly by herself, as if lost in thought.

Summer shared her wonderful experience of the *Hair* production in *Ordinary Girl: The Journey* and recalls that the musical was a success and the leads, of which she was one, became 'local celebrities'. She even performed a few songs in German.

Continuing her musical theatre career, she began working in the studio, recording the soundtrack to the show *Haare* (*Hair*) in 1968. Her first recordings in German were 'Wasserman' and 'White Boys'. The track 'Schweben Im Raum' was recorded with other cast members. The cast recording of *Haare* charted circa March 1969 at no.4 in Germany. The album stayed in the German Top 40 for sixty-four weeks.

Summer's follow-up was for *Ich Bin Ich* (the German version of *The Me Nobody Knows*) in 1971, and she recorded the ballad track 'How I Feel'. The album has been released in two versions, one in German and one in English.

Her second musical recording was in 1971 for 'Sweben Im Raum', 'Oh segne Gott mein' Seel' and 'Du Bist Das Licht Der Welt' with some other cast members from *Godspell*.

Donna Summer continued to work in the studio and in 1971, she released the single 'Sally Go 'Round The Roses'. The song was a cover from a girl group named The Jaynetts, who had a no.2 hit in the *Billboard* Hot 100 in 1963. Summer's version sounded more raw than the original, which had a cheerful, happy-go-lucky, up-tempo feel. This fabulous cover was to be the first demonstration of the young Donna Summer's ability to take on a song and give it her unique signature. Summer also recorded the track 'So Said The Man', a down-tempo melody for the B-side of 'Sally Go 'Round The Roses'.

The single was produced by Vincent Malouney and released under the label MCA/Decca. This early recording has circulated among lucky fans for years.

Summer answered a question from Gary Trust for the website annecarlini.com about whether lucky individuals can make money if 'Sally Go 'Round The Roses' is in their possession? Summer answered 'probably'! In an article 'Donna Summer: The Empress Of Herself', Summer remembers that Vince Melouney, the former drummer of The Bee Gees, recorded 'Sally Go 'Round The Roses' with her in London. She said that perhaps somewhere in one of the studios in London the tape is 'sitting on someone's shelf'. It seems somebody out there may not realise the hidden master copy is just waiting to be rescued! Reminiscing about the day she recorded the track, Summer remembered 'the whole thing'. From Germany, Summer went into the studio in London. They also recorded 'So Said The Man'. According to Summer, the song was a 'bizarre' composition 'about meeting like a prophet ... just some guy who could tell the future ... and it was a kind of an odd song.' However the songs 'didn't work out' and Summer moved back to Germany.

Nonetheless, 'Black Power', the song credited to P. Thomas and G. Fran-cropolus was arguably to be considered her first successful English studio work. Summer could have recorded the track while she was working in the Hair production. 'Black Power' is the first track of hers to be featured in a TV series – this is an achievement for Donna Summer in her own right. The song appeared commercially for the first time in a German compila-tion album titled 'Peter Thomas – Moonflowers & Mini-Skirts' in 1998. The track was taken from a German television thriller mini-series titled *11 Uhr 20* in 1969. A young Summer vocal is presented here, displaying her big voice – a great experience for fans that own the track. This is a very early recording and the immaturity can be heard clearly, but the presence of that big powerful voice is clearly there. Fanatical fans evidently loved it, and the production track is worth getting one's hands on, but it is not up to the quality of her best work.

When the song was played to Paul Gambaccini, he evaluated 'Black Power' as a mess of a recording and believed one must see the song in the context of 1969. The Black Power sound started in 1968 with James Brown, most definitively in the song 'Black And Proud'. Gambaccini points out that Donna Summer's background is not deep R&B, having come from Boston and not some sort of ghetto environment. Summer is a pop person and she was a musical theatre personality. In his view, the 'Black Power' sound displays a lot of period influences such as Latin and jazz and the beginnings of funk. In Paul Gambaccini's own words:

'Ironically, the strongest part of the song was her entrance right at the beginning. She said the title, you get the title, you get the concept. It loses its conceptual strength and becomes a grab bag of ideas ... But she is not a genre vocalist here at this time. She doesn't appear particularly at one with funk. She can live with funk but she's not funky. So she doesn't make the impression that she's going to make with Giorgio Moroder.'

Before Summer met Giorgio Moroder for studio sessions while working in Austria, she met and married a good-looking actor, Helmut Sommer, in 1972. They had a beautiful daughter, Mimi.

Donna Summer continued her musical theatre career in Germany, sang background vocals on records and cut some demos. She released a single 'If You Walkin' Alone', credited as Hans Hammerschmied and Donna Gaines in 1972. The song has a cheerful sound – suitable for beautiful spring weather and reminiscent of the era's style and colourful outfits, the guys with the leather jacket and undone shirt button and the ladies with the short mini-skirts and a designer hat, dancing the 'go-go'!

Paul Gambaccini said the song is interesting because it is in the category of a showbusiness belter! Oxford University degree-holder Gambaccini recalled that Linda Clifford had a big hit song with a similar feel a couple of years later with a version of 'If My Friends Could See Me Now' from the musical *Sweet Charity*, a theatrical song that became a disco hit.

Listening to 'If You Walkin' Alone', Gambaccini noticed that Donna Summer's vocal opens up at the end of almost every line:

'She wants to belt but she doesn't know exactly where, so she belts everywhere to let you know that she can be forceful and that is something that sounds like a forerunner of Donna Summer hits . . .'

The second song, 'Can't Understand', again credited as Hans Hammerschmeid and Donna Gaines and taken from the same single, has a slower introduction which then builds up to a full orchestral arrangement from the middle to the end of the song – Summer's powerful voice is presented here. The song 'Can't Understand' was Summer's very first with her own lyrics. Summer acknowledged in 'Disco Queen Is Just An Ordinary Girl' by A. Scott Galloway that she wrote the 'pretty simple' song when she was fourteen years old. As she acknowledged, she was a typical moody teenager at the time. She started writing poetry, then moved on to writing music. This time the single was released under the Philips label but the producer is unknown. It was a good song and listening to the two tunes will take listeners back to the late 1960s and early 1970s. 'Can't Understand' continues the funk theme. *Hair* was having a big year in 1969 and this sounds reminiscent of the musical, except that its writers, according to Gambaccini, would have written 'more organised songs'. This one is in fragments; he found it impossible to latch on to it. Paul Gambaccini said the beginning of the funk sound is more evident on 'Can't Understand', but even on this, it is still theatrical. Personally, he can imagine 'Can't Understand' being in a show – the composition tries to master the elements of street music but according to Gambaccini, is not quite there yet. The funk reminiscent of James Brown, which was about to make a big impact in the early 1970s, was gaining strength and can be heard in 'Can't Understand'.

Her earlier tracks had influences of rock, hippie and folk in the late 1960s and early 1970s. At this time the credits were for Donna Gaines. It was a great experience to have shared a music listening session with Paul Gambaccini. He listened for the very first time to 'Black Power' and 'Can't Understand' and noted with interest the cheerful funk sound of 'If You Walkin' Alone'. It's in this one of the three that he can hear the inherent style of Donna Summer. This is the closest to a hit of the three but Gambaccini added that 'If You Walkin' Alone' could only become a hit at the right time. The song would not be a hit at the time it was released.

To date, the recordings are still little known by fans and the music-buying market. Not even many entertainment figures know about these songs! However, thrillingly for Donna Summer devotees, in 2011 an album titled 'Funky Fräuleins Vol. 2' was released. 'Can't Understand', credited as Donna Gaines, was included in the compilation project. Thomas Worthmann, the album's producer, wrote in the liner notes:

'The rare single is an absolute collector's item, fetching around 400 Euros. On the sleeve, Philips dropped the E from her surname and made a grammatical blunder ('You' instead of 'You're'), but the music remained first-rate on both sides. The flipside cut, 'Can't Understand', is a psychedelic-hypnotic monster, chugging along with funky guitar and bass, fluttering violins and Donna's enchanting, powerful vocals, rising inexorably to a bolero-style crescendo. Priceless – and not just for collectors!'

Donna Summer's 1971 single 'Sally Go 'Round The Roses' would apparently fetch between 100 to 300 Euros on a bidding site. Does this mean that these early recordings are great songs by Summer's standards? Not quite! Summer herself might want to forget about the songs but some music fans are fascinated with the tunes. They are collectable because they are rare. The music itself might not be valued but their rarity means that the 'hardcore' fans want to get their hands on them!

In 1973, Summer recorded with a group called The Veith Marvos Red Point Orchestra, who recorded one album. This album was re-released in 1983, retitled 'Donna Summer And Friends'. The vocal production is focused on Summer's voice, the other cast members vocals faded out using a voice cancelling system, which minimises the volume of the voices the producer doesn't want us to listen to. Music fans can hear Summer's powerful voice clearly in this bizarre vocal remix but it sounded very out of tune! Not due to Summer's vocal but as a result of the sound engineering being focused on her voice. The re-released album was also marketed under a different label.

This same album has, amazingly, gone by a number of titles including 'Reflections Of Donna Summer', 'I Love To Dance', 'Fun Street', 'Shout It Out', 'Gold', 'Donna Summer Live', 'Nice To See You', 'Pearls Of The Past', 'Millennium Edition' and in 2000 it was titled 'Remix And Earlier Hits' and so on . . . have mercy!

For fans, it was a fantastic discovery to have found a 'lost' album. It was relatively easy to find once you knew all the various titles it was released under. However, the inevitable disappointment comes with finally listening to the album. Many fans wondered how this could have been released in the first place – it simply wasn't up to the standard that they expected from a Donna Summer recording. She was said to be less than pleased with the release and she and her team did manage stop the production. However, once one title was stopped printing, another 'title' appeared. Summer has claimed it was not her in the record. Would you blame her? The vocal, technically remixed and retouched to find the background vocal alleged to be 'Donna Summer', should never have been produced! It was reported that the original was kept and 'available' when it was first pressed onto a CD format. This would have been good for Donna Summer collectors if she ever contributed on the vocal! Surely someone out there 'In Another Place And Time' has the original album. It is time to clear it up!

Although these were not the best examples of Donna Summer's allegedly 'contributed' work, most of her truly dedicated fans thought that these below par productions were worth collecting. Bizarrely, some fans quite liked what they heard! On a better note, a seven inch by The Veith Marvos Red Point Orchestra titled 'Nice To See You' with 'Do What Mother Do' was released in 1975 – a genuine original. A warning for fans; it was also circulated that a track called 'Why' was recorded at the same time as the above album. There is no evidence to support this claim.

It was during a demo session in the early 1970s for the group Three Dog Night, on a song 'Mama Told Me Not To Come', that she met producers Giorgio Moroder and Pete Bellotte. 1974 saw the birth of the 'Denver Dream' single, composed and written by Bellotte, a beautifully crafted song and vocal arrangement. This release was Donna Summer's first official collaboration with the two producers. The single also included a second track, 'Something's In The Wind'.

'Denver Dream' was released under the Lark label with her name being anglicised. It was reported that no one at the record label bothered to check the original spelling, which was 'Sommer'. Donna Summer said in her autobiography that changing the spelling was part of a general 'make-over' for her in Europe. 'Denver Dream' was only issued in Holland and did not make a big impact on listeners, but in actual fact it was good material.

Donna Summer and the team carried on their studio work and later a single taken from the 'Lady Of The Night' album, 'The Hostage', was released reaching no.2 in Germany in 1974. 'The Hostage' was a Top 5 hit in France, Holland and Belgium. But it was in Holland and Belgium that the single spent the most time in the charts – nine weeks. The second single from the album entered and peaked at no.2 in The Netherlands. However, the single only made no.40 in Germany and 'Lady Of The Night' stayed in the charts merrily for seven weeks! On 30th November 1974, the single entered the Belgian chart, got to no.2 and was in the chart for fourteen weeks. In 1976 the single peaked at no.6 in Austria for seven weeks.

Each country and culture has its own preferred music style and Paul Gambaccini said that the single 'Lady Of The Night' would never be a hit in America because it wasn't 'black' enough. American music at that time was influenced heavily by funk and swing and had lots of rhythm. 'Lady Of The Night' did not have these elements. However, some records that were hits in Britain at that time had a similar sound. Gambaccini pointed out that it was clear that listeners could tell from the vocal that it is Donna Summer. The problem is listening to the song now, as it sounds dated. He also said that it's hard to hear how it would have sounded when it was fresh. Gambaccini, sharing his experience after listening to 'Lady Of The Night' said:

'. . . it would have a fighting chance to be a medium chart record in Britain. Because there were some things then were not missed in America by black artists because England didn't miss the funk element, it didn't like the funk element, it still liked the more melodic element. So whereas in Europe at that time they weren't funky at all, they would have liked more of the oompah in there.'

The 'Lady Of The Night' album represented the pop-rock-folk concept. Pete Bellotte produced the album under the Groovy label. Giorgio Moroder and Pete Bellotte were credited together as songwriters, apart from 'Domino', 'Let's Work Together Now' and 'Sing Along (Sad Song)' which were solely credited to Bellotte. 'Lady Of The Night' went to no.27 in The Netherlands.

'Lady Of The Night' was re-issued in 1995 with a new cover sleeve and in 1999 the original album cover was reintroduced. Interestingly, the track 'Full Of Emptiness' was omitted from the CD re-issue. 'Full Of Emptiness' was included in the 'Love To Love You Baby' release in 1975.

There were mixed reviews for 'Lady Of The Night'. Enthusiastic Donna Summer followers agreed that it was a moderate European pop sound with a bit of folk flavour. Yet fans were thrilled to own a copy of an early pre-disco composition of Giorgio Moroder and Pete Bellotte for Donna Summer. Fans enjoyed the tracks – it was Summer's first full-length musical recording.

The songs in 'Lady Of The Night' tell a story, which is what Summer's songs are popular for. An example is 'The Hostage' which is introduced by a ringing phone followed by a catchy tune; the story of a kidnap gone wrong. The ballad 'Friends' is about two children who grow up together but as they get older, one party wants their relationship to be closer.

'Domino' is the story of a girl who goes to a carnival and meets an attractive man wearing a mask, but never gets to find out who the person was.

'Lady Of The Night' showcases her vocals and her natural and powerful range, helped by Moroder's coaching and her experience in the theatre.

It was said in *Donna Summer: Her Life And Music* (Josiah Howard, 2003) that 'The Hostage' was Summer's least-favourite European release. Donna Summer acknowledged in an interview back in 1995 that the song was poor, and she would sue somebody if the track was ever released in America. Whether the 'diva' was serious or not, there has been no confirmation that she would really do it. She may have just made the comment as a joke or she may have been misrepresented.

'The Hostage' may have been a 'juvenile' song to some listeners and music critics, but actually it has a catchy tune and is lyrically interesting.

Listen to it with an open mind – it could be a four-minute movie! The telephone call starts the scene and the story unfolds from there.

Donna Summer may not be too keen on the song, perhaps due to the fact that the track was offered to almost every label in Europe, but no major recording companies were interested. Finally, it was released by Groovy Records. Even though it was not Summer's favourite track, 'The Hostage' became a no.2 hit in Holland and a very successful single in France. The single first appeared in the Belgian hit parade on 17th August 1974 and later entered the Top 5, staying in the charts for ten weeks (noted by Robert Collin in his 1993 'Het Belgisch Hitboek 1954 – 1993 40 Jaar Hits In Vlaanderen'). The persistence of Giorgio Moroder had paid off and Donna Summer's fame began to soar.

Donna Summer, in *Ordinary Girl: The Journey*, said that for some reason 'The Hostage' was a hit in Holland. She did live shows and appeared in the local clubs. It was hard work. Powered by the driving force of Ton Van Den Bremer, Tony Berk and Frans De Wit, it was then that things started to happen for Summer. Bremer, in the article 'Summer In Munich' for *Billboard* magazine told Ellie Weinert that the first time he listened to 'The Hostage' he 'got goosebumps'. Van Den Bremer had faith in the song and 'started working on the record'. He visited every single radio station in Holland and also recorded jingles to promote 'The Hostage'. Bremer received his first positive response from Radio Veronica.

The jingles were to promote Donna Summer, introducing herself to listeners and to the radio stations. The history of 'The Hostage' is interesting; while the single became popular in Holland and supposedly in Germany, it was taken off the playlist of Germany's radio stations a result of the kidnapping of a prominent Berlin politician by terrorists. The title was deemed unsuitable for airplay. As a result, the single did not make any impact in Germany. Van Den Bremer came up with the bright idea of putting Summer on a television show to compensate for the lack of support by radio DJs. Luck was on their side; Summer was called for a TV appearance and performed 'The Hostage' on a comedy disco show titled *Disco Corner*. The comedy sketch was very well received and a request for a repeat from viewers was granted making the song a hit – the record started to sell! The clip of the young Donna Summer's performance was first just circulated between fans but is now available on the Internet.

Tony Berk told *Billboard* in 1994 that he was happy to give the credit for Donna Summer's break to Ton Van Den Bremer.

Several other European hits followed after the release of 'The Hostage'; 'Lady Of The Night' in 1974 and 'Virgin Mary' in 1975. The single 'Virgin Mary' was not taken from an album. These singles were not released in the US or UK.

Many dedicated fans of Donna Summer will have these recordings of their favourite star's earliest sounds but it's not that widely known that she recorded European singles and an album. For some fans, the first time listening to 'If You Walkin' Alone', 'Virgin Mary' and 'Lady Of The Night' was an experience beyond excitement. Everyone will have their own view of the songs, with some saying that they will keep it in their 'Pandora's Box'!

Most fans outside the US and UK are still in the loop when it comes to Donna Summer's earlier records. These tracks are hard to find and only the lucky ones have obtained the original releases of 'Sally Go 'Round The Roses', 'If You Walkin' Alone', 'Denver Dream' and 'Virgin Mary'. Many fans share the tunes with each other, rightly or wrongly.

Hardcore collectors will be thrilled to hear Donna Summer herself mention in an interview with Gregg Shapiro for the *Windy City Times* that her very first professional recording session involved singing three Aretha Franklin songs. The diva recalled two tracks as 'Respect' and 'Dr. Feelgood'. The tape should be somewhere out there! There must be many demo recordings and studio sessions that might come to light in future. Let's hope!

In *Ordinary Girl: The Journey* Summer wrote that the recordings with Moroder 'were invaluable'. They recorded the songs as many times as possible in order to get the presentation, melodies and atmosphere exactly the way Moroder imagined them. Apart from getting Moroder's compositions right on the final cuts, the experience in the studio also allowed them to develop their professional creative relationship.

Even some loyal fans are not aware of the existence of these tracks. Fortunately, the musical soundtracks of *Hair*, *Godspell* and *The Me Nobody Knows* were re-issued in 1998 in Europe. Yet Summer's earlier solo efforts remain on the shelf. Perhaps these tracks might feature in a compilation album someday in the future?

Donna Summer undeniably learned a lot from her experience at the theatre and during her earliest recordings. The potential of her voice can be clearly heard. It was still an immature voice that later, as her experience grew and with the guidance of Giorgio Moroder and Pete Bellotte, developed into the voice we know and love today.

Moroder, Bellotte and Summer continued their magic with demos, working on new sounds and ideas. Fans were now able to trace the evolution of her style from the early theatre days through 'Lady Of The Night' and imagine what the future might hold.

4

Disco Phenomenon

In 1975 three creative forces, Giorgio Moroder, Pete Bellotte and Donna Summer continued to work their alchemy, creating the majestic 'Love To Love You Baby', an idea originated by Donna Summer.

In *Off The Record: An Oral History Of Popular Music*, Joe Smith said that when Summer came up with the catch phrase 'Love To Love You Baby' she went straight to Moroder's office and presented her ideas. Moroder immediately loved Summer's cute line and within days of the initial presentation, Summer was collected by his girlfriend to work in the studio.

Summer went into Moroder's office and sang the tune 'Love To Love You Baby'. The rest is history. Dick Leahy, then MD of GTO records in London had previously heard Moroder's own track 'Son Of My Father', a 1972 no.1 single in the UK, recorded by the band Chicory Tip. He loved what he heard and asked to hear Moroder's newest composition. The following year, Leahy and Moroder met up at the Marché International du Disque et de l'Edition Musicale, the world's largest music industry trade fair, held annually since 1967 at the Palais des Festivals in Cannes. Moroder played 'Love To Love You Baby' and they made a deal immediately! Leahy enjoyed the uniqueness of the melody and was surprised at how good the lead vocal was. They released the song but it got a poor response. The single was released as 'Love To Love You' in Europe and it climbed to no.17 in the Netherlands.

Summer told *Penthouse* in 1979 that it was released twice but failed in Europe! Maybe the mainstream European market wasn't ready for disco. Luckily, the late American executive Neil Bogart spotted the track and was completely captivated with the sound.

Fred Bronson, in the *Billboard* article 'Endless Summer', wrote that Neil Bogart, President of Casablanca Records, felt 'something very special' about the song. He acknowledged that it was not only Summer's voice but 'the overall sound' of the composition.

When he played the song at a dinner party, it received a very encouraging response and Bogart knew he had something great. He licensed it in the US to his Casablanca Records label. He quickly realised that both the song and Summer were not just 'smash-a-roo', 'rise 'em to-the-top-of-the-charts' hits. The party apparently became a little raunchier and Bogart wanted a version of the song that he didn't have to replay so often! He later suggested to Moroder that the track needed to be much longer – Moroder agreed it was a fantastic idea.

Paul Gambaccini noted that the extended 'Love To Love You Baby' received two edits, one for Europe and one for the UK. The songs were a huge success both in the US and the UK.

The author of *Turn The Beat Around*, Peter Shapiro, explains that Moroder stretched out his composition by using and introducing 'a new bassline as a tidal bridge between segments, creating waves that surged, climaxed and crashed every four minutes'. Shapiro acknowledged that with his creative mixing ability, Giorgio Moroder delivered a sound that 'permanently changed the character of music'.

As a result the super-sexy, sultry disco diva exploded into the public's consciousness and music was never to be the same again. Summer recalled in *The Telegraph* that the idea of having a sexy image was very strange. Being a sex symbol was just a joke to her and she wondered how to portray such an image. Summer may be beautiful and sexy, but she never thought of herself in that way. As Giorgio Moroder once told her, if she can act, why not take the role and just play the part?

During a conversation with Paul Gambaccini about Summer's image created by Casablanca, Gambaccini pointed out that "in no way did Donna Summer ever consider herself as a sex symbol".

However, the actor Donna Summer did play the role! Summer had taken the character of a sexy new American singer and took it back to her native land all the way from Germany. At that time, the image fitted in with the industry, the media, the public and music fans perfectly.

In 1994 Tony Berk, the MD for Basart Records who worked with Donna Summer at the beginning of her career, told Ellie Weinert in the *Billboard* article 'Summer In Munich' that Donna Summer had the charisma to be a star (3rd September 1994). Tony Berk knew that with his 'small company', his team 'couldn't have launched her in a worldwide career'. He knew the best man to propel Summer's career was Neil Bogart. He and Casablanca Records could provide Donna Summer with the glamour, fame and 'star status' she deserved.

Paul Gambaccini commented on Summer's rise to international super-stardom with the track 'Love To Love You Baby':

'It isn't that she was looking for the superstardom because she thought she was an actor. But she happened to be a perfect example of the right person meets the right circumstances.'

Summer's life changed dramatically after she signed to Casablanca, not just professionally but personally too. Her marriage to Helmut Sommer ended in divorce in 1976. However, they remain in close contact to date.

On the 3rd November 1975, Neil Bogart's letter to welcome Donna Summer home also told her that there had been many changes in the five years since she left the US. He praised her achievements in Europe and told her that *Billboard* magazine rated her as 'one of that year's most refreshing new artists'. Bogart explained that her album had become no.1 for the disco charts and sold over 300,000 albums within five weeks of its release. Finally, Bogart 'saluted' Summer, Oasis Records, Bellotte and Moroder.

On 6th December 1975, just before her divorce, 'Love To Love You Baby' entered the *Billboard* chart at no.55 and on 7th January 1976, it peaked at no.2. The single was in the US Top 100 chart for eighteen weeks.

'Love To Love You Baby' was the highest new entry in *Billboard* Top 100. That week, the no.1 was by Fly with the single 'Fly, Robin' and at no.2 were K.C. & The Sunshine Band with 'That's The Way (I Like It)'. That year, ten acts reached no.2 in *Billboard*, including Summer.

'Love To Love You Baby' first entered the UK Top 40 on 17th January 1976 at no.37 and peaked at no.4, spending nine weeks in the chart in total. The single was an instant hit in the UK and achieved Gold status (19th February 1976) in her native land, which required the sale of 500,000 copies at the time. Neil Bogart was pleased with the singles chart placing in the US and the UK.

'Love To Love You Baby' was a hit in Canada, reaching no.2 in February 1976 for two weeks and spending fourteen weeks in the chart. The single was certificated Gold by the CRIA (1st May 1976) signifying sales in excess of 50,000 copies in Canada!

In Germany, the country where Summer made her very first recordings, the single reached no.5 in February 1976 and spent five months in the chart. In New Zealand, the single reached no.8 in April 1976 and stayed for eleven weeks in the country's official chart. It was a no.4 hit in Australia, no.11 in Ireland and no.17 in The Netherlands.

Neil Bogart suggested that 'Love To Love You Baby' should occupy one entire side of the album. Its success affected Bogart's career in many ways.

American Popular Music And Its Business: The First Four Hundred Years 1900– 1984 Vol.III observed that Neil Bogart, because of his promotion of disco music, starting with Summer, was soon to be known as 'a pioneer of sex rock'.

The success of the song showed that the public were tired of elongated, self-obsessed guitar solos and 'prog rock'. Music fans wanted 'mood music' and they wanted to feel as good as the star when they listened to their songs.

The album 'Love To Love You Baby' reached no.11 in the US and stayed in the album chart for thirty weeks. It peaked at no.16 in the UK, spending nine weeks in the chart. Summer's seductive album was loved in Europe reaching the Top 10 of the charts in France, Italy, Norway, Austria and Sweden. Surprisingly, it only managed no.23 in Germany.

Although 'Love To Love You Baby' developed the early disco sound and was debatably the first twelve inch extended record, the other numbers on the album displayed Summer's range of musical styles on songs such as 'Whispering Waves', 'Pandora's Box', 'Full Of Emptiness' and 'Need A Man Blues'.

Summer's vocals had evolved compared to those on the 'Lady Of The Night' album that made the most of the power of her voice. The track 'Full Of Emptiness', which was included on the US and UK release of 'Love To Love You Baby', was originally from the 'Lady Of The Night' album. 'Love To Love You Baby' was marketed with different track listings for the European market. The single 'Virgin Mary' was selected for the Dutch release and the French release featured 'The Hostage'. Both 'Lady Of The Night' and 'The Hostage' were chosen for the German version. In Asia, all of the European releases were marketed. The original Dutch, French and German releases are no longer in production. The only available version now is internationally standardised and does not include 'The Hostage', 'Virgin Mary' or 'Lady Of The Night'.

In 1975, the single 'Virgin Mary' was released in Europe with 'Pandora's Box' as the B-side.

Ironically, despite the success of 'Love To Love You Baby', none of the other tracks from the album were marketed as singles. Only 'Need A Man Blues' was issued as the B-side for the single 'Love To Love You Baby' in its first edition. The 'Love To Love You Baby' single released in 1975 with the label and code 'Oasis 401' was essentially the first mix of the song.

'Love To Love You Baby' has been compared by some music fans and the media to the infamous single by Jane Birkin and Serge Gainsbourg, 'Je T'aime (Moi Non Plus)'.

Despite all the success, Summer's parents were not too pleased that their daughter had recorded such a sexually suggestive song. Her mother told the TV programme *A & E Biography* that it took a while for them to calm down once they realised the song had been recorded and released. In a radio interview with Tom Ashbrook for *Donna Summer: Trying To Be Free* (April 2010), Summer laughingly said that while recording the song she thought that her 'father will kill her'! One can understand how Summer's parents felt. They might not have been as pleased as Casablanca Records were, but they couldn't resist the legendary 'Love To Love You Baby Cake', specially baked to celebrate the success of the song. The cake was flown by plane, taking up two first class seats, and was escorted by ambulance to the Pierre Hotel in New York. Summer, her parents and siblings struck a pose and smiled with the cake, which featured a reproduction of the album's back cover. The cake was apparently as delicious as the song!

'Love To Love You Baby' did cause a stir of excitement but, according to Larry Harris in *And Party Every Day: The Inside Story Of Casablanca Records*, it wasn't US radio that made the breakthrough but clubs in Florida which played the song continuously, followed by clubs in the northeast. Harris, writing the radio play for 'Love To Love You Baby', says that in actual fact Frankie Crocker, a DJ at WBLS in New York was the first to give the single airplay. Crocker broadcast the long version 'every night after midnight' and made 'Love To Love You Baby' a hit – 'it grew exponentially once the hype had begun.'

Still not everyone was pleased with the suggestive content. The weekly news magazine, *Time* noted in 'Show Business & TV' that the Reverend Charlie Boykin of Tallahassee set fire to $2,000 worth of rock records. Boykin had previously burnt some pop records after 'a poll of North Florida high schools revealed 984 of the 1,000 unmarried girls sampled had become pregnant' simply because they listened to pop music – 'during fornication, of course'. He also wanted to restrict airtime for these records. From *Time* (29th December 1975):

'On the average, 15% of air time devoted to songs like "Do It Any Way You Wanna", "Let's Do It Again", "That's The Way I Like It" and "I Want' A Do Something Freaky To You". Radio's hottest song right now is also the most lubricous: "Love To Love You Baby". Donna ... wrote the lyrics herself. They are stunningly simple – mostly five words repeated 28 times. Donna's message is best conveyed in grunts and groans and languishing moans. Her goal is to make an album "for people to take home and fantasized in their minds." ... She and her promoter, Neil Bogart ... are being hailed as the sex rock pioneers'.

The suggestively erotic vocals resulted in numerous radio stations around the globe banning 'Love To Love You Baby', including the BBC. I have contacted the BBC and they confirmed and noted that they had discontinued playing 'Love To Love You Baby' on 20th January 1976:

'We have researched your query and been informed . . . Donna Summer's . . . "Love To Love You Baby" was banned from the Radio 1 chart rundown, the Sunday Top 20 show and TV's *Top of the Pops*. The controller of Radio 1 and Radio 2, Charles McLelland is quoted as saying "It is thought to be unsuitable for programmes which attract very large family audiences."'

'Love To Love You Baby' was not the first, or last, track to be banned by the BBC. This censorship has been practised since the earliest years of the organisation's existence. Despite, or because of this, the song became a huge success that propelled Donna Summer to international stardom.

American song writing legend Cole Porter had the classic songs 'All Of Me' and 'Let's Do It, Let's Fall In Love' banned because the lyrics were thought to be 'suggestive'. In 1966 The Troggs song 'I Can't Control Myself' got into trouble with the BBC because of the sexually suggestive sounds made by the lead vocalist, Reg Presley. Even The Beatles' 'A Day In The Life' was banned by the BBC because of its alleged promotion of drug use, a claim denied by John Lennon and Paul McCartney. Interestingly, George Martin later commented that the BBC suspicions were probably correct! The infamous 1969 track 'Je T'aime (Moi Non Plus)' by Serge Gainsbourg and Jane Birkin is another classic example.

Ironically, banning a song and the accompanying publicity usually adds to its popularity and success, with the public curious to know what all the fuss is about. A ban also adds an element of edginess and rebellion to a song that naturally attracts teenagers, who make up the majority of the singles-buying market. Most of these banned songs inevitably become accepted for airplay as time moves on and social norms become ever more liberal.

The publication *Continuum Encyclopedia Of Popular Music Of The World: Vol.1* comments:

'. . . raunchy songs were recorded nearly as often as love songs and laments, although lyrics might vary between live and recorded performances . . . The fake orgasm has been one of the main ways of communicating sexually explicit elements in pop, as Yoko Ono's "Kiss, Kiss, Kiss" (1980), Led Zeppelin's "Whole Lotta Love" (1971), Lil' Louis' "French Kiss" (1989) and P.J. Harvey's "The Dancer" (1995) evidence. The male orgasm, as heard on the Led Zeppelin track, is a relative rarity within pop, a fact that adds weight to claims that rock essentially gives expression to a macho credo.'

The 1967 Velvet Underground track 'Venus In Furs' is supposed to be loaded with 'sexual fetishism' and the iconic Roxy Music's 1973 'In Every Dream Home A Heartache' tells the tale of a sexual relationship with a blow-up doll. 'Long John Blues', created by Tommy George and performed by Dinah Washington in 1948, purported to be about a visit to the dentist. It describes how Long John had a 'golden touch' and when he started to drill it thrilled her and she declared she 'needed' Long John 'very much'. It is in fact an explicitly sexually lyric:

'He took out his trusted drill. And he told me to open wide. He said he wouldn't hurt me. But he'd fill my hole inside.'

Sue Kerridge, assistant to the BBC Head Of Music, in a communication with me on 17th May 2010:

'... we no longer "ban" records on Radio 2 or 6 Music even though the situation for some songs and "Love To Love You Baby" might have been the case many years ago'.

As stated in the *MTV Pop And Rock World Records 2011*:

'As a government-owned public service, the BBC long felt obliged to ban – temporarily or permanently – records it found distasteful or too controversial. This usually involved explicit sexual content, overt political posturing or foul language.'

The book provides a list of Hit Records Banned By The BBC, including The Rolling Stones' 1967 'Let's Spend The Night Together'; The Beatles' 'Lucy In The Sky With Diamonds'; Jose Feliciano's 1968 'Light My Fire'; Wings' 1972 'Give Ireland Back To The Irish'; The Sex Pistols' 1977 track 'God Save The Queen'; 'Glad To Be Gay' by The Tom Robinson Band in 1978; in 1979 'Killing An Arab' by The Cure, followed a few years later by The Police's 1981 song 'Invisible Sun'. Frankie Goes To Hollywood had their sexually suggestive 'Relax' banned in 1984. Also banned were The Pogues' 'Fairytale Of New York' in 1987 and The Shamen's 'Ebeneezer Goode' in 1992.

Donna Summer, during 'Later With Jools Holland' in 2004 , a live-audience UK music show, said she was grateful for the UK ban of 'Love To Love You Baby' which helped the album became a huge success in the UK and the US.

'Love To Love You Baby' may be relatively tame by today's standards but in 1975 it was 'groundbreaking'. Summer has acknowledged she became uncomfortable with the 'image' given to her. Nevertheless, the song's erotic presentation made history in the pop world. The lyrics and vocal style are relatively restrained and sophisticated compared with the more obvious approach of modern songs.

Although the presentation and sexy reputation of the song grabs all the headlines, it is the musical production that was arguably the most interesting aspect. With its cutting edge electronic beats and chorus, the song is beautifully crafted over the track's entire 16.48 minutes. The famed moaning is key to the ambience of the track – not every singer has the ability to make a genuine sexy and sultry sound. With Summer's gifted vocal presentation and Moroder and Bellotte's great musical craftsmanship, the track has stood the test of time.

Paul Gambaccini admitted that he had a soft spot for 'Love To Love You Baby'. An artist's breakthrough record always catches his attention, particularly when a good tune becomes a favourite. Gambaccini said these songs sound 'true' as they are composed without any high expectations. 'Love To Love You Baby' thrills him most when the song reaches the chorus echo and the orchestral music comes up – a moment of musical accomplishment.

Nick Coleman wrote in *1000 Songs To Change Your Life* (Time Out Guides) about 'Love To Love You Baby':

'Programmed into mathematically precise sonic helixes by Giorgio Moroder in that well known haven of down 'n' dirty funk, Munich, Donna Summer's 'Love To Love You Baby' was not the first record to make use of sequencer technology ... The programmed beat, with all its implications for DIY musicianship, portability, manipulability, economy and interface, took off like an aesthetic rocket and came to dominate pop music across the genres for the next twenty-five years, as the electric guitar and drum kit dominated the first twenty-five.'

The lyrics to 'Love To Love You Baby' are not, in actual fact, particularly explicit. It is simply a story about two lovers lying close to one another and celebrating their feelings of love. The song, which celebrated the female sexual orgasm, goes:

'... there's no place I'd rather you be, than with me here ... Do it to me again and again. You put me in such an awful spin. In a spin ... '

Donna Summer recorded her smash hit when she was a married woman and a mother. In *Penthouse* (1979) the star said that during the recording session she 'had more romantic' thoughts going through her mind. In an interview with Elliott Mintz, Summer said that 'there are ecstatic moments in life that are physical, that are like an orgasm.' She explained as a mother that having a child is a miracle in itself – 'there are moments ... that are ecstasy.' She approached the song as an actor approaches a part, imagining it as a script about two people in love who see each other for the first time.

Summer knew then that she had achieved what she needed to deliver from brief to completion. Releasing disco concept albums, Summer found herself at the height of her recording career.

British Hit Singles (Guinness, 1995) by Tim Rice, Paul Gambaccini and Jonathan Rice says:

'Donna Summer was number one on the *Billboard* Hot 100 once in 1978 and three times in 1979.'

It's a shame that the song had been 'brushed up' in 1994 to sound less 'erotic'. The original sound, with its seductive, sultry 'moaning and groaning' was now unremarkable by modern standards. Summer's approach to the sound was widely acknowledged to be creative, brave and ahead of its time. Over the years many recording acts 'borrowed' the style yet failed to achieve the original seductive sound that Donna Summer created for 'Love To Love You Baby'.

It was the perfect soundtrack for lovers. In 2009 in an interview with BBC Radio 2 for the show *Feelin' Love: The Donna Summer Story*, Summer joked, with regards to the sixteen-minute version of the song, that 'Love To Love You Baby' had to be more than four minutes unless one was very quick! Apparently, back in the days, her fans used to seek her out back stage after her shows to share with her their sexy experiences while listening to the song! And, she says, 'thank her for helping them discover how finally to let go'!

Interviewed by Charles L. Sanders for *Ebony* magazine in 1977, Summer recalled the comments from fans:

'. . . Girl, I put on "Love To Love You Baby" when I get together with my man, and it really helps me get down and enjoy myself and tell him what I want done.'

Although Summer thought this was great, she also explained that sexuality is not just about getting into bed having sex. It is also about understanding and knowing who you are and knowing your own body.

Sex can also have some health benefits, other than just being about pleasure. Stuart Brody, Professor of Sexual Psychology at the University Of The West Of Scotland, said that sex can lower the blood pressure and reduce stress.

The Sun, in an article in their health section titled 'Twenty-Four Hours To Beat Depression' (4th November 2010) quoted research published in the journal *Biological Psychology* which showed that people who had 'sex the previous night responded better to stressful situations.' According to Professor Stuart Brody it was linked to the 'soothing effect' caused by the touch of the partner. The study revealed that after sex, people seemed to be 'happier the whole of the next day.' Brody noted that there was an immense amount of research showing that 'touch' has a major comforting effect, whether as part of sex or not. The professor said that being touched at length by a person one cares about increases the effect.

The Virgin Encyclopedia Of 70s Music (Colin Larkin, 2007) says:
'... "Love To Love You Baby" in 1975 ... the title track was a ground-breaking recording, technologically ahead of its time and aimed squarely at the thriving disco scene ... typified by New York's thriving clubs, such as The Gallery, The Paradise Garage and Studio 54.'

Epic Records, in publicity material released for Donna Summer's project with the label in 1999, stated with regards to the track:
'The success of "Love To Love You Baby" triggered a series of Donna Summer albums that would brilliantly blend the primal groove urgency of disco and funk with symphonic strings and soaring, dramatic vocals.'

In the interview 'In Tune With Britain's Disco King' for BBC Online, Pete Bellotte told Tom Bishop:
'When it took off for us, it was just serendipity.'

Thirty-three years after the release of the song, *Listverse*, an online journal, placed 'Love To Love You Baby' at no.19 in a list of the Top 20 Greatest Love Songs. On 22nd September 2008:
'Definitely on the lusty side of the love song genre, but it's clear she truly, deeply and passionately loves her man ... fantastic expression of her love.'

The Billboard Hot 100 Annual had Summer as one of their top debut artists for 1976. The success of the 'Love To Love You Baby' album saw a certified Gold in the US on the 19th January 1976 and the UK on the 1st January 1977.

After the success of her sexy signature album, Donna Summer recorded the disco album 'A Love Trilogy' in 1976. This was her first full-length disco album and was produced by Giorgio Moroder and Pete Bellotte.

The vocal on the album continued in a style that fans were familiar with, although they may have noticed that Summer's delivery was slightly less sensual than previously.

The Coretta Scott King Award-winning author, Jim Haskins and writer of the TV programme *That's The Spirit*, J.M. Stifle, co-wrote in *Donna Summer: An Unauthorized Biography* that the presentation of 'the high, whispery vocals, the simple, repetitive, slightly suggestive lyrics, and the synthesized orchestration' from Summer's first international release gave her followers what they wanted – a disco standard. This made the 'Love To Love You Baby' album, which showcased and introduced just one 'disco track', a success.

Summer and the team maintained the seductive sound from 'Love To Love You Baby', which can be heard in 'Prelude To Love', the introduction piece composed and written by Moroder, Bellotte and Summer, through to her version of 'Could It Be Magic', a cover of Barry Manilow's 1975 no.6 *Billboard* hit. The cover sounded more manufactured and less heart-felt than the original but Summer gave it her best, resulting in a dance song that is popular to this day.

In an interview for the BBC Radio 2 programme *Feelin' Love: The Donna Summer Story*, Manilow admitted that at first he was surprised and cagey, knowing Summer and Moroder wanted to cover his song as a disco number. However, after listening to the result he was pleased and felt it could work. The Manilow song was a personal favourite of Summer and the star herself asked if she could record it, a request Moroder agreed to. The single debuted on 1st May 1976 in the US chart and reached no.52, spending eleven weeks in the chart. 'Could It Be Magic' first entered the UK chart on the 29th May in the same year, peaking at no.40 a few weeks later. Even though it did not get to the Top 20 in the US or the UK, 'Could It Be Magic', remains one of Donna Summer's most popular songs.

Ian Levine, in Martin Roach's *Take That: Now And Then (The Illustrated Story)*, noted that Summer's version of 'Could It Be Magic' was 'revered' as 'a god-like record' and American gay clubs loved the song. 'Could It Be Magic' was their 'anthem'. For DJs at Heaven during that time, Summer's cover was a favourite on the playlist 'at the big party nights'.

Although 'Could It Be Magic' was popular for parties and in clubs it could not compete with the success of 'Love To Love You Baby' in the UK and US. 'Could It Be Magic' fared much better in Europe reaching no.2 in The Netherlands, no.3 in France, no.5 in Belgium, no.14 in Austria and no.23 in Germany. *Goldmine* magazine proclaimed Summer's version and vocal expression to be more appealing than Manilow's, saying that Summer's presentation of the song was bolder.

The single 'Wasted'/'Come With Me' was the first release from 'A Love Trilogy' failing to make it into the pop chart but it was a hit on the dance floor, reaching no.7 in the US dance chart. The track 'Try Me, I Know We Can Make It', released in the US only, peaked at no.80 on the 10th July 1976 – a disappointing result. But again it enjoyed greater success in clubs, reaching no.1 in the US dance chart. 'Try Me, I Know We Can Make It', co-written by Summer, Moroder and Bellotte, was a beautiful disco track that played for almost eighteen minutes. The concept combined three distinct songs with a similar theme – 'Try Me (Just One Time)', 'I Know We Can Make It' and 'We Can Make It (If We Try)'.

Pete Bellotte told *Sound On Sound* publication in October 2009 that he was 'always the ideas man'. They started to use themes in Summer's disco albums. He explained in 'Donna Summer "I Feel Love" Classic Tracks' that he was the person that came up with the idea of three songs to be combined into one.

The album reached no.21 in the US spending twenty-seven weeks in the chart and no.41 in the UK with ten weeks in the chart. Giorgio Moroder considered the project a moderate success. In Spain and Italy, it was a no.1 album and reached no.4 in France spending seventy-one weeks in the chart! In Austria it reached no.8 and in Sweden it spent twenty-one weeks in the chart, peaking at no.18. The album was a success on a global level, achieving Gold album certificates from the US and the UK. But the single releases failed to emulate the success of 'Love To Love You Baby' in the regular pop charts. What 'A Love Trilogy' did do was cement Summer's image as a sexy love goddess, giving her the title 'First Lady Of Love'.

Paul Gambaccini said:

'This is all pretty well remarkable ... she started as an American in Germany. So she couldn't have thought that she would have international popularity. But Giorgio Moroder of course turned out to be this genius. For a while, everybody he touches became popular. She was the most popular.'

In the same year, Casablanca Records released 'Four Seasons Of Love', which climbed to no.29 in the album chart in the US, achieving Gold status (11th November 1976). It was a success, spending twenty-six weeks in the *Billboard* album chart. It did not enter the UK album chart but was still awarded Silver status by the BPI on 31st January 1977. 'Four Seasons Of Love' reached no.1 in Italy and in France charted at no.4. The album was Summer's first story concept; a year's love affair – Spring, Summer, Autumn and Winter. It was also the first album on which Summer was credited as a writer on all the tracks along with the producers. The album was very well packaged with a glossy fold out calendar of Donna Summer and a colour lyric sheet. Summer was also credited for the album sleeve design with Joyce Bogart and Susan Munao.

The 'Four Seasons Of Love' tracks presented a very sophisticated disco sound. The smooth up-tempo tune of 'Spring Affair' was the first single release and entered the US chart on the 18th December 1976 at no.80, eventually reaching no.58 on the 22nd January 1977 with title 'Spring Affair'/'Winter Melody'. Strangely, on the 29th January 1977 it became 'Winter Melody'/'Spring Affair' and climbed to no.52!

According to Joel Whitburn, the owner of Record Research and a writer and expert on the *Billboard* chart:

'... "Spring Affair" was a big disappointment because it didn't live up to "Love To Love You Baby" and "Could It Be Magic". Casablanca got real scared . . . and released "Winter Melody" because it was wintertime and decided to put "Spring Affair" as the B-side. They put both songs on the radio throughout the country, hoping it would take off, but it didn't.'

Even though the singles didn't take off, the songs in the album were well put together. The tunes 'Spring Affair' and 'Summer Fever' ran non-stop and blended very well. 'Summer Fever' is a fantastic melody with a great vocal and is the finest of the four songs.

The only very sentimental track on the album was 'Winter Melody'. The track entered the US Top 50 at no.43 on the 12th February 1977 and stayed for eight weeks in the Top 100 chart. The single was to be Summer's third UK hit, finishing at no.27 on Christmas day, 1976. 'Winter Melody' is still often heard on the radio and in department stores during the Christmas season. It has also featured on several Christmas compilation albums.

All fans have their own stories to tell about listening to Summer's work. One fan, Stor Dubine, says 'Four Seasons Of Love' is his favourite album! The story starts one day when his sister played the record. Perez remembered how his ears began to feel the language of the song as he watched his sister dance to the rhythm of 'Winter Melody'. The album helped him discover the magic of music. Perez says:

'Because I was born partially deaf, I could only hear with two hearing aids and I learned to lip read; now I got a new dimension of sounds and images. The sound of music was very confusing at first. With Donna's album I learned to understand every word, lyric, emotions and senses, and I learned to hear. From "Four Seasons Of Love" I started to buy Donna's LPs.'

Award-winning singer Jody Watley, in an official internet page conversation with me about Watley's music and this project, said that her favourite Summer album is 'Four Seasons Of Love'. The Grammy Award winner comments:

'. . . I was a dancer on Soul Train the first time Donna Summer performed on the show. She had the best albums and album covers – my fave is 'Four Seasons Of Love'.

The 'Four Seasons Of Love' project was also marketed as a Club Special Edition/Club-Sonderauflage in West Germany on the Atlantic Records Label, as printed in Wikipedia site, last updated on the 28th August 2011.

Endless stories and inspiration can be gained from Summer's music and album art work. For example, the 'Four Seasons Of Love' album sleeve colour palate is like a room with dark solid wood flooring! Summer's coat on 'Winter Melody' conjures up a warm room with a deep textured cream rug to soften the floor. The continuous music play and Summer's sensual voice is reminiscent of the ergonomic shape of a 1971 classic 'Bocca' seating that was itself inspired by a Salvador Dali painting, 'The Face Of Mae West'. The song choruses are the essence of spring, with pinks, blues, and yellows providing a palate for the walls. Summer's version of Marilyn Monroe's 'The Seven Year Itch' scene with its billowing white dress is the silk curtain that falls to the floor, creating a sense of drama and romance when the summer winds blows from the window.

After 'Four Seasons Of Love', Donna Summer teamed up with the late John Barry, the hugely influential British composer, for the soundtrack album to the movie *The Deep* in 1977. Summer recorded the track 'Down, Deep Inside'. This represented a departure from her usual disco sound.

Her follow-up album was 'I Remember Yesterday' in 1977, the first production that did not feature 'Love' in the title. It was also the first project that didn't have a predominantly disco theme. Although the tunes 'Take Me' and 'I Feel Love' are firmly disco, the other songs were a new departure. Tracks such as 'I Remember Yesterday', 'Love's Unkind' and 'Back In Love Again' evoked the sounds of previous decades. Summer used the melody from 'Something's In The Wind', the B-side of her 1974 single 'Denver Dream' but with new lyrics added. The track 'Black Lady' presented the soul sounds of the 1970s and showcased the transition of Summer's vocal style from the usual soft, whispering, seductive sound to a more funky, attitude-filled style. Moroder, Bellotte and Summer composed and co-wrote seven tracks on the album with 'Can't We Just Sit Down (And Talk It Over)' credited to T. Cauley. The album took critics by surprise, and they started to take notice of Summer's strengths and possibilities. Her image was rather more toned down in 'I Remember Yesterday'.

In an article for *Sound On Sound*, Pete Bellotte said his idea of the album came after he had read *A Dance To The Music Of Time* by Anthony Powell. In the article, Bellotte said he was 'peeved' when the idea for the album title 'A Dance To The Music Of Time' was changed to 'I Remember Yesterday';

'. . . I really wanted it to be called "A Dance To The Music Of Time" – and continued with a bit of rock, a Tamla Motown number and so on, and then brought it up to date with disco, before the final, futuristic song was "I Feel Love" . . .'.

Summer's new sound helped make 'I Remember Yesterday' a success. It reached no.18 in the US and no.3 in the UK album chart, staying in the US chart for forty weeks and the UK chart for twenty-three. 'I Remember Yesterday' brought a satisfying result to Casablanca and many music fans. The Italians loved it, pushing it to no.1. In Norway it peaked at no.5 and it entered the Top 20 album charts in The Netherlands, Sweden and New Zealand.

'Can't We Just Sit Down (And Talk It Over)' is a beautiful ballad from 'I Remember Yesterday' and was released as a single. Casablanca marketed the single because they wanted Donna Summer to have a hit with a ballad. Unfortunately 'Can't We Just Sit Down (And Talk It Over)' did not make it into the UK chart and only reached no.104 in the US, but was much more successful in the US R&B chart reaching no.20. It was the B-side, 'I Feel Love', that generated a huge amount of interest, especially amongst radio DJs. The track presented Summer as the public expected her to be – a sexy disco queen. This resulted in 'I Feel Love' moving to the A-side of the single. The single debuted in the US in first week of August 1977 and reached no.6 on the 3rd September. It stayed in the Top 100 for twenty-three weeks.

The song first entered the UK chart on the 9th July at no.15 and reached no.1 on the 23rd July in 1977, staying in the top spot for a month. 'I Feel Love' stayed in the UK chart for eleven weeks and was her second single release to reach the Top 10 in both the US and the UK.

'I Feel Love' was the very first global no.1 hit single for Donna Summer. The UK and Europe welcomed the futuristic sound accompanied by the simple but sensual chant in the summer of 1977.

'I Feel Love' was a no.1 hit in Holland, France, Austria, Belgium and New Zealand where it spent fourteen weeks in the chart. In Canada it reached no.4, enjoying twenty-two weeks in the chart. In South Africa it reached no.6 and was in the country's official chart for ten weeks. 'I Feel Love' was the first Donna Summer single to enter the Zimbabwe chart; entering on 15th October 1977; the single peaked at no.9 and stayed in for ten weeks in total.

Pete Bellotte was thrilled with the sound of 'I Feel Love' and recalled in a 2004 interview with the BBC:

'We had no idea it was going to sound so special!'

In an interview for *Sound On Sound*, 'Classic Tracks: Donna Summer "I Feel Love"' Bellotte shared the story of the song. They knew that what they were working on was 'part of a good album'. They posted their compositions to Neil Bogart in Los Angeles and the Casablanca President immediately suggested that the track should be the first single – 'it needs three edits and these are the edits.' Pete Bellotte said:

'Doing these immediately improved the fluidity of the track no end. He was that kind of a record man. And, of course, those edits no longer exist, because they would have been sliced from the quarter-inch master and simply thrown on the floor. That's how it was then. If you ever did any editing, the floor was cluttered with all the stuff you didn't use. We never saved anything; it was just discarded. However, because of his uncanny feel for music, Bogart knew exactly where the track should be edited and, of course, the improvement was fantastic.'

The single was awarded Gold in the US (9th November 1977) and became Summer's first Gold single in the UK (1st August 1977). 'I Feel Love' received Summer's first Platinum award from Canada (1st November 1977).

Speaking to Joel Whitburn about the success of 'I Feel Love', he said:

'... "I Feel Love" was very popular, also big in the R&B chart. She was on track to become a major star after "Love To Love You Baby" ... Following up that with the right song would make a point. You can loose the star pretty quickly unless you follow up with something a little different ... 'I Feel Love' delivered a fantastic beat that hit right through you ... a mysterious song ... well presented synthesizer with the rhythm that jumps right out ... just a good song. Casablanca was a good label for her ... she worked very well with the label.'

The new European synthesizer-based techno-pop sound of 'I Feel Love' remains one of Summer's most popular tracks and marked a new development in the history of pop music. 'I Feel Love' is still one of the favourite tracks on any club's playlist. It is said that the late John Lennon thought the song was the future! He also apparently rushed to the record store to purchase the record and played it non-stop!

Chuck Eddy, author of *The Accidental Evolution Of Rock 'N' Roll,* who has written many music reviews, writes that the song is a few words sung continuously with the presence of 'machine beats' from the start to the end. Eddy also noted that Summer's 'voice was no monotone'. It is sensual; 'it had sex in it, and so did Giorgio Moroder's electronics'. He observed that the song is not an easy record to produce. Some critics may have said that 'I Feel Love' is just repetitive 'chanting', but Eddy maintains that 'nobody else had ever sung that way before'.

British author and music journalist Paul Du Noyer says in the *Enclyclopedia Of Singles*:

'...."I Feel Love" pushed the disco genre to its metronomic best, sitting at no.1 in the UK charts ... selling over half a million copies ...'

Tim Letteer, a dance music producer from New York, has spoken of his feeling for some of Summer's songs:

'...."I Feel Love" was the beginning of modern electronic music and probably the first trance track years before anyone defined it. "I Feel Love" didn't showcase her vocal range, but the way she sang it and the synthesising was just hypnotising.'

Although a massive hit, the song was not universally well-received by critics. Robert Dimery in *1001 Songs You Must Hear Before You Die* wrote that the track seemed to ignore its genre origins in black soul music. The hit was criticised by music critic Nelson George as being suitable for people with no sense of rhythm.

The success of 'I Feel Love' was more than just a disco hit; it was ahead of its time, a glimpse into the future. Colin Larkin, author of *The Virgin Encyclopedia Of 70s Music* declared:

'. . . (it) was an electronic production masterpiece, especially considering the technology available at the time. It was another apex in disco's history and confirmed Summer's unintentional rise to the role of disco "prima donna" . . .'.

In 2008, 'I Feel Love' was included in the book *1000 Recordings You Must Hear Before You Die* by Tom Moon. The song is an evolutionary point in the history of modern pop music, not only propelling Summer to superstardom, but also establishing Giorgio Moroder as a master of electronica.

In *The Rough Guide To Soul And R&B*, Peter Shapiro comments:

'Even more of a landmark was 1977's "I Feel Love", which had more fake-orgasm vocals from Summer set against an entirely synthesized background. Introducing both the syn-drum and the galloping Moog bass line that would come to categorise the strain of disco called Hi-NRG, "I Feel Love" was a masterpiece of mechano-eroticism.'

In the 'Disco Playlist' section of *The Rough Guide To Soul And R&B*, the single 'I Feel Love' is described as:

'The cocaine chill of the "Me Decade" in a nutshell.'

In the article 'Giorgio Moroder: Electric Dreams with Donna Summer', Richard Buskin wrote:

'Continuing to produce Summer's albums, Moroder also composed more hit singles in the same vein. "I Feel Love" attracted the attention of film director Alan Parker, and this led to Moroder composing and producing the score for the highly acclaimed 1978 movie *Midnight Express*, which gained him his first Academy Award for Best Original Score.'

In a TV interview, Giorgio Moroder mentioned that when 'I Feel Love' became popular, things changed in music-making. 'Violins disappeared' and the music production moved towards the 'technical' and 'techno' sides. Moroder said 'I Feel Love' was the first song where he didn't write the melody before he wrote the tracks. This happened because of the use of the synthesizer; Moroder said that 'it was very difficult to get the bass line' as it was all electronic.

Giorgio Moroder created 'I Feel Love' especially for Donna Summer and for the album 'I Remember Yesterday'. Moroder's aim was to create a conceptual album which contained songs from different eras, from the 1950s through to the future. 'I Feel Love' was the song from the future. In 'Giorgio Moroder At Future Music' (1996) he says:

'At that time I was a little fed up with synthesizers which I'd started to use in early '71, but the only way to get futuristic sounds was to use synthesizers – that wouldn't work now.'

Talking to *Attitude* magazine (2004) for the article 'Any Queries?' Donna Summer said:

'... when Pete Bellotte and I began writing that song we started with a lot of words and then we hit on "I Feel Love" and realised that was it. It was a chant. And the rest we wrote in two minutes ... "I Feel Love" was just one of those songs where we knew it didn't need too much humanity to do it because it was about the technology.'

Tom Moon says in '1000 Records To Hear Before You Die':

'... "I Feel Love" is minimal – a few lines of lyrics, an ingratiating beat, simple keyboards ... her cooing vocal hook seems to just float on top of the arrangement. This track showed that Summer, then a rising star, had some artistic range.'

David Sheppard, the author of *On Some Faraway Beach: The Life And Times Of Brian Eno*, says that 'I Feel Love' was 'the product of German recording culture', particularly the 'technically advanced Musicland studios in Munich.' He added that the song consisted of 'little more than a staccato electronic' rhythm with Summer's ecstatic voice fundamentally repeating the title. Brian Eno first heard 'I Feel Love' on a bright morning while 'strolling up Notting Hill's Portobello Road.' When Eno heard the song 'from an open window', the catchy tune stopped him 'in his tracks.' Sheppard writes:

'Combining a robotic, propulsive synthesizer backing with a yearning, sensual female vocal, it sounded like disco-soul music as Kraftwerk might have imagined it. He heard it again in an Oxford Street record shop, where he learned that it was Donna Summer's 'I Feel Love'. Eno, like millions of other record buyers, fell instantly in love with it, purchased a copy and proceeded to announce to all and sundry that he'd heard the musical future.'

Sheppard goes on to say that Eno was so inspired by 'I Feel Love' that he abandoned the album he was working on at that time 'in favour of something slicker' with a 'Moroder-esque' flavour. Eno and David Bowie were said to have 'synchronized' on matters of tuneful modernism. When

Brian Eno was in Berlin he routinely claimed that the song, with its energetic 'electronics and hot-blooded sensuality', represented the 'seeds for a whole new strain of club music' culture.

Brian Eno was joined in his admiration of 'I Feel Love' by Moby, in an interview for the website 'about.com' by DJ Ron Slomowicz. He said the song was responsible for his love affair with dance music and he was mesmerised on first hearing it.

Marc Almond, in his book *Tainted Life*, writes that during a night out with some friends in a club, they noticed that a new record was being played when they took to the dancefloor:

'This had an electronic pulse rhythm to a machine beat with spaced-out, other-worldly vocals that sounded cold yet sensual at the same time. It was the entrancing, ground-breaking "I Feel Love", and was to herald a new age of music, an electronic dance phenomenon: disco.'

Andy Bell from the British group Erasure, in his official webpage biography, says that he first heard the beautiful tune at a gay venue called The Embassy Club. On his first night out there he says 'I couldn't believe the men were so good looking and the music was so fantastic . . . "I Feel Love" by Donna Summer'.

Although 'I Feel Love' was highly praised, synthesizer based recording was already being used in a major way by groups including Kraftwerk, Tangerine Dream, Emerson Lake & Palmer and Tonto's Expanding Head Band. Still, 'I Feel Love' made the electronic sound a massive success, reaching no.1 on the *Billboard* disco chart for three weeks, no.6 in the pop chart and no.9 on the R&B chart in the summer of 1977.

Peter Shapiro, in his book *Turn The Beat Around,* says:

'With Summer's mock-operatic fake-orgasm vocals set against an entirely synthesized background of syndrums, stereo-panned percussion effects and a Moog playing that galloping bass line from "Do What You Wanna Do", "I Feel Love" was a masterpiece of mechano-eroticism . . . Summer sings about the pleasure of the flesh as if she was disembodied, or at least lying back and thinking of Munich . . . On the other hand, though, never before had a record throbbed so tremulously, so basely, yet at the same time been so rapturous that there was almost a holy purity about it.'

By the end of 1977, Summer's no.1 hit single was in third place for the most weeks at the top of the UK charts, sharing the number three position with David Soul's 'Don't Give Up On Us', Rod Stewart's 'I Don't Want To Talk About It/First Cut Is The Deepest' and Abba's 'Name Of The Game'. They all spent four weeks at number one in 1977.

'I Feel Love' was at no.7 for the Top 10 Best Selling UK Singles of 1977. It was arguably the first mass appeal disco song and its production techniques were well ahead of their time.

Continuum Encyclopedia Of Popular Music Of The World: Vol. VII (2005) *Europe* states that the combination of Moroder, Bellotte and Summer delivered lucrative results. First with the epic 'Love To Love You Baby' and then with 'I Feel Love'.

In *An Essential Guide To Music In The 1970s*, Summer's 'I Feel Love' was the song of the month for July 1977:

'The disco genre was now fighting off the challenge of punk rock for the attentions of the teenage pop market. However, one new release soon towered over all its competitors when Donna Summer finally sailed to the top of the British singles list with the dance floor favourite, "I Feel Love". This smash hit showcased the synthesizer sound as Giorgio Moroder supervised the creation of this modern pop classic. Summer's semi-orgasmic vocals are a key component in an item which must be a candidate for the best chart-topper of the decade.'

After the huge success of 'I Feel Love', the UK was introduced to the single 'Down, Deep Inside' from the movie *The Deep*, which Summer had recorded with the late John Barry earlier after 'Four Seasons Of Love'. 'Down, Deep Inside' was written by Summer and composed by Barry. It reached no.5, staying in that position for four weeks. 'Down, Deep Inside' first entered the UK chart at no.50 on 20th August 1977, hitting the no.5 spot in the week ending 10th September and staying in the UK chart for ten weeks in total (Silver certification on 1st October). 'Down, Deep Inside' was not released as a single in the US but it was a no.3 hit in the dance chart there. The single reached no.16 in South Africa, no.5 in Belgium, no.6 in The Netherlands and no.10 in Ireland.

The song has a smooth up-tempo melody with seductive lyrics. It still contained Summer's trademark orgasmic moaning but was more low-key than her previous disco efforts.

From the *Continuum Encyclopedia Of Popular Music Of The World: Vol.1* (2003):

'Seventies disco in particular dealt in material that could be regarded as soft-core pornography. Donna Summer's most explicit song, "Down, Deep Inside" (1977), contained the line "Something warm is sliding inside of me" and a faked mid-song orgasm.'

The original soundtrack album contained 'Down, Deep Inside (A Love Song)', a slowed down version of the single. Unfortunately the album has not been released in CD format for general sale to date, making the track hard to come by for fans, who need to find the original vinyl in order to hear the album. In 2010 the soundtrack of *The Deep* was marketed as a limited two CD edition of three thousand prints only! It was produced by Intrada under the label's 'special collection' releases.

In 1977 Casablanca also took the opportunity to place an advertisement promoting their 'goldmine' acts and releases. The classified advert titled 'Spring Into Summer: A Casablanca Record And Film Works Production', included ten full colour pages with three full pages dedicated to *The Deep*.

The advertisement in *Billboard* printed in May 21st 1977 announces:

'... coming attractions. Millions have read, seen or heard about it ... and now Casablanca has it on record.'

The record label's major star, Donna Summer, had one full page to herself, with the notes proclaiming:

'... all the heat of Summer.'

Summer's complete album covers were displayed in full colour – 'Love To Love You Baby', 'A Love Trilogy', 'Four Seasons Of Love' and 'I Remember Yesterday'. The success continued when the title track from the album 'I Remember Yesterday' was released as single, peaking at no.14 on the 22nd October 1977 in the UK.

The single 'Love's Unkind', which was not released in the US, first appeared in the UK chart on 3rd December 1977 and climbed to no.3 six weeks later. It was kept off the top spot by Wings' 'Mull Of Kintyre'. The single became one of Summer's biggest hits, staying in the charts for thirteen weeks. On 1st January 1978, 'Love's Unkind' was certified Gold by BPI. It was a no.2 hit in Ireland and in Germany, Austria and Belgium the single peaked at no.18.

The concept of 'I Remember Yesterday' was to represent time passing. It opened with retro-styled 'I Remember Yesterday' and finishes with the futuristic electro-funk of 'I Feel Love'. The tracks 'Take Me' and 'I Feel Love' feel out of place with the other tracks of album, which evoked the sounds of the 1940s to the 1970s. 'Take Me' represented the current vogue for disco while 'I Feel Love' represented the future. 'I Remember Yesterday' remains Summer's most successful album in terms of the UK chart position to the present day.

The album reintroduced Summer to the Top 20 of the album charts both in the UK and in the US, a position she had not held since 'Love To Love You Baby'. The album was successful around the world; it reached no.2 in Zimbabwe and no.3 in both Austria and Italy. It spent seventeen weeks in the chart in Norway, twenty-four weeks in Sweden and an astonishing seventy weeks in the French album chart!

Rolling Stone noted that Summer's sexual 'breathiness' had evolved musically. The magazine acknowledged that the project had totally succeeded in propelling Summer, as both singer and song writer, beyond disco.

Pete Waterman, one of the producers behind Summer's 1989 hit album, acknowledged that her vocal is one of the key elements that has made her a successful recording act, loved by many fans around the world.

Here he comments on what makes Summer unique:

'... Her voice! Fantastic voice! Very few people have really distinctive and brilliant voices and she does. Not just a brilliant voice but it's so Donna Summer. You would hear it, you just go "that's Donna Summer"!'.

This distinctive voice inspired the UK dance/trance act Inanna to pursue her dreams in music, discovering Summer's music through her elder sister who constantly played her records. She believes it's Summer's fabulous songs and vocal range which make her 'one of a kind'. Of all her work 'I Remember Yesterday' is Inanna's favourite.

Summer's voice is undoubtedly her greatest asset. One of Summer's peers, Gloria Gaynor, shared the same opinion as Waterman and Inanna, praising Summer's vocal ability:

'The uniqueness of Donna Summer is her voice quality. She has a very different voice ... when I hear ... I have no doubt that's Donna Summer. I don't care what she sings, I recognise her voice because she has a unique ... rich and strong voice.'

Every singer has their own distinctive vocal style. It is a matter of individual preference as to what sound you prefer. The timbre of a singer's voice is the characteristic that most easily distinguishes one from another.

Phil Ball said in his comprehensive work *The Music Instinct: How Music Works And Why We Can't Do Without It*:

'Timbre is arguably the most personal characteristic of music. When it comes to singing, timbre often holds the key to our preferences.'

Ball referred to the extremely distinctive vocal tones of legends such as Billie Holiday, Frank Sinatra, Nina Simone and Bob Dylan.

For example, Madeleine Peyroux's vocal on her 'Careless Love' album was remarkably reminiscent of jazz legend Billie Holiday. Donna Summer's timbre is certainly identifiable to listeners. No other acts at the time of writing can be identified as having a similar vocal timbre to that of Summer.

Not only was the vocal in 'I Remember Yesterday' praised, the album was recognised for its overall achievement. It was certified Gold in the US by RIAA in July 1977, and likewise in the UK by the BPI in August 1977. The album's concept and production means it still sounds fresh even today.

Just months after 'I Remember Yesterday', Summer recorded 'Once Upon

A Time', a Cinderella-style fairytale which was Summer's first double concept album (originally to be titled 'Cinderella'). 'Once Upon A Time' was the first album to credit all the songs to Summer, Moroder and Bellotte. The album was her first non-stop recording, which added an interesting effect to the production. The project did not take too long to record. In *Donna Summer: For The Record* Craig Halstead asserts that it took just four night-time sessions. Donna Summer and Pete Bellotte also wrote the entire lyrics within 'just a few days'.

The 1998 *The Encyclopedia Of Albums* claims that Summer was the most 'artistically ambitious' singer of the time. The album did not become Donna Summer's best selling project, although it did sell well when it was released.

The album received positive reviews, hitting no.26 and spending fifty-eight weeks in the US album chart and reaching no.24 in the UK with thirteen weeks in the chart. 'Once Upon A Time' reached no.9 in Norway and was also popular in Italy, reaching no.2. In France it managed a no.3 position and stayed in the chart for an amazing seventy-seven weeks!

In an interview carried out in 1982, Donna Summer said that, structurally, the album was the best she ever done at that time.

The disco tune 'I Love You' debuted in the US on 19th December 1977 and reached no.37 on the 28th January 1978. The romantic dance tune was first introduced to UK fans on 10th December 1977. Five weeks later the single reached no.10. Several weeks later another single was marketed. 'Rumour Has It' missed the Top 40 in the US, entering the chart on 4th March 1978 and reaching no.53, but it was a hit in the UK, reaching no.19 in the singles chart on 18th March 1978.

Interestingly the track 'Rumour Has It', recorded and written by Adele Adkins with Ryan Tedder in 2011, has a similar formula to Summer's tune. The chorus and the high energy beat focuses on the words of the title and is repeated many times whereas Summer focuses on the phrase 'There's a rumour, rumour has it'.

The team, Moroder, Bellotte and Summer revisited the style of their colossal hit 'I Feel Love' with 'Now I Need You', 'Working In The Midnight Shift' and also 'Queen For The Day' all making use of electronic programming. 'Queen For The Day' was recorded to produce a big, spacey sound. The music, once again, sounded ahead of its time. Chuck Eddy, in his 1997 book *The Accidental Evolution Of Rock 'N' Roll*, wrote that Summer used 'massive cathedral gospel and catacombic choruses' on 'Now I Need You'. Whether or not they were influenced by 'Now I Need You', this sound was recreated later by the group Enigma on their UK hit 1990 single 'Sadness Part 1'.

The album also introduced a new vocal direction for Donna Summer, with slightly different vocal tone stylings in songs such as 'Say Something Nice', 'Sweet Romance', 'Rumour Has It' and 'If You Got It, Flaunt It'. Listening to the album's four sides, Act One to Act Four, her vocal gradually changes, mimicking the metamorphosis of a young girl into a woman. 'Once Upon A Time' also introduced music fans to the sentimental side of Summer with two slow tunes, 'A Man Like You' and 'Sweet Romance', both beautifully performed.

'Once Upon A Time' was a creative double concept album that marked a high point on Summer's musical journey. In *Donna Summer: Her Life And Music,* Josiah Howard writes:

'In 2001, *Mojo* magazine placed it among the Top 100 Soul Albums of All Time.'

The album exceeded its aim, which was to provide music fans with a modern musical fairytale love story. Beautifully put together, the lyrics tell the story of a girl who goes from having nothing, leading a lonesome life, to finally finding the love that she had been waiting for and living 'Happily Ever After'. Its success earned it Gold status in the US, UK and Canada.

Summer also released several compilations, which were well received by the public. 'The Greatest Hits Of Donna Summer' album was only released in the UK on the GTO label and reached no.4 in the chart. The hits package was well received by Summer's UK listeners and stayed in the album chart for eighteen weeks, receiving Gold certification from the BPI on the 6th December 1977.

A single from 'The Greatest Hits Of Donna Summer' titled 'Back In Love Again' peaked at no.29 on the 6th May 1978 in the UK. The song was originally from 'I Remember Yesterday'. 'Back In Love Again' combines Donna Summer's trademark of disco beats with a dash of the 1960s. In Europe, a compilation album titled 'Donna Summer: Greatest Hits' was also marketed. This package was an added bonus for devotees of the 'Queen Of Disco', including the European hits 'Virgin Mary', 'Lady Of The Night' and 'The Hostage'. It was only available outside Europe by import.

In 1978, Summer recorded three songs for the soundtrack album 'Thank God It's Friday' including 'Last Dance', 'With Your Love' and a cover of the 1960s hit 'Je T'aime (Moi Non Plus)' as a special bonus track for the album. The cover lasted fifteen minutes and forty-seven seconds, following in the footsteps of 'Love To Love You Baby' and 'Try Me, I Know We Can Make It'. The song was released as a seven inch single in Brazil and other parts of the globe but not in the US or the UK. The twelve inch promo was in fact pressed in 1977 before it went into the soundtrack project.

Although Donna Summer recorded a few tracks for the project, she also co-wrote a disco number with Bruce Sudano and Joe Esposito for the group Sunshine called 'Take It To The Zoo', which was included in the 'Thank God It's Friday' album.

The single from the soundtrack 'Last Dance' entered the US Hot 100 on the 13th May 1978. It was a success in the US, reaching the Top 40 on the 3rd June and making it to no.3. Shockingly it only managed no.70 in the UK on the 10th June 1978. 'Last Dance' re-entered the UK chart but still only managed to climb to no.51 by 24th June 1978. Even though the single was not as popular as in the US, 'Last Dance' managed to stay in the UK chart for nine weeks. In France it peaked at no.2 for five weeks; it reached no.3 in New Zealand, spending ten weeks in the chart. 'Last Dance' hit the no.8 spot in Holland and Belgium and stayed for eleven weeks in their singles chart.

'Last Dance' is considered to be the first track that Summer sang using her full vocal range. Everybody in the record company, and Summer herself, knew that it was time to make a change in Donna Summer's singing style. 'Last Dance' is also considered one of the first disco songs to feature slow tempo parts.

In the same year she released a live recording titled 'Live And More', another exciting development for her fans and her career. The concert album was recorded live at the Universal Amphitheater, Los Angeles in 1978.

'Live And More' reached the top of the chart in the US and no.16 in the UK. The album also included a studio recording of a cover of 'MacArthur Park'. It spent a colossal seventy-five weeks in the US charts and a more modest sixteen weeks in the UK chart.

'Live And More' was her first live double album and Summer broadened her musical repertoire by experimenting with more jazzy numbers such as 'The Man I Love' and 'I Got It Bad And That Ain't Good', performed as the 'My Man Medley'. Summer had performed the medley as early as 1976 at Don Kirscher's Rock Concert.

'The Man I Love', a popular standard by George Gershwin, was part of the 1927 score for the Gershwin anti-war musical satire called *Strike Up The Band*, but the song was removed from the 1930 version of the show. The late 'love songbird' Helen Morgan was reported to be the first to make the song popular. It was subsequently recorded by the jazz legends Billie Holiday, Ella Fitzgerald, Sarah Vaughn and by British icon, Kate Bush. 'I Got It Bad And That Ain't Good' was introduced in 1941 by the late Ivie Anderson in the West Coast musical *Jump For Joy*. In October of that year

Duke Ellington recorded the track featuring Anderson with Johnny Hodges and it became a hit. The song has also been covered by stars such as Nina Simone, Frank Sinatra and Peggy Lee, each with their own particular interpretation.

On 'Live And More' Summer covered Barbra Streisand's song 'The Way We Were'. However another cover, Leon Russell's 'A Song For You' that reportedly received good reviews, was not included for the live album. Fans were surprised and thrilled to hear a beautiful new song that was dedicated to her daughter, titled 'Mimi's Song'. Summer ended by introducing her daughter to the audience at the concert.

The studio single 'MacArthur Park' went to no.1 in the US, her first no.1 in her native land. It hit the top spot ten weeks after entering the chart on the 9th September 1978 at no.85. 'MacArthur Park' was also well received in the UK, debuting on 14th October 1978 and climbing to no.5 position two weeks later. It was a big hit for Summer, staying in the US Top 100 for nineteen weeks and ten weeks in the UK chart. 'MacArthur Park' remains a favourite among fans around the world.

'MacArthur Park' reached no.1 in Canada on the 29th November 1978 and stayed in the charts for eighteen weeks. In New Zealand the single peaked at no.4, spending ten weeks in the chart. It reached no.9 in Holland and no.11 in Belgium.

As Ian Birch wrote in *Melody Maker* in October 1978:

'A gloriously daft string quartet and beefy choir stand Donna as she warbles about cakes in the rain and so forth. Then – yeees! – a synth drum twitches into life, Donna screams "aaah!" and we're off . . .'

'MacArthur Park' was written by Jimmy Webb and it was first recorded by Richard Harris in 1968. The Four Tops recorded it in 1971, their version entering the *Billboard* chart on the 11th September that year. The tune has been performed or recorded by singers as diverse as Frank Sinatra, Tony Bennett, Ed Ames, The Three Degrees, Elaine Paige, Andy Williams, Diana Ross & The Supremes and Liza Minnelli. It has also received the big band jazz treatment by Maynard Ferguson, Stan Kenton and Woody Herman. But the track is best known to pop music lovers as Summer's 1978 disco hit.

Paul Gambaccini enjoyed 'MacArthur Park' musically, especially the way Summer pronounces the words 'MacArthur Park', which he describes as 'cute'. As for the song, he thinks Summer's version is great. The original was excellent and because of the charismatic melody it delivers, the covers by other acts also sound good.

In an interview with Malaysian record producer and Summer fan Roslan

Aziz, he says he first heard of 'MacArthur Park' through a local live band performance:

'... I was a teenager in school when I heard this mind-blowing song played by the then popular club band Discovery. I was blown away ... the song arrangement was superb!'

Aziz later asked one of the band who the song was by, and later got hold of the tune. Aziz was overwhelmed by what he had heard and Summer instantly became one of his favourite artists; her upbeat melody was played in every hot spot in town. Aziz has a huge amount of respect for Summer's talent and 'MacArthur Park' still inspires him today. He claims to feel 'rejuvenated' every time he listens to the song's introduction.

Malaysian star Francissca Peter says Summer's live version of 'MacArthur Park' was remarkable and no other act has performed a better version. Summer delivers the song full of emotion and it was her live version that Peter loved, with a medley of songs that showcase her energy and powerful voice. The melody that Peter describes was probably the 'MacArthur Park Suite', a medley of 'MacArthur Park', 'One Of A Kind', 'Heaven Knows' and 'MacArthur Park (reprise)'.

Dance music producer Tim Letteer said that 'MacArthur Park' made him fall in love with Donna Summer's voice. Letteer enjoyed her live version and the 'MacArthur Park Suite' was 'to die for'. The first album Letteer owned by Summer was 'Live And More' and following this he started to collect Summer's recordings from around that era.

During the 1970s, disco dominated the *Billboard* charts. In 1978, there were nineteen singles that reached no.1 besides 'MacArthur Park'. The non-disco singles included 'Three Times A Lady' by the Commodores, 'With A Little Luck' by Wings and 'Miss You' by The Rolling Stones. The Bee Gees dominated that year with 'Night Fever' and Andy Gibb's solo work 'Shadow Dancing' spent seven weeks in the chart. Chic's 'Le Freak' finished the year at no.1.

Giorgio Moroder told Josiah Howard, author of *Donna Summer: Her Life And Music*, that even though 'MacArthur Park' was not his song, it was probably his best work with Summer; it was one of his and Pete Bellotte's favourites. He told how the idea to re-work the song was in his mind for years and knew that the melody could become a catchy number. Moroder was justifiably pleased with the outcome.

The hit singer of 'Never Can Say Goodbye', Gloria Gaynor, also has 'MacArthur Park' down as her favourite Summer track. According to Gaynor, it really shows off her voice and she did a wonderful job with the song. Gaynor also said that the track is one of the few worthy of Summer's talent.

In the 1978 Christmas issue of *Melody Maker*, the magazine ran a chart of the year's greatest-selling albums. Donna Summer was one of the fifteen biggest selling artists in that year.

The 1999 *Melody Maker History Of 20ᵗʰ Century Popular Music* comments: 'The list of artists made it seem as if punk had never happened: The Bee Gees (Saturday Night Fever), Abba (The Album), ELO, Fleetwood Mac, Boney M, Genesis, Kate Bush, Thin Lizzy, Bob Dylan, Meat Loaf (Bat Out Of Hell), Rod Stewart, The Rolling Stones, Blondie, Donna Summer and Elton John ... the best-selling album artists ...'

Billboard presented the ten top artists in the US for 1978. These were Andy Gibb, The Bee Gees, Donna Summer, Barry Manilow, Chic, Olivia Newton-John, Billy Joel, Player, Paul McCartney and Wings and Foreigner.

On the 20th January 1979, a catchy song called 'Heaven Knows' peaked at no.4 in US, achieving Gold status. This track originally appeared as part of 'The MacArthur Park Suite', a medley that was first heard on the 'Live And More' album in 1978. The released seven inch 'Heaven Knows' was recorded with a male group Brooklyn Dreams and stayed in the Top 100 for nineteen weeks. 'Heaven Knows' was later released in the UK reaching no.34 on the 10th March 1979, spending eight weeks in the chart. The single reached no.2 in Canada achieving Gold, no.15 in Australia and no.14 in New Zealand.

In the 1990s, the album 'Live And More' was re-issued but fans were disappointed to find that the 'MacArthur Park Suite' was replaced by the twelve inch version of the single 'Down, Deep Inside'.

The reason for the change was the requirement for the re-issued package to be contained in a single compact disc. However, the Japanese re-issue did include the 'MacArthur Park Suite' with slightly shorter time. Fans were disappointed that the original front cover artwork was omitted. Instead, the original artwork from the inside of the gate-fold album cover was used as the new front cover of the re-issued compact disc. The accompanying insert was also very limited.

In a question and answer session for *Billboard*, Summer told Craig Rosen that it was often said that disco acts couldn't sing, that it was all down to the technology and the producer's magic touch.

In *Off The Record: An Oral History Of Popular Music*, Joe Smith wrote that Summer observed that following the release of 'Love To Love You Baby', only a handful of music fans thought the star could really sing because of the whispering technique that she used on the song. However, once she finally opened up her vocals to full throttle it became clear that she really could sing, and then some!

The idea that disco acts can't sing is clearly a little ridiculous. Famous disco star, Gloria Gaynor, agrees that the public can hear whether an act can sing well or not, and music fans can make up their own minds as to whether or not the producer contributes more to the sound than the singer's vocal. In her own words, during a conversation with me on 15th May 2010, Gaynor said:

'Certainly none of the reasons were because the artist couldn't sing. There are many people out there who can sing; why would a producer put someone onto the recording who can't? Nowadays . . . you do get that sometimes. I think that they chose the person who can't necessarily sing that well because their forte is being a performer rather than being an actual singer.'

Gaynor, like Summer, is beyond all doubt a great singer. Unlike Summer, Gaynor made use of her full vocal range from the outset. Summer, on the other hand, limited her style to suit the image created by the record label and the 'Love To Love You Baby' concept. Summer's background in musical theatre trained her to be a performer and a singer and it was time for her to demonstrate the experience she had gained in Europe. Gaynor suggested that maybe the producers thought that disco fans were more interested in the music then the singer.

Summer's live performances changed this perception permanently. Casablanca knew it was important for her to produce a live album in order to showcase her vocal abilities. 'Live And More' was certified Platinum in America on 19th October 1978 and the album went Gold in the UK on 16th November 1978. In Canada, the album achieved Double Platinum on 1st March 1979.

In the late 1970s, Summer was at her zenith. Her star never burned quite as brightly again. The disco movement, of which she was queen, was at its peak.

In *The Virgin Story Of Rock 'N' Roll* (1995) the writer Paul Du Noyer wrote:

'1978 was one those years when rock styles that had come to the fore in the previous twelve months proved their styling power and became part of the establishment. Punk and New Wave continued to thrive, with bands emerging and returning to obscurity on a monthly basis, while disco and disco-influenced pop continued to be well presented by Donna Summer, Abba and Boney M – the fact that these acts had been the best-sellers of the previous year too goes to show how much pop music stood still in 1978.'

The thrill of that time is captured in Summer's autobiography, *Ordinary Girl: The Journey*. The year 1978 was a remarkable time for Summer, winning her first Grammy for the Best Female R&B Vocal Performance for the song 'Last Dance', taken from her first film role. The song also won a Golden Globe and had been nominated for the Academy Awards that year in the Best Song category. In 1979, 'MacArthur Park' was awarded a Grammy Award for the female category of Best Pop Vocal Performance. Summer said she was thrilled to perform 'Last Dance' at the Academy Awards ceremony in spring of 1979.

In *And Party Every Day: The Inside Story Of Casablanca Records*, Larry Harris observes that Summer delivered a series of huge hits for Casablanca. Again, 1978 was a great year with the success of 'Live And More' album, not forgetting the singles 'MacArthur Park' and 'Heaven Knows', both hits from the live album. By 1979 Summer 'had unquestionably reached superstar status'.

Summer continued recording live with the track 'Mimi's Song' for the album 'Music For UNICEF Concert: A Gift Of Song' released in 1979. Summer donated the royalties from the song to UNICEF. Elsewhere in the world, *New Zealand Music Charts 1966–1996 Singles* by Dean Scapolo, has Summer at no.12 for the Top 20 Artists 1978, no.1 for the Top 20 Artist 1979 and no.12 for the Top 40 Artists of the 1970s.

Donna Summer continued her creative work with the team. The 1970s disco phenomenon saw Summer deliver hit after hit. She also began to explore a new musical direction, celebrating dance floor rhythms with more rock influences introduced into her new sound.

5

The Hot Beep Goes On

The 1970s was unquestionably a demanding time for Donna Summer, being constantly in and out of the studio.

A new project 'Bad Girls' was released in 1979, a double concept non-stop music recording. The double Platinum album debuted in the *Billboard* album chart on the 12th May 1979. The project received the reaction Casablanca wanted – no.1 and in the chart for forty-nine weeks. In the UK album chart, 'Bad Girls' debuted on the 2nd June 1979 and peaked at no.23, staying for twenty-three weeks in total, with Silver certification by the BPI. The album was, not surprisingly, a hit globally. In parts of Europe the project entered the Top 5; a better result than in the UK. 'Bad Girls' was a no.3 hit album in New Zealand. In Japan, it charted at no.9 and even did well in Zimbabwe's chart, reaching no.15.

Billboard noted that Summer was; 'The hottest female vocalist' in the entertainment world and was 'prolific'. The release of 'Bad Girls', her third double album, ensured that Summer 'remained consistently strong'. The magazine reviewed the album on 5th May 1979:

'...("Bad Girls") represents somewhat of a departure, in that the first two sides at least are more rock-oriented. Summer's vocals not only are more powerful and sexy but multi-dimensional. The music strength carries over to all four sides. Based on a "bad girl" concept, Summer comes across in a seductive vein in vocal delivery and even through the album's graphics ... The musicians behind her supply her with pulsating and energetic fire-power with some guest players also helping.'

'Hot Stuff' was the first hit single from the album. The single debuted into the Top 40 on the 28th April 1979, peaking at no.1 in the US. It reached no.11 on the 2nd June 1979 in the UK. The song was a new departure for Donna Summer, having more of a rock-edged influence including guitar and an upbeat dance tune which had not previously been used in any of Summer's single releases. 'Hot Stuff' was certified Platinum by the RIAA and remained at no.1 on the *Billboard* Hot 100 chart for three consecutive weeks in 1979. It was a commercially successful project and critics praised it as one of the best Summer albums. From disco, Summer had moved effortlessly to a more rock-orientated concept. That the tunes were great was undeniable, but some fans who loved Summer for her 'disco' sound were a bit disappointed with their diva's transformation. They thought the song was too rock-flavoured and missed Summer's sexy, smooth, camp disco touch. Naturally, fans had a range of views, with many loving the new sound.

Paul Gambaccini recalls the time when he listened to WNEW Radio in New York while DJ Dave Herman introduced 'Hot Stuff' to his listeners. Gambaccini said Herman thought that because the song featured a hard rock guitar solo, it was a rock record. Paul Gambaccini said Herman introduced 'Hot Stuff' by saying:

'I'm now going to play you, which will surprise you ... it's by Donna Summer, but I think it's rock!'

Gambaccini explained that, of course, the radio station phones lit up with callers both praising and complaining! Dissatisfied callers asked how Dave Herman dared to contaminate the airwaves with disco music! But it was such quality material that made the disco-cum-rock concept that 'Hot Stuff' became popular in both genres.

The album also borrowed the technique of 'Once A Upon A Time' by having a continuous set of sentimental songs. This time, fans were treated to four slow-motion melodies, 'On My Honor', 'All Through The Night', 'There Will Always Be A You' and 'My Baby Understands'. These were emotional tunes from Donna Summer.

In an interview in 1994 with Capital Radio in the UK, Summer said that there were many of her songs that she loved listening to now and then, but the ballad 'There Will Always Be A You' was one of the favourites that she had composed and co-written, as well as 'I Feel Love' and 'Hot Stuff'. The beautiful, romantic tune was written for her sweetheart at that time, Bruce Sudano, now her adored husband.

Summer was now firmly established as a major star in the US. 'Bad Girls' was a no.1 (US Platinum single) and another single, 'Dim All The Lights' shot to no.2 (US Gold single) in the *Billboard* chart. However, the two singles were less successful in the UK market with 'Bad Girls' making it to no.14 (BPI certified it Silver) and 'Dim All The Lights' only managing a no.29 position. But 'Bad Girls' was a hit around the world, entering the Top 10 in Canada, New Zealand, Switzerland, Norway, Belgium and Holland.

The success of 'Hot Stuff', 'Dim All The Lights' and 'Bad Girls' overshadowed the other dance tracks on the album; 'Our Love', 'Sunset People' and 'Lucky' are solid up-tempo tracks with good lyrics, but did not receive the same acclaim.

Interestingly, 'Bad Girls' was rejected by Neil Bogart. After a demo presentation to Bogart, he decided that Cher should record 'Bad Girls' as he felt it wasn't the right material for the Queen Of Disco, but Summer was having none of it and decided to shelve the song as she had written it for herself.

In *Ordinary Girl: The Journey,* Summer famously tells how when Bogart suggested that the track should be offered to Cher, Summer stormed out of the office with her demo tape. She had nothing against Cher but 'Bad Girls' was her song!

Summer explained that although she loved Cher, 'Bad Girls' was for her and not anyone else! She had based the lyrics of the song on an actual event. A young secretary in the PR department of her record label was mistakenly identified as a 'working girl' while she went out for her lunch break. A police officer made the error while she was walking in an area known for its street girls. Summer was so annoyed that she wrote the lyrics for the now famous track with Eddie Hokenson, Bruce Sudano and Joe 'Bean' Esposito. Now she would have to put it aside and wait before recording it. Alice Echols in *Hot Stuff: Disco And The Remaking Of American Culture* (2010) says that Summer recorded the 'Bad Girls' demo in 1977.

Some years later, as many fans may know, the demo was found by engineer Steve Smith in a studio in Los Angeles. Later the team brushed it up and added the now classic Summer 'toot-toots' and 'beep-beeps'. It was presented to Neil Bogart and was finally approved for recording.

Paul Gambaccini notes that there was a song in 1960s called 'Bang Bang' by The Joe Cuba Sextet with some similarities to Summer's catchy 'beep-beeps'. When I did my own research and listened to 'Bang Bang', the phrase 'ahhh beep-beep' can be heard at ten to twenty-five seconds and repeated at one minute thirty-seven to one minute fifty-six seconds. They sang it towards the end of the song in some of their live performances.

The Puerto Rican musician passed away in 2009. Gambaccini said it was either one of the world's most amazing coincidences, or 'Bad Girls' borrowed 'ahhh beep-beep' from this song. Continuing, Gambaccini suggested it didn't matter due to the fact that most people are not familiar with Latin music. It worked well and music fans took it as an original idea.

The original, rare demo version of the track (which did not feature the 'beep-beeps') was included in the release of a special Deluxe Edition in 2003. 'Bad Girls' sounded raw and funky with rock influences. The demo delivered the sound of a live studio band recording. Creative, full of attitude and with a soulful feel, it is a must-listen for all music lovers; a true tour de force! In November 2004, a year after the remastered 'Bad Girls' was marketed, 'Hot Stuff' was ranked at no.103 in *Rolling Stone* magazine's list of The 500 Greatest Songs Of All Time.

Gavin Martin wrote in the *NME* in May 1979:

'Dirty, aggressive, she-slut Donna, on heat and working up an appetite: the guitar solo is excruciating, but it's still an irresistible single. Donna's not just a sex symbol, y'know.'

Talking in *The Hot Ones* radio interview in 1983, Summer said 'Hot Stuff' was a real hot number because the fans would demand she sing it three or four times in a row. The energetic star would jump all over the stage, then at the end of performances she felt 'zapped' and had to just lie down on the floor. She said she realised that she was too old to be doing this, after all she wasn't seventeen anymore!

Many years later, in 2010, *Mojo* magazine placed 'Bad Girls' at No.55 in their list of The 70 Best Soul Albums Of The 1970s! From 'The 70 Best Soul Albums Of '70s! Soul 70' by Jon Savage in his review of the album:

'Summer's third double album in two years, and her imperial move with two US no.1's – "Hot Stuff" and "Bad Girls" – a side of ballads and three tracks of pure electronic dance music: "Our Love", "Lucky" and "Sunset People". No.1 in the US for six weeks: disco at its zenith.'

A stunning success! Abandoning the mellifluous vocal styling, Summer was propelled away from the seductive disco oeuvre. A stronger woman here, she still delivers the love interest but this time the songstress is a dance-rock-R'N'B sexy chick! For the first time, Summer was the sole composer and lyricist for 'Dim All The Lights', 'There Will Always Be A You' and 'My Baby Understands'.

There were many talented individuals involved in 'Bad Girls'. The three musketeers – Summer, Moroder and Bellotte – this time had separate song credits, and other names appeared alongside including Harold Faltermeyer, Keith Forsey, Eddie Hokenson, Bruce Sudano, Joe 'Bean' Esposito, Bob Conti and Bruce Roberts, all helping to make 'Bad Girls' such a success! It was a definitive moment in Summer's musical development.

Summer's career was highly productive at this point. Fans were presented with another album 'On The Radio: Greatest Hits Volumes I & II'. Everything was going well, with her work adored by her fans, music lovers and the media. 'On The Radio: Greatest Hits Volumes I & II', a well packaged and designed compilation of disco hits, was in the US album chart for thirty-nine weeks (double Platinum) and in the UK equivalent for twenty-two weeks (Gold).

Three singles were marketed from this album. The first single, out before the album was released, was a duet with Barbra Streisand. The song entered the US Top 40 chart on the 27th October 1979 and was called 'No More Tears (Enough Is Enough)'. Listeners instantly fell in love with the tune and it later went to no.1 in the US and success followed soon across the Atlantic. On the 1st December, 'No More Tears (Enough Is Enough)' hit no.3 in Britain. In the UK, the track was competing with 'When You're In Love With A Beautiful Woman' by Dr. Hook at no.1 and the Queen hit 'Crazy Little Thing Called Love' at no.2. The following week, ending 8th December 1979, the two 'queens' were blocked from the top spot by a huge 'brick wall'. Fans tried to take Summer and Streisand to the top, but the Police's 'Walking On The Moon' landed at no.1 first and Pink Floyd sat at no.2 with 'Another Brick In The Wall'.

Even though the single did not get to no.1 in the UK, 'No More Tears (Enough Is Enough)' presented Donna Summer not only as a winning solo recording act but also as a successful collaborator, able to hold her own against the megastars of the entertainment industry. It was tears of joy for Summer and Streisand's record labels. 'No More Tears (Enough Is Enough)' entered the Top 5 in the *Billboard* chart while 'Dim All The Lights' was still at no.2. Adored by fans, 'Dim All The Lights' was possibly disadvantaged by the rapid climb up the charts of the duet. Although it was of course fantastic that 'No More Tears (Enough Is Enough)' was a no.1, Summer wanted to get to the top with her own composition. Not for vanity or to prove to the industry that she could, but for personal satisfaction. Paul Gambaccini's outlook on 'Dim All The Lights', which starts with a slow tempo and gradually introduces a dance flavour, was that it was a great example of disco composition. This showed Summer as more mature and creative in her productions. As Giorgio Moroder said in Josiah Howard's *Donna Summer: Her Life And Music,* by 1979 Summer started getting involved in the production and arrangement side of things.

The duet from two of the hottest names in music needed to be a US no.1 hit. Casablanca could not gamble and wait, they wanted to take advantage of the high chart profile of Summer. The release of 'No More Tears (Enough Is Enough)' before the album was necessary at that point. Recording the duet offered Summer valuable experience, interesting memories of the recording session and a massive hit record. Artistically speaking, it was noted that the two divas had some differing points of view in the studio.

In the words of the Haskins and Stifle, authors of *Donna Summer: An Unauthorized Biography*:

'There was a great deal of gossip surrounding the recording session ... Rumour had it that the session was a near-disastrous collision of two monstrous egos, with each singer bent on imposing her own will ... that might sound more interesting than what really happened.'

The author of the biography says that Donna Summer dismissed the rumours, saying she found the work process 'interesting'.

There were two hardworking stars in the studio with independent opinions and creative ideas. Whenever artists work together there will be different ideas, but this is not necessarily a negative thing. At Streisand's request, the song was composed with consideration for her natural territory. The slow introduction and the lyrics linked the song to Streisand's solo album 'Wet' and enabled it to sit comfortably with the other tracks on that album. At the time of recording both artists were firmly established stars. The final product produced by the late Paul Jabara and Bruce Roberts complemented both stars' natural styles although the song, as a disco number, was comfortable territory for Summer. Streisand was certainly not on familiar ground here, and observers no doubt formed their own opinions of the relationship between the two divas. As several rare studio session demo recordings that have been circulated among some fans and two short sessions obtained by me prove, the stars were professional. Fans will have to make their own minds up about what was heard on record.

In *Ordinary Girl: The Journey*, Summer states that working and performing with one of her 'true heroes' was an amazing experience and an 'opportunity and privilege' that she could cherish for a lifetime.

Summer's fans have been surprised that Streisand has not to date given much of an outlook on the recording. They have noted that, in a conversation between Streisand and her audience about her duets during Streisand's 2001 'Barbra: Timeless – The Final Concert', 'No More Tears (Enough Is Enough)' was not mentioned. Streisand talked at length about her work with other stars. She has recorded with: Celine Dion 'Tell Him' in 1997, Barry Gibb 'Guilty' in 1980, even Neil Diamond 'You Don't Bring Me Flowers' in 1978. Perhaps Streisand saw the tune primarily as a Summer work and, as a middle of the road 'easy listening' act, she might not feel that it was an important work for her fans. In a publication, *Donna Summer: For The Record* (2011) by Craig Halstead, Streisand allegedly said she enjoyed her work with Summer. She liked the result and said it was 'sort of the other side of a love song'. It was not clear where and when the quote was taken. According to Streisand, her experience with Summer 'was the least painful of all the duets' she has released. Streisand said that perhaps because both the divas felt 'intimidated by each other' she and Summer were on their 'best behaviour'!

For the mischievous, Clay Cane from *Pride Source* once asked Donna Summer if a Streisand drag queen had a battle with a Summer drag queen what advice would Summer give to 'her' drag act? The star said 'go' for 'Streisand's' nose! So if fans really want the two great stars to fight then let's get frocks out!

Barbra Streisand has had many hits in her long and glittering career. She is quite within her rights to talk, or not talk, about whatever bits of her career she wishes to. The bottom line is that the track was recorded by two music icons, both strong personalities. It is a feminist celebration, a hymn to independent strong-willed women everywhere which also happens to have a great beat. The track is a perennial favourite in clubs all over the world.

Twenty-four years later *The Telegraph* produced a special feature on the 50 Best Duets Ever, with a poll of the finest collaborations from pop history. 'No More Tears (Enough Is Enough)' came in at no.43. From the *The Telegraph* Online dated 8th November 2003:

'With a running time of 11.40, this rapturous meeting of divas is rarely played from beginning to end, but it's worth listening to every second ... Key moment: after what seems like a lifetime of tear-drenched lamentation, the duo throw off their ballady chains and go forth with the first exultant "Enough is Enough" chorus.'

Enthusiasm for Summer's 'No More Tears (Enough Is Enough)' continues. Malaysian singer Salamiah Hassan, stated during an interview that when she hears Summer's tunes, the songs bring back memories close to her heart. The lyrics of 'No More Tears (Enough Is Enough)' are meaningful to her and the Malaysian singer shared it with her daughter, also a popular singer. Hassan added that Donna Summer is a soulful singer and was her idol.

After the success of 'No More Tears (Enough Is Enough)', Summer released 'On The Radio'. Initially Summer had wanted Sudano to write the lyrics to Moroder's great melody. However, Sudano apparently didn't really feel inspired by the music and took so long to get round to composing the lyric that Summer just wrote them herself and then recorded the tune.

'On The Radio' debuted in American chart on 26th January 1980, reached no.5 and stayed for seventeen weeks in the *Billboard* chart. In the UK, the track first entered the chart on 16th February 1980 and a week later peaked at no.32 (spending six weeks in the chart). The final single from 'On The Radio: Greatest Hits Volumes I & II', titled 'Sunset People', was released only for the UK market and debuted on the 21st June 1980, reaching no.46 and staying in the chart for five weeks.

'On The Radio' also featured in the soundtrack to the film *Foxes* in 1980. The album included the extended soundtrack mix and a sentimental version of the song. 'On The Radio: Greatest Hits Volumes I & II' was produced by Moroder and Bellotte. The albums featured a non-stop mix that slickly blended the tracks into each other. The electronic synthesizer sound was displayed at its best in a pure celebration of disco.

Recalling the disco era with its novel electronic sound, Juan Atkins, one of the originators of techno music, told *Bleep 43* magazine it was Summer and Moroder's use of electronics in their productions that got him interested in the sounds; it was a new and different idea at that time. Summer's album sleeve mentions 'The Microcomposer'. It was a music technology at that time with an upbeat and catchy electronic sound that had been produced for Summer's music. Atkins saw Summer's song not just as a 'disco' melody. It was a *sound* that he enjoyed. He argues that 'Sunset People' has a similar sound to that of 'I Feel Love'. Although Summer was his idol, he was also heavily influenced by Giorgio Moroder's productions. While he loved 'Sunset People' and 'I Feel Love', Atkins also had a big crush on Summer! Atkins told Dan Bean of *Bleep 43*:

'Those were great tracks. There's something about 'I Feel Love', it's quite melancholy. When I hear it, it makes me feel a certain way.'

Atkins two favourite tracks were included in 'On The Radio: Greatest Hits Volumes I & II'. The album was full of gigantic hits such as 'Love To Love You Baby', 'Try Me, I Know We Can Make It' and 'Bad Girls'. The disco mix B-side finished with 'Sunset People', fantastic for DJs and Summer lovers! The C-side came with two new extended pieces. Most importantly, Summer was credited exclusively for the album cover concept. The album was certified double Platinum in the US and Gold in the UK. In 1984 'On The Radio: Greatest Hits Volumes I & II' was re-issued on Casablanca Records.

Chuck Miller, in *Warman's American Records, 1950–2000: Identification And Price Guide* (2001), describes Summer as the 'most popular female disco singer'; from the 'sultry beat' of the single 'Love To Love You Baby' and through all her hits, Miller rates Summer's songs as 'must-hear'. Her songs were not just huge disco hits but 'I Feel Love', 'Hot Stuff', 'Bad Girls', and 'On The Radio' also represented the beginning of 'successful forays into techno-pop and social commentary'.

By the late 1970s, Summer had scored three no.1 albums in the US. The albums were; 'Live And More' (1978), recorded at the Universal Amphitheatre, showcasing Summer's talents as a live performer. 'Bad Girls' (1979), introduced fans to Summer's dance-pop-rock flavours and finally 'On The Radio: Greatest Hits Volumes I & II' (1979), an anthology of her selected disco hits.

Summer's highest Top 10 UK album position was at no.3 with 'I Remember Yesterday' (1977) and 'The Greatest Hits Of Donna Summer' (1977) at no.4. Most of her albums reached the Top 40 in the UK in the 1970s. Her albums reached higher positions in other parts of Europe. 'Four Seasons Of Love', 'I Remember Yesterday' and 'Bad Girls' were Top 5 hits in Norway, Austria, Italy and France. As for 'Love To Love You Baby', 'A Love Trilogy', 'I Remember Yesterday' and 'Bad Girls', they were all Top 10 hits in France, Norway, Sweden, Austria and Italy.

This period is acknowledged by both fans and critics as Summer's most prolific and successful period, commercially and artistically. It included the recording of a successful film theme for *The Deep*. With a string of US no.1 albums, Summer's singles also achieved top positions in the chart. She scored four no.1 hit singles in US with 'MacArthur Park', 'Hot Stuff', 'Bad Girls' and 'No More Tears (Enough Is Enough)'. Summer had only one no.1 single in UK with 'I Feel Love'. *The Rolling Stone Encyclopedia Of Rock And Roll* asserts out that 'I Feel Love', her first synthesiser recording, had extended Donna Summer's stylistic range. In 1999 the song was placed at no.36 for the Top 100 Singles Of All Time in the UK.

Nowadays, ratings can be based on physical sales, airplay or Internet downloads. Summer's songs may not always make the *Billboard* Top 40, but most of her tunes still climb to the top spot of the *Billboard* dance chart.

As reported in *Record Collector* magazine in 'Special Pressings Price Guide' released in May 1990:

'Donna Summer had a lot to smile about during the late Seventies when her disco anthems made her one of that era's most successful female singers.'

Her popularity led to titles such as 'Queen Of Disco', 'Goddess Of Sex Rock' and 'Lady Of Love' being bestowed upon her. It is often said that Gloria Gaynor sang the first disco record. Gaynor recorded the hit song 'Never Can Say Goodbye' in 1974 which charted at no.9 on the *Billboard* chart and stayed in the US Top 40 as long as ten weeks. It was a no.2 hit in the UK, enjoying thirteen weeks in the charts. 'Never Can Say Goodbye' was also the first disco number to be played on AM radio in the US. Gaynor had already experienced success as a disco artist while Donna Summer was in Germany. In the UK TV programme *When Disco Ruled The World*, Gaynor's record was noted to be the first disco set that consisted of three tracks segued into non-stop play. The same concept was used on Summer's

A-side of the 'A Love Trilogy' album. Gaynor said the idea to have contin-uous recording was developed by her, the producer and Tom Moulton, the album's mixer. The segued recording had encouraged DJs to play the record in clubs and this ultimately led to the extended remixes seen later, including Donna Summer's long play 'Love To Love You Baby'. Gloria Gaynor recalls her 1974 recording:

'I thought it was a wonderful idea because I love to dance. At that time a normal recording was about three minutes at the most ... if you are a dancer, three minutes is not nearly enough to dance. So when you have this recording with three songs ... non-stop you have an opportunity to really dance to your satisfaction.'

That same year 'The Hustle' by Van McCoy became a no.1 hit in the US and reached no.3 in the UK. The song 'Rock Your Baby' by George McCrae, which represented a softer disco sound, was hailed as the first national anthem of disco and started the disco craze. The song went to no.1 in the US and in the UK and was a global success. With the new sound gaining popularity, many more performers and producers recorded disco albums. 'I Will Survive', by Gloria Gaynor, is arguably the greatest disco classic of all time. The single was a no.1 hit both in US and the UK in 1979. Summer performed 'I Will Survive' live at the Grammy Awards on 27th February 1980 at Shrine Auditorium, Los Angeles as part of a medley alongside country singer Kenny Rogers. When it was referred to during an interview in May 2010, Gaynor said she was honoured to hear that Donna Summer had sung her hit single at the high-profile ceremony. It was the first time Gaynor had heard about the performance:

'It's an honour! I mean Donna Summer is a great singer ... she did a good job with it because she is a wonderful singer.'

Perhaps it is this performance that has led to the erroneous belief by some people that 'I Will Survive' is a Summer track. 'I Will Survive' will always be Gaynor's anthem. Many acts have covered the song but, most fans agree, the original is still by far and away the best. In a conversation, Gloria Gaynor said she liked all the covers but Chantay Savage's version wins her heart. Donna Summer told ABC News in 2008 on *Nightline Playlist*, that the public thought 'I Will Survive' was her song. Summer has used Gaynor's hit in her own life 'playlist' and it has helped her in difficult times, but she has never claimed it as her own work.

Disco stars such as KC And The Sunshine Band, Van McCoy, George McCrae and Gloria Gaynor were all favourites in the New York club scene, yet in 1976 Summer was hailed as the first to lead the way as America's first disco superstar.

Peter Shapiro writes in *The Rough Guide To Soul And R&B*:

'Disco is producer's music par excellence, and with Donna Summer disco found its ultimate blank canvas.'

That canvas would not have been as vibrant without Giorgio Moroder and Pete Bellotte. Gloria Gaynor said in a BBC radio documentary *Feelin' Love: The Donna Summer Story* that in any pop music genre there will be great and not-so-great songs. Moroder made sure that the best music was provided for Summer. Many music fans thought Summer's music was the beginning of disco, but in reality the first hit disco songs were sung by George McCrae and others such as Carl Douglas with his catchy 'Kung Fu Fighting' in 1974; the first recognised female disco singer was Gloria Gaynor. During the early stages of the disco movement (1975 – 1976) the big disco hits were dominated by male voices: Van McCoy, KC And The Sunshine Band, The Bee Gees, Leo Sayer and The Real Thing. Only later came the female vocalists in groups such as LaBelle and of course Donna Summer.

Paul Gambaccini said the fact that Donna Summer was a beautiful iconic figure meant that she made a perfect figurehead and her vocal talent matched the productions of Moroder. When Donna Summer joined the Casablanca label, they knew it was a perfect pairing which was ready to make an impact! The labels picked up on it and very quickly positioned their fresh acts in the 'disco' category. Then along comes Donna Summer and wipes everybody off her territory.

The marketing and packaging of Donna Summer by Casablanca Records went beyond that of other acts at that time. Some delightful examples of Donna Summer's songs are 'Try Me, I Know We Can Make It', 'Could It Be Magic', 'Summer Fever' and 'Spring Affair'. Most of these disco standards revelled in their campness; soft disco which suited her sultry image at that time until the arrival of 'Hot Stuff' in 1979. Donna Summer's career boomed in 1979, which proved to be her greatest year in the music business. *Billboard* certified her as Disco Artist Of The Year for the fourth year in a row. Summer was also named Top Overall Female Artist, Number One Pop Singles Artist, Number One Pop Female Album Artist, Number One Pop Female Singles Artist, Pop Female Vocalist Of The Year and Top Overall Singles Artist. The poll, which was based on record hits, resulted in Summer being the first female singer to capture this spot since Diana Ross in 1976. *The Warner Guide To UK & US Hit Singles* had Summer at no.3 for the Top US Artists in the UK 1970 – 1979. Donna Summer was also one of the acts that spent most time in the charts in 1979 in the UK. The *Billboard* Top 25 Artist By Decade Seventies (1970 – 1979) poll placed Summer at no.17 with 1068 points and the album 'Bad Girls' at no.15.

Summer was the no.1 Billboard 1979 Top Artist, with The Bee Gees at no.2, Peaches And Herb at no.3, Village People at no.4, Earth, Wind And Fire at no.5, The Doobie Brothers at no.6, The Knack at no.8, Chic at no.9 and at no.10, Blondie.

Due to the success of the album, 'Bad Girls' was remastered and re-released in 2003 as part of the US Universal Music Company deluxe edition series of legendary albums. It is sometimes said to be the end of Summer's heyday, representing the height of her creativity.

Paul Gambaccini points out that fortunately for Summer, in the 1970s recording acts released records far more prolifically than now. Donna Summer and her team could produce a double album worth of greatest hits. The present-day artist releases an album on average once every three years. Gambaccini also suggested that 'Bad Girls' is the disco equivalent to 'All Things Must Pass' by George Harrison. The album was his first after Harrison left The Beatles. Gambaccini explained the creativity of Moroder when producing Summer's double albums linked to the artistic output of Harrison:

'George Harrison had so much pent up material that it was a triple album. Two studios and a jam session disc which included all the songs that couldn't go into a Beatles' album. Obviously, Giorgio Moroder had lots of ideas he was waiting to get out. It was perfect for 'Bad Girls'. This is a phenomenally successful record.'

Releasing a double album live recording, two studio albums plus a compilation hits package was a major venture. The late 1970s period is a fantastic reminder to young music fans of when Donna Summer was the Madonna, Janet Jackson, Beyonce, Britney Spears, Christina Aguilera, Mary J Blige, Rihanna and Lady Gaga of her day all rolled into one. Time will tell how many of these acts will survive the long haul. While busy with her own career in the late 1970s, Donna Summer went into the studio to work on another album, this time for Twiggy. Summer and Juergen Koopers were the producers of Twiggy's 1979 project 'Heaven In My Eyes' but the album wasn't released until 2007, to fans' delight, with four new remixes.

In 1980, Summer won best female rock vocal performer for 'Hot Stuff' at the 22nd Annual Grammy Awards. Summer was thrilled to receive the award but the crowning glory of her career was, and remains, 'Last Dance', the Oscar winning Best Film Song from the movie 'Thank God It's Friday'. She won 'Best Rhythm & Blues Vocal Performance Female' and 'Best Rhythm & Blues Song' at the 21st Annual Grammy Awards for 'Last Dance' in 1979. Added to the achievements above, the song was a 'Favourite Disco Single' at the 'American Music Awards'.

Marc Almond wrote in his autobiography, *Tainted Life*, that at the time he wanted songs about good times, danceable tunes that one could get drunk and 'high' to, and disco created that for him. He recalled that while transvestite singer Sylvester's song 'You Make Me Feel (Mighty Real)' featured on the TV screen urging fans to feel real, Donna Summer had taken him and fans even higher with her work with Giorgio Moroder on the astonishing song 'Once Upon A Time' and the fascinating 'MacArthur Park'.

In *She Bop: The Definitive History Of Women In Rock, Pop And Soul* (1996), Lucy O'Brien writes:

'. . . American companies manufactured twelve inches first as a promotional tool, then by 1976 as commercial releases. Summer's extended mixes were among the first of the new breed, with hits such as "I Feel Love", "Heaven Knows", "MacArthur Park" and 1979's "Bad Girls" becoming disco classics of the pioneering work she did with Moroder . . .'

Donna Summer explains in the same publication that obviously during the 1970s, things were different. Summer was pleased and grateful that she was 'the person it was designed for'.

The disco phenomenon had a big impact on music fans of that era, with Summer's fans finding a particularly close connection with her songs. The Malaysian singer Francissca Peter says that 'Last Dance' is one of her – and her fans – favourites. Now grown up and successful, many had been young music fans in the 1970s and the song reminded them of their youth.

Of all Donna Summer's smash hit songs in the 1970s, 'Last Dance' seems to be the one most personally connected to Summer. It becomes a 'poignant song', dedicated to the memory of people who are special to her. Summer closes nearly all of her concert performances with 'Last Dance'.

6

Life On The Screen

Donna Summer not only sang 'Last Dance' in *Thank God It's Friday*; it was also her debut on the big screen. She played Nicole, a young singer anticipating her big break. From movie press releases:

'. . . a Columbia Pictures release, it is a contemporary comedy with the music of disco life.'

The press material for the movie promoted *Thank God It's Friday* as: 'A high-spirited, light-hearted film . . . depicts the comedic adventures of a group of colourful characters out for a rollicking Friday night'.

The blurb emphasised that the movie, based around The Zoo Club, was not primarily about 'disco', but instead about 'human behaviour', a comedy about the lives of club 'denizens, the chic and the freak'. The movie was the first major film to use the ambiance of a modern club. Disco was huge and was the new trend being followed by the young and vibrant.

From the *The Cambridge Companion To Pop And Rock* (2001) by Simon Frith, Will Straw and John Street:

'The central challenge for the recording industry was that disco, to a far greater degree than earlier dance music, circulated primarily in clubs.'

Disco became so big that established stars such as James Brown and Isaac Hayes produced disco-inflected songs. A movie based on the phenomenon was the next logical money-making step. Unfortunately, *Thank God It's Friday* didn't set the world on fire.

In an article titled 'Donna Summer: What's She Like?' in *Attitude* magazine, Paul Burston said the film *Thank God It's Friday* was possibly 'one of the worst movies of all time'. He criticised the production of the movie as 'a cynical attempt' to compete with the fame of *Saturday Night Fever*.

The BBC TV show *When Disco Ruled The World* examined the craze and its origins. Author John-Manuel Andriote said:

'What *Saturday Night Fever* did for disco, Elvis Presley did for rock and roll. There were black people for years and suddenly you put a white face on it and it became the hottest thing in the world, and the same thing happened to disco.'

Thank God It's Friday and its soundtrack couldn't compete with *Saturday Night Fever*, but Summer still recorded three great songs for the movie that remain classics. In *1000 Record Covers* (1985) by Michael Ochs:

'The splintering rock scene of the seventies was united commercially with the release of the disco-dance film *Saturday Night Fever*. The accompanying album could not be manufactured fast enough to meet the demand and with 25 million copies sold, soon became the biggest selling soundtrack album of all time. Gloria Gaynor, The Village People and Donna Summer helped disco attain a popularity with all ages not seen since "The Twist" . . .'

The *Thank God It's Friday* soundtrack made it to no.10 in the US, and was certified Platinum. It first hit the British Album Chart on 20th May 1978 at no.40 and stayed for five weeks. The record featured popular stars from the labels Casablanca and Motown. The soundtrack, although successful in the US, was still nowhere near as successful as the *Saturday Night Fever* soundtrack.

Summer's first film role did not bode well for a successful future film career. Her acting failed to convince and the only times when she seemed to be natural and believable was when she was about to sing, a part she was well qualified for! There were occasional convincing moments in her role, but overall the lack of direction in the film and the poor acting were disappointing.

Donna Summer admitted in her autobiography that her experience filming *Thank God It's Friday* was a disappointment, adding that all her time developing her acting skills in Europe was wasted. Summer thought she would have had a better part allowing her to showcase her ability and springboard her into a movie acting career – fulfilling her earlier dreams! But she was offered the part of young girl dreaming of becoming a singing sensation.

In the chapter 'About The Music', the Columbia Pictures press package booklet says:

'Donna's voice provides a good deal of the musical excitement of *Thank God It's Friday* and when she gets her moment in the spotlight to sing "Last Dance" she is positively <u>electric</u>. "Try With Your Love" and "Je T'aime" also fill The Zoo disco with the sounds of Summer, just as they have entertained discotheque audiences the world over.'

The press material points out that Summer made her debut in the film as a special guest star in a role that was perfect for her. They noted that it was 'a dream Donna Summer knows well, since she made it come true for herself'. They salute her recording success and acknowledge that 'Once Upon A Time' was awarded Gold and that she 'has established herself as a major recording star'. Summer was the perfect star to be featured in their disco-themed film.

Summer's introduction to movie sound tracks was with the theme she co-wrote with the late John Barry to *The Deep*, also a Columbia Pictures release and a UK success. Summer's 'acting' stint was perhaps an attempt to promote the soundtrack and her songs rather than primarily a serious attempt to forge a new career path. Maybe the team knew that her acting was not the best but were afraid to risk offending the biggest star of the very phenomenon that the movie was portraying! With a better movie, Summer may have been able to turn in a great performance, which could have opened up further movie roles. This movie debut however did not take her acting career any further.

Summer would liked to have pursued further her interest in acting but, in *Ordinary Girl: The Journey* she acknowledges that following the part in the movie she was unlikely to get any other roles. She was essentially seen as a singer, not an actor, and as a result she would concentrate fully on her career as a singer.

It was also reported that she preferred the feedback of a live audience. Yet Summer was still eager to appear in a movie, making her dream to become an actor a reality.

In an interview with Graham K. Smith in *Record Mirror* on October 15th 1983, Summer was asked whether she had any other movie ambitions. She replied:

'There's a comedy that might be made, and a biblical story I'd like to do. Moses' second wife was a black woman and I'd like to play her life story.'

Summer has not acted in any other movies to date but her name has been associated with several productions. In 1993 she was name-checked in a scene from the film *Tina: What's Love Got To Do With It?* when Ike Turner, played by Laurence Fishburne, tells Angela Basset's Tina Turner that she is no 'Donna Summer'. In a scene from *The Dead Boys Club*, directed and written by Mark Christopher (1993), while sorting out the belongings of a recently-deceased friend, a young man asks what they should do with the old LPs. His older companion replies that the young man can take the rest of the LPs but the 'Donna Summer' is all his. The young man, surprised, asks why. His older friend, hugging the album close to his chest, replies that the younger generation will never know what they have missed. In the biopic *Selena*, the young Selena tells her father that instead of performing Latin songs she would prefer to emulate her idol Donna Summer and sing like her. Selena was an American singer and songwriter, and was one of the most successful Latin artists in the US. She was named 'Top Latin Artist Of The 1990s' and also 'Best Selling Latin Artist Of The Decade' by

Billboard magazine. At the first release of her no. 1 album 'Dreaming Of You' in 1995 the album sold as many as 330,000 units. Sadly in the same year, at the height of her success Selena was shot dead on 31st March 1995 two weeks before her 24th birthday by a lady that worked with her and had embezzled money from her fan club. The movie also stars Jenifer Lopez as the older Selena, miming 'Last Dance' and 'On The Radio' on stage, songs that were covered by Selena.

Summer continued her acting efforts, appearing in the 1994 US sitcom *Family Matters* for two series, in the role of Aunt Oona from Altoona. The first episode that Summer appeared in was directed by Gary Menteer and was titled *Aunt Oona,* in season five on 6th May 1994. In one episode, *Pound Foolish*, originally aired on 25th April 1997 and directed by Jason Batman, Summer plays a newly-overweight Aunt Oona. While visiting her nephew and the Winslow family, and obviously embarrassed by her weight, she agrees to try an 'invention' of her nephew, Steve, played by Jaleel White, hoping to gain the confidence to meet the Reverend Fuller, the man she fancies (and who fancies her in return). Successfully transformed into the sultry Summer that fans know, she attends church where she suddenly expands back to her extra-large size. Horrified, she runs back to the Winslow home. All ends well when the Reverend confesses that he likes her, whatever her size. Summer's acting skills can be seen convincingly in the kitchen scene before she goes into the 'weight loss' machine. Her acting was promising, delivering the part smoothly. She also sang two gospel numbers 'Rejoice' and 'Amazing Grace' with 'She Works Hard For The Money' played at the end of the sitcom. This was her last acting role to date. Summer showed promise as an actor in the series and maybe, given the right opportunity, could still develop a career in acting. Who knows?

Summer remains a popular point of reference in the world of entertainment. In a special 2002 Christmas edition of the hit BBC comedy series *Absolutely Fabulous* titled *Gay*, which also featured Whoopi Goldberg, Jennifer Saunders' character Edina 'Eddy' Monsoon, a rich London fashion victim, is thrilled to hear that her long estranged son, Serge, played by Josh Hamilton, is gay. After finally meeting the grown-up Serge, who turns out to be rather dull and straight-laced, she tells him that she always wanted him to be gay which is why she played Donna Summer songs to her swollen abdomen constantly during the pregnancy! It was fascinating for Summer fans that their diva's hit song was name-checked in an episode of the TV series *Drop Dead Diva*, entitled *The Dress* which aired in the US on 13th September 2009. Summer's names comes up when a lawyer 'Jane Bingum', played by Brooke Elliott, is having a discussion with her lawyer colleague about suing a boutique that did not stock bigger size clothing and had 'politely' thrown her out of the shop due to her size. Unhappy with this second rate treatment Elliott's character says '... at some point, enough is enough ... is enough.' Her colleague 'Kim Kaswell', played by Kate Levering, replies 'Thank you Donna Summer, but you can't sue for hurt feelings'. Interestingly, Summer's chart success inspired a scriptwriter of a popular TV series, *Supernatural* in an episode entitled *Slash Fiction* (season seven, episode six) to write 'the quickest climb up the chart since Donna Summer'. The show aired in the US on the 28th October 2011.

Not generally known is the fact that Donna Summer once appeared in a cameo role as a disco diva singing in a bar, for a German TV production *11 Uhr 20* aired on the 11th January 1970. Her small singing part, which was not credited, appeared in episode three of *Tod In Der Kasbah* (Death In The Kasbah). She also showcased her acting skills, in an introduction to the 1984 music video 'There Goes My Baby'. In between singing in the music video, snippets of Summer's acting without any speech (a typical video style) were convincing!

Disco regained some popularity in the middle to late 1990s with a handful of movies made to celebrate the golden years of disco. The films *54* and *The Last Days Of Disco* were released in 1998. Ironically, neither of the film's soundtracks featured songs from the biggest star of the era! To the delight of Summer's fans, their idol's name was mentioned in the film *54* during a monologue by Ryan Phillippe, playing 'Shane O'Shea', that Anita Randazzo, a character played by Salma Hayek, wanted to be the 'next Donna Summer'. To complement the dialogue a copy of the LP 'Live And More' was displayed on the record shelf in the background during a scene in the movie. Her songs may not have been featured but Summer's popularity during that era was celebrated. To date, her name and music continue to be mentioned or featured in many films and TV productions.

7

New Life After Disco

Disco first began as an underground movement in New York. Songs by Gloria Gaynor, George McCrae, KC And The Sunshine Band and Donna Summer simply introduced disco to the mainstream.

Jim Haskins and J.M. Stifle, writing in *Donna Summer: An Unauthorized Biography* observed that popular music venues, far from disappearing, just moved underground after the 1960s, supported by minority groups in the urban centres of the US. They noted that 'these groups nurtured a new, more vital, grass-roots disco movement, one that would have a wider appeal than its predecessor.'

Young white audiences, tired of watching their 'rock' icons perform live in concert, were searching for other forms of entertainment. Instead of being passive observers they wanted to be the stars, be watched by others. The underground disco scene fulfilled these fantasies and the movement exploded.

After a few years as the dominant popular sound, people began to get bored. The music had become formulaic, a parody of itself. In the US, people who had never liked the genre, took advantage of this disaffection with disco music and a campaign against it was promoted strongly by Steve Dahl. A rock radio DJ, Dahl who was dismissed from a previous position when the radio station changed their format from pop rock tunes to 'disco', his show apparently not getting enough listeners. Dahl was hired by another radio station and it was there that he took his revenge on disco music, promoting the 'disco sucks' movement.

An infamous event took place at a baseball game between the Chicago White Sox and the Detroit Tigers in the interval between two games. Disco records by Donna Summer, Chic, KC And The Sunshine Band, Gloria Gaynor and many more acts were set on fire.

Craig Werner writes in *A Change Is Gonna Come: Music, Race And The Soul Of America*:

'On July 12, 1979, straight American took its revenge. Between games of a doubleheader at Chicago's Comiskey Park, the throng, gathered in support of DJ Steve Dahl's anti-disco crusade, joined in a thunderous chant of "Disco sucks!" … Dahl approached a wooden box overflowing with disco records doused in lighter fluid … set the altar ablaze, igniting a drunken rampage that trashed the field and resulted in the cancellation of the second game.'

In conversation, Gloria Gaynor said it was astonishing that any individual could hate disco music so much that they would feel the need to take part in an organised event to burn discs containing the offending music. Paradoxically, Dahl's followers who went out and burned the disco albums seem to have had these records in their own collections!

It has been claimed, online, that some people even took records belonging to their families to the 'event'. They may have never been forgiven. People also purchased the records in order to get a little discount on the entrance fee to the stadium. A fan of the game said that he remembered bringing both a Donna Summer and a *Saturday Night Fever* record to gain admission. He recalled being cut by all the broken records flying around! Many true fans of the game, who were not aware that the event was taking place, were ashamed at what had happened in their stadium.

During 'Disco Demolition Night' things got out of control as the 'mob' surged onto the field and a near-riot ensured. For Gloria Gaynor, disco music was the first and only music style to appeal to people of every age group, every nationality, every race and gender. Disco music could have helped to bring people together in all kinds of ways.

Alice Echols wrote in *Hot Stuff: Disco And The Remaking Of American Culture*: that this marked the end of an era:

'The day after Disco Demolition, Chicago's dedicated disco station, WLUP, played Donna Summer's 'Last Dance' for twenty-four hours straight, then pronounced disco dead and started spinning Top 40 rock songs.'

Twenty-two years later, on 12th July 2001, Mike Veeck, one of the 'key' individuals responsible for Disco Demolition, apologised to Harry Wayne Casey, the lead singer from KC and The Sunshine Band in a brief ceremony before the Florida Marlins' home game. Casey was chosen because he was one of the original disco acts in America. In the book *Slouching Towards Fargo* (2000) Veeck writes that the second he saw one of the audience shimmy down the outfield wall, he knew that his life was over! As a result of the debacle, Veeck and his 'partners in crime' were allegedly blacklisted from Major League Baseball for quite some time after his father, Bill Veeck the former owner of the White Sox, retired in 1981. Although the apology didn't make up for what happened, it was a contrite act and a decent thing to do.

Pete Bellotte recalled the 'Disco Sucks' movement in a 2004 interview with the BBC, saying that when he saw the derogatory graffiti plastered everywhere in New York he realised that it was the final curtain for the disco movement.

Despite the backlash against disco in the US, in the UK, Europe and other parts of the world the music was still popular. As music fans know, disco never been disappeared, it just evolved into 'dance'.

In *The Rough Guide To Soul And R&B*, Peter Shapiro wrote:

'Whatever its critics may have decreed at the time, disco has had a profound influence on popular music from the way it is produced to the way it sounds. House, techno, trance, drum 'n' bass and garage wouldn't exist without disco, and it's entirely possible that hip-hop wouldn't either. Contemporary production techniques like remixing, editing and mash-ups were all pioneered by disco producers and DJs.'

While US music may have been conquered by hip-hop, 'disco's evil twin', Shapiro believes that seventy percent of charts in Europe would sound a great deal more diverse if it were not for disco. He maintains that disco is an intrinsic part of the soul tradition.

Gloria Gaynor believes that disco music is still alive and well and living in the hearts of music lovers around the world – 'the name has been changed to protect the innocent.'

To this day, fans have still not heard any comments from Donna Summer about the infamous Disco Demolition Night. However, at the time her career was at its most hectic and she may have simply just not have noticed the animosity directed at the genre by some people or simply believed it was just another change in fashion. She had by that time already explored different styles, examples of which included the new material showcased in 'Hot Stuff', which introduced a more guitar rock-based style with additional dance beats. The ballad 'My Baby Understands' showed a more sentimental side.

Donna Summer has said that the greatest contribution disco has given to the world was 'Staying Alive', The Bee Gees song in *Saturday Night Fever*. In an interview with Scott Galloway for the *Sacramento Observer* in 2003, Summer described disco as a form of escapism from the harsh realities of everyday life.

The end of the disco era provided an opportunity for many acts to broaden their musical horizons and explore different styles of composition, and Donna Summer was no exception, although she played a crucial part in the disco movement. According to *The Virgin Story Of Rock 'N' Roll*. Donna Summer and Marvin Gaye helped to push the boundaries of 1970s music; 'Love To Love You Baby', 'I Feel Love', 'Hot Stuff' and 'Bad Girls' are good examples of this.

Thirty-two years after the 'end' of disco, Jeremy Kinser from advocate.com wrote in 'You Should Be Dancing' that disco music would 'never die'. Kinser celebrated two of Summer's songs, 'Last Dance' and 'No More Tears (Enough Is Enough)' to be included amongst fifteen dance songs that he selected as ever-popular and timeless.

A new phase in Summer's career began in 1980 with the ABC network. Summer's first television special titled *The Donna Summer Special* aired on January 27th 1980. The one-hour show, recorded at the end of 1979, was produced by Summer's own production company, Summer Nights Inc. The network executives insisted that the programme focused on her singing. Summer also had difficulty persuading the network chief to let her have her own special. The desire to have more control over her show had meant that *The Donna Summer Special* was to be the first and last aired by the ABC network. It could also have been the result of a lack interest from the viewers in disco music. Despite the lack of support from the network, Donna Summer enjoyed working on her first TV special.

In *Ordinary Girl: The Journey* Summer describes how she was busy and excited preparing for her first network television special for ABC. She also got to meet up with an old colleague from her days in Austria, Robert Guillaume, with whom she performed in *Porgy And Bess*.

One thrilling moment for Summer was to be able 'to involve Mimi' in her TV show. She said she introduced her daughter 'in a unique way' – Donna Summer performed 'Mimi's Song' to her daughter on camera.

Josiah Howard, author of *Donna Summer: Her Life And Music*, wrote that even though the show had a promising start, the rest of the TV special failed to present Donna Summer 'at her best'. Howard also observed that the programme 'looked cheap and second-rate', with 'B-list' guest stars – Robert Guillaume, Twiggy, Pat Ast and Debralee Scott.

Although Summer had achieved what she had set out to achieve, she felt miserable and was not happy with her career. In the 1970s Summer had developed an addiction to prescription pills and was on the verge of suicide. She could not cope with her overnight fame. Secretly, Summer was not happy with an image that did not have many good lessons to offer, primarily being used as a sex emblem. Although at first it started out as a bit of a joke, the public seemed to think that what they saw was the real Donna Summer.

Ironically, it was because she played the part so well that her rise to stardom was so rapid, helped of course by the talent of Moroder and

Bellotte. Summer wrote in her autobiography that with her strong religious faith, to portray a false image to music fans was wrong. She had talent and wanted the public to see her as more than just a sex symbol!

In *Ordinary Girl: The Journey*, Summer says that 'sex is a beautiful thing in the right context'. However, the industry's presentation of her as a sex symbol, whilst understandable at the time as a marketing technique, in retrospect went against all of her core beliefs.

She also felt everything that was going on around her was superficial, not really a surprise in the world of popular music. The sexy image wasn't all put on; Summer was a naturally beautiful and sexy woman. It is obvious that the public persona of Summer is just one side of her personality, and her private life and persona will remain just that; private.

One of Summer's oldest friends, Dagmar, who worked with her in the early days on *Hair*, said that she was thrilled to see how Summer had grown up and become a swan; she had once called herself an ugly duckling!

Summer had some good times in the 1970s. Musically, it was a crazy and hectic time for the star and she managed to avoid the more extreme elements of the showbiz culture. But at some point she made a fundamental decision about the direction she wanted her life to go in. Metaphorically, Summer surrendered to God and embraced the teachings of Jesus Christ. From that day, her life had changed.

In January 1980, Donna Summer sued her manager Joyce Bogart and Casablanca Records for undue influence, misrepresentation and fraud. From the *New York* magazine article 'Can Disco's Bogart Play It Again?' (18th February 1980):

'. . . Donna Summer, by far Casablanca's most profitable act, is suing the company for $10 million, claiming she was inadequately represented by her manager . . .'

Larry Harris, the author of *And Party Every Day: The Inside Story Of Casablanca Records* said that Neil Bogart wanted to 'have a great deal of control over' Donna Summer's career. The only way to 'control' their 'emerging' superstar was by appointing Joyce Bogart (at that time having a romantic relationship with Neil Bogart) as co-manager 'to work with' Summer's then manager, Dick Broder. Ideally, Bogart would be able to have control over Summer's career without her 'manager getting in the way'. Also, Moroder was living in Germany and would not be able to take part in the day-to-day management process.

Harris mentioned that Neil Bogart thought this arrangement would also be 'helping the company' and 'it would benefit' the star herself. According to Harris, Joyce Bogart made twenty-five percent of Donna Summer's income. That is 'a very sizable' profit for a manager.

Obviously, Casablanca Records promoted Summer heavily but finally she realised the situation; there were too many conflicts of interest. Luckily, Summer had people that were concerned about her career and well-being. She finally understood what needed to be done but she didn't even have a lawyer at that time. In *Ordinary Girl: The Journey*, Summer wrote that she felt great affection for Neil Bogart and was without a doubt indebted for all his hard work and creative ideas, pushing her career to superstardom. She also felt overly controlled by him; caged in.

Eventually, she was released from her contract with the record company. By this time, half of Casablanca was sold to PolyGram. Summer parted company with Casablanca Records, the label that had made her.

In the *The Rolling Stone Book Of Women In Rock: Trouble Girls* (1987), Barbara O'Dair writes:

'Summer was then free to record elsewhere provided she delivered two more albums over the next three years to Mercury/PolyGram, which now owned the remainder of her contract.'

Later, Summer signed to David Geffen's new record company, the first singer to be contracted to the label. Geffen, the founder of Asylum Records, told *Rolling Stone* magazine that in his view, the music people are doing 'it' imperfectly and he thought he could do it better, so he launched his new label, later signing Elton John and the late John Lennon.

In *Donna Summer: An Unauthorized Biography* Jim Haskin writes that when it was official that Summer had signed to Geffen she was hit with a lawsuit claiming an astounding $42 million from Casablanca and Bogart. It claimed 'breach of contract' and aimed to prevent Summer recording with any other label. This undoubtedly had an effect on her creative efforts.

On 16th July 1980, Summer married Bruce Sudano, a writer and musician with the group Brooklyn Dreams. Their joint venture, 'Heaven Knows' had been a hit in 1979. The union resulted in the birth of their two beautiful daughters, Brooklyn and Amanda Grace.

In September, *Donna Summer: An Unauthorized Biography* noted that the demand from Casablanca Records to ban Donna Summer from making future records with any company was denied by 'a superior court judge in Los Angeles'. In November, the album 'The Wanderer' was released, Summer's first project with Geffen. Her work had branched out with pop-rock and New Wave flavours, away from her traditional disco base.

Summer co-wrote three songs, 'The Wanderer', 'Looking Up' and 'Grand Illusion'. Two tracks, 'Running For Cover' and 'I Believe In Jesus' were solo efforts. It received mixed reviews from fans expecting another 'Bad Girls'-styled album. Disco was no longer cool. Musical styles had changed and artists needed to move with them.

Summer had changed her singing style. 'Grand Illusion' had her singing in a high-pitched, squeaking vocal. According to *The Accidental Evolution Of Rock 'N' Roll,* the track got its title from Styx and its vocal quacking from Rush. She also returned to her musical roots and shared her renewed religious belief by recording a gospel track, 'I Believe In Jesus'. 'The Wanderer' was a success, earning Gold status on the 12th December 1980 in the US. However, it didn't sell as well as her earlier albums.

The groundbreaking musical collaboration of Moroder, Bellotte and Summer had come to an end. The Eurodisco sound that fans loved so much was not to be heard in this project. It was difficult for fans to adjust to this change. The overtly religious 'I Believe In Jesus' simply didn't blend in with the pop-rock-New Wave project. Her belief was clearly important to her, but she was trying to sell popular music to fans, not convert them to Christianity.

Summer wanted to take her life in a different direction, both personally and musically. In an article for a Christian publication titled 'Donna Summer Announces New Album, US Tour', she observed that to get a 'gospel label' was actually difficult. Summer was faced with a lot of negative reactions:

'Instead of being more forgiving, or whatever it takes, and saying, "Hey look, this is a person who could potentially sell a lot of records", we didn't get that reaction ... We prayed over it, and it didn't come through that way. So we felt it wasn't right. I know that anything I have needed from God that is right for me always comes. I totally rely on that. And when that didn't come through, we realised that it had to be God's desire for it ... to be the record that it was.'

In *Donna Summer: An Unauthorized Biography* it is said that Giorgio Moroder had not been too enthusiastic about including 'I Believe In Jesus', but Summer insisted it should go in. 'The Wanderer' was well-produced and Summer's performances were excellent. She captured the character in 'Running For Cover' and 'Cold Love' perfectly. But 'I Believe In Jesus' saw Summer stand out in the role as she delivered an inspirational performance!

Would this appear to be something out of the norm for Summer's musical creativity? Not likely! Summer's performance of a gospel number had been showcased since the disco era. Summer had performed gospel with Tom Jones and Dolly Parton and also sang with Mac Davis 'Sounds Like Home' live on his show on 26th April 1977.

Jim Haskins and J.M. Stifle eloquently put it in *Donna Summer: An Unauthorized Biography* that Summer seemed to be taken aback when the 'single recording of that song did well'. Pleased with the result and feeling grateful, Summer 'could not help but believe that the song had struck a responsive chord in the hearts of her fans.' The recording star knew her fans would love to listen to more songs of a similar nature.

To include a religious song on an album was not a new idea. They had appeared in various musical productions. In 1970 George Harrison recorded 'My Sweet Lord' (a successful single) for his 'All Things Must Pass'. Even in the jazz world Nina Simone's 1978 release 'Baltimore' included 'If You Pray Right'. Whitney Houston merrily sang 'Jesus Loves Me' on 'The Body-guard' soundtrack. 'Jesus Promised Me A Home Over There' can be heard in Jennifer Hudson's self titled album in 2008. On the other hand, even though Donna Summer's 'I Believe In Jesus' did receive promising reviews, at that time the majority of her fans were not ready for her to perform such a melody; she was a dance act after all!

Long gone was the whispered, breathy cooing and moaning. The new, 'mature' Summer delivered her message to music fans with dignity. No more longing for one-night steamy affairs. All inappropriate thoughts were to be abandoned. She had been there, done that! Now it was the beginning of a beautiful new journey, and acceptance of the born again Summer's new musical identity.

The album hit no.13 in US but only reached no.55 in the UK. In the US, 'The Wanderer' stayed in the album chart for eighteen weeks, but only managed a poor two-week residence in the UK chart. Although a flop in the UK, it did better in Sweden, peaking at no.15 and spending seventeen weeks in the chart. It was also a no.18 hit in Norway managing to stay in the chart for fifteen weeks.

None of the singles from the project were released as twelve inch remixes or extended versions. 'The Wanderer', 'Cold Love' and 'Who Do You Think You're Foolin'' were released as ordinary singles. Fans had expected the release of at least one remix or long single version. 'Rumour Has It' that the remixes were produced but not released.

'The Wanderer' was in the US charts for twenty weeks and the title track single entered the charts on 20th September 1980. It rapidly climbed from its debut position at no.43 to no.18, finally peaking at no.3. The single only managed no.48 in the UK on the 18th September 1980 (six weeks in the chart). Sweden liked it more, making it their no.9 single and keeping it in the chart for fifteen weeks! In South Africa, it climbed to no.5. The single was a hit in Canada, climbing all the way to no.2 and staying in the chart for thirteen weeks. In Zimbabwe it reached no.10, with nine weeks in the chart in total.

The second single 'Cold Love' entered the American chart on the 29th November 1980. It debuted in the Top 40 a few weeks later on 10th January 1981 but only managed no.33. In the UK, the single peaked at no.44 on the 24th January 1980. The last single from the project, 'Who Do You Think You're Foolin', debuted on 28th March 1981 and peaked at no.40. The single was not released in the UK.

Summer's departure from disco paid off – in the US at least! She was nominated for a Grammy for Best Female Vocal Rock Performance and the gospel song 'I Believe In Jesus' received a nomination for Best Inspirational Performance.

The performances on the 'The Wanderer' were not as grand as her other albums. In an interview with the *NME*, Summer said that the album did great and she was not disappointed with the reception and the sales outcome. 'The Wanderer' was not as comprehensively promoted by Summer as her past projects. There were no road tours, TV or radio appearances. She was busy with, amongst other things, the lawsuit with Casablanca and on a happier note, she was getting used to her new life as a wife and a mother.

The writer Christian John Wikane observed that 'The Wanderer' was an important project which transformed Summer's image from that created during her time with Casablanca. It was an image more in tune with pop-rock recording acts, as envisioned by Moroder, Bellotte and Summer. It was a bold move for Summer, especially on the self-penned track 'Running For Cover'. Showing great affection for 'The Wanderer', Wikane believes the star's vocal quality can be heard on every song.

'The Wanderer' was ranked by *Rolling Stone* as the no.2 album of 1980 behind Bruce Springsteen's 'The River' and awarded the album four stars out of five.

Many of Summer's fans were in their twenties or thirties when they discovered her music through 'The Wanderer'. Some fans said that the album's more personal tone attracted them to it, this tone being why they think it's her finest album. The fact that the image and the sound were so different from her past albums helped to make it more interesting. Existing pop-rock fans were really pleased with the theme and the more 'hardcore' tunes. 'The Wanderer' didn't have the impact of 'Bad Girls', yet it still achieved Gold status in the US. In *Hot Stuff: Disco And The Remaking Of American Culture* Alice Echols wrote that Dave Marsh, a rock critic, celebrated it in *Rolling Stone* as the 'most mature and satisfying effort in large measure'. He was convinced that Summer was a rock 'n' roll artist at heart.

Before 'The Wanderer' came out, Casablanca Records released 'Walk Away – Collector's Edition (The Best Of 1977–1980)', the first part of the contracted project agreed by Summer to be released by Casablanca. The album made it to no.50 and stayed in the album chart for fifteen weeks in the US but did not get into the album chart in the UK. The single 'Walk Away' debuted in the American chart on the 13th September 1980 and later peaked at no.36.

While Summer moved away from the disco beat, Motown queen Diana Ross still produced disco-orientated songs. She had a hit with 'Upside Down', which reached no.1 in the US and no.2 in the UK, and 'I'm Coming Out', a no.5 in the US and no.13 in the UK. Other groups continued to have disco inspired hits on both sides of the Atlantic including Lipps Inc. with 'Funky Town' and Olivia Newton-John with 'Xanadu'. The disco sound still had life in it.

The *Billboard* Top 20 Artists poll for 1980 put Donna Summer at no.13 – just below Diana Ross at no.12.

A year later, Summer recorded 'I'm A Rainbow', a double-record pop concept album. The album followed the model of 'The Wanderer'. Clean-cut, middle-of-the-road pop; long gone was the energy and edginess of 'Bad Girls'.

Summer talked about some of her sensual and suggestive songs in the interview for the article 'Donna Summer Announces New Album, US Tour'. In the article, she expresses regret about the style of her earlier work but accepts that it is part of her past. She goes on to explain that she just needs time to build up a new body of work that is more compatible with her beliefs.

Unfortunately, to the horror of fans, 'I'm A Rainbow' was never commercially released by Geffen. It would have been her final album with Moroder and Bellotte. Apparently a bootleg print entered circulation pretty soon and was a topic of discussion for fans for years to come.

The decision not to release 'I'm A Rainbow' wasn't made public at that time. According to Jim Haskins and J.M. Stifle in *Donna Summer: An Unauthorized Biography*, one reason for the non-release was because the world was facing economic recession. Record companies also had to pay attention to their costs and 'I'm A Rainbow' was deemed unlikely to make an adequate return by the record label.

In retrospect, critics believed the album lacked commercial value and did not highlight Summer's vocal talents. Perhaps Geffen Records did not want to take a risk after what had happened to 'The Wanderer'. Geffen was very dissatisfied with the 'I'm A Rainbow' concept and suggested that Summer did not work with Moroder and Bellotte any more. Maybe the team had lost that magic touch after being together for so long. Most of the songs are mediocre. Some critics said that it was probably a wise decision to shelve the project.

Josiah Howard, in *Donna Summer: Her Life And Music*, rates 'I'm A Rainbow' as 'uninspired and forgettable', just a repeat of 'The Wanderer'. He supported the decision of Geffen not to release what in his view would almost certainly have been a commercial failure. This might not have been the view of Summer's fans.

Alan Light, writing in the booklet that accompanied 'The Donna Summer Anthology' album, said that 'I'm A Rainbow' was more of an introspective record that covered many issues facing Summer at that time.

Summer was disappointed when the album was not released. She had said in 'On Nashville, Christmas, Barbra And Image-Breaking', an article in *Billboard*, that David Geffen did not think there was enough dance material in the project; it wasn't what he was looking for. Summer had not gone into the studio to have an album canned. There have been many questions asked about why the project was withdrawn. Pete Waterman said in an interview that Geffen had a completely different view of Donna Summer from everyone else, whether it was music producers, the public or die-hard fans.

'I'm A Rainbow' was said to have been a very personal favourite of the star. The recording sessions 'reportedly cost $200,000' according to Jim Haskins. Even though it was not released, some of the tracks were licensed and released by other recording acts such as The Real Thing, Anni-Frid of ABBA and Amii Stewart.

Howard's *Donna Summer: Her Life And Music* tells how Geffen 'hurled' the demo 'across his office' in anger and frustration. In the same publication, Giorgio Moroder himself agreed that it wasn't particularly good and didn't really contain any sure-fire hit singles. If Moroder thought this, why, as the producer, didn't he raise the issue with Summer and do something about in the studio? Moroder does go on to explain that if he could turn back the clock, he would record it as a single album with 'the ten best' tracks; he thought 'Don't Cry For Me Argentina' was the 'only good' melody on the album. Moroder himself was credited on seven tracks and Bellotte on ten. Summer shared credits on six tracks and Sylvester Levay contributed to several. 'I Believe (In You)' and 'Leave Me Alone' were credited to Harold Faltermeyer and Keith Forsey. The beautiful rendition of the title track was composed by Summer's husband, Bruce Sudano.

Speaking to *Mojo* magazine about the departure of Moroder, Summer said when Geffen Records told Giorgio Moroder he was no longer going to produce her work, Moroder wasn't pleased! Moroder had every right to express his dissatisfaction. The shared history between him and Summer went beyond that of producer and singer. Summer said they had 'a very tight and deep union'. But, as Summer admitted, Geffen 'was paying the bills'. He wanted a 'blacker' sound, more R&B, funkier and more dance-orientated. Donna Summer in *Mojo*, 2004:

'Giorgio wanted to do what was right for me, and he had many other projects going on and many hits without me; he was enormously successful in his own right. I think for both of us it showed that we were entities unto ourselves, and able to be ourselves. But the break was really very painful.'

The failure of 'I'm A Rainbow' might have had a positive side. That an album of hers had been rejected was a shock – a wake-up call that challenged Summer's 'star' status. It may have made her a stronger person spiritually and motivated her to work harder.

The sentimental 'Don't Cry For Me Argentina' was said to be Donna Summer's favourite from the album. It also could have been a hit as a single had it been released back in 1981. Summer recorded the track beautifully and in an interview with *Billboard*, she said the song belonged to her. Summer didn't mean it to sound presumptuous, she just felt such a connection to it.

On the 13th May 1996, a message was sent to Donna Summer's fans by William Meisinger from PolyGram and publicly shared in The Donna Summer Internet Zone:

'The album has been digitally mastered for over a year, and includes eighteen tracks ... an essay has been written for the CD jacket, but the primary hold-up is the missing cover artwork ... My impression is that in the interest of releasing the album, they will eventually do something creative just to get the album out to us fans.'

After many years, 'I'm A Rainbow' was released in 1996 by PolyGram and is considered to be amongst her finest and most personal musical achievements to date. The project included several different musical styles: 'Leave Me Alone' is pop-rock; 'Don't Cry For Me Argentina' sentimental; 'To Turn The Stone' uses traditional Scottish instruments; both 'Highway Runner' and 'Romeo' were originally used in the movie soundtracks for *Fast Times At Ridgemont High* and *Flashdance* respectively, following the failure of the album to be released.

Fans had thought that the album contained nineteen, not eighteen tracks as released. However the confusion was due to some bootleg copies which also included 'Walk Hand In Hand'. It was confirmed in 1996 by Bill

Levenson from PolyGram that 'I'm A Rainbow' had 'only' eighteen tracks in its original form. The original artwork for the album could not be found and PolyGram couldn't locate the photographer David Alexander, who did the photo shoot. Summer didn't have the original photographs herself; it is said that the original artwork might have been used for the 'Donna Summer' album in 1982.

In 1982, the self-titled album was released, produced by Quincy Jones. The album exhibited a smooth blend of the traditional Donna Summer sound and the jazz funk-based pop that was the producer's signature. Summer was not involved in selecting her producer and it had not been her idea to work with Quincy Jones, yet she was excited by the prospect.

Quincy Jones contributed to two tracks on 'Donna Summer': 'Love Is In Control (Finger On The Trigger)' with Rod Temperton and Merria Rossa and 'Living In America' with Summer, Rod Temperton, David Foster and Steve Lukather. The singer was also credited on two tracks, the other being 'Love Is Just A Breath Away' with Temperton and Foster.

Two intriguing tracks, 'Lush Life' and 'State Of Independence', explored new territory for Summer. The album also featured a pop-rock tune titled 'Protection' created by Bruce Springsteen. Summer was thrilled by the chance to work with Springsteen. In *Ordinary Girl: The Journey*, Summer reveals that her husband was Springsteen's 'number one fan'. 'The Boss' sang 'personally' just for her before the actual recording session took place.

The track 'Protection' clearly had the stamp of the rock star but with the touch of Summer mixed in. Summer's vocal style is clearly more rock-oriented in his track. The single was not released either in the US or the UK, but music fans in Japan were luckier. Perhaps they even had the opportunity to get their hands on a 'Dance Contemporary' DJ promo pack, considered very rare! The seven inch release says 'Dance Contemporary' on the sleeve, but keeps its original sound.

'Lush Life' is a great jazz number that has been recorded by countless legends. The lyrics and music were written by Billy Strayhorn. It is said the song was only performed privately by Strayhorn until he and vocalist Kay Davis performed it sometime in 1948 with the Duke Ellington Orchestra at Carnegie Hall. The beautiful 'jazz' piece was recorded by Ella Fitzgerald, Chet Baker, Nancy Wilson and Nat King Cole to name a few. Recording it showed that Summer could sing a jazz standard. It was a smart move by Quincy Jones, especially at a time when the team were moving away from disco-dance tunes. Some critics thought the track was a little 'forced', Summer herself admitted in an interview with Barney Hoskyns that the song was really hard and almost broke her 'chops' trying to sing it because she had to complement the backing without overwhelming. Recording the song became a real labour of love for her.

In *Attitude* magazine, she explained that she normally recorded a track very quickly. She would study the song, make up the character for herself and record the material. She would not sing the track several times because, in her personal view, the spontaneity and 'magic' of the song would be lost. However, Quincy Jones was adamant that she got the jazz track down precisely. He came from a background where, if necessary, the singer would record the same track six hundred times until they got it right. Summer did not see it that way; she was bored and increasingly lost interest. But the final result justified the effort. 'Lush Life' works beautifully and Summer's hard work and Quincy Jones' attention to detail was indeed worthwhile. The track would fit in perfectly in any jazz compilation.

Summer, talking about 'Lush Life' in her autobiography, *Ordinary Girl: The Journey*, said that it was one of the most difficult sessions she had ever had to go through. Jones was a perfectionist and made Summer sing the demanding piece over and over again until he felt it was just right.

'State Of Independence' was yet another triumph. The song was actually a cover of a song by Jon Anderson and Vangelis, originally released as a single in 1981 then re-released in 1984 when it reached no.67 in the UK charts. But Summer's version remains the most well known.

The clever, catchy chant was written in the lyrics as:

'Shablamidi, shablamida; Shablamidi, shablamida; Shablamidi, shablamida'.

The meaningless words constitute a form of 'word painting'. The song featured an all-star choir including Dara Bernad, Dyan Cannon, Christopher Cross, James Ingram, the late Michael Jackson, Peggy Lipton Jones, Quincy Jones, Kenny Loggins, Michael McDonald, Lionel Richie, Brenda Russell, Dionne Warwick and Stevie Wonder. Stevie Wonder also created a new lyric that can be heard at the fade out at the end of the track. It would have been amazing to be surrounded by all those stars in one studio, and Summer felt suitably honoured that they all took part – but the main star wasn't there!

Answering a question in *Attitude*'s 'Any Queries?' in 2004, Summer recalled she was not present during the choir session. She was 'heavily pregnant' and also at that time had 'a severe stomach virus'. Summer's sister acted as a substitute and, according to Summer, 'was in her element'.

Summer's world-music inspired, spiritually-flavoured 'State Of Independence' spurred Quincy Jones to create the charity project 'We Are The World', which again featured many big recording names, although Summer was not included in that high-profile single.

In *1001 Songs You Must Hear Before You Die,* author Robert Dimery says that in 2008 Chris Martin from Coldplay said that 'State Of Independence' is Brian Eno's favourite tune. Martin said Eno played the song on a regular basis. Eno described the single as 'one of the high points of twentieth-century art'.

Summer said that 'State Of Independence' was at that time the one song that best expressed her true feelings.

Summer states in *1001 Songs You Must Hear Before You Die*:

'It's got an optimism and sense of purpose that is based in reality.'

Robert Dimery notes that when the single was released, the reception it got from the public was average compared with the album's first single, 'Love Is In Control (Finger On The Trigger)'. It subsequently became 'widely celebrated'.

'Donna Summer' peaked at no.20 in the US, lower than 'The Wanderer'. However, it remained in the album chart for thirty-seven weeks. The UK public were far more interested in 'Donna Summer' than 'The Wanderer', the album reaching no.13 in the UK and spending sixteen weeks in the chart. 'Donna Summer' was a global success, reaching no.2 in Sweden (eighteen weeks), no.3 in Norway (fourteen weeks) and no.17 in France, where the album spent thirty-six weeks in the chart!

The funky 'Love Is In Control (Finger On The Trigger)' was the first single release and went straight to no.10 a few weeks after it debuted in the US chart on the 26th June 1982. In the UK, it peaked at no.18 by the 14th August 1982. The single was a massive hit in Europe. In Spain it hit no.1 and reached no.3 in Norway, no.5 in Switzerland, no.6 in The Netherlands and no.11 in Ireland. The instrumental version of the twelve inch had a saxophone solo by Ernie Watts. The seven inch version included a beautiful ballad, 'Sometimes Like Butterflies,' on the B-side which was not included on the album. Summer told *Attitude* that 'Sometimes Like Butterflies' was written at David Geffen's house in one afternoon with Bruce Roberts. She pretended to be Bette Midler and recorded the tune in 'a kind of raspy voice'.

Many years later the track was released in CD format on the compilation album 'Different Love' by Mark Tara. He had always loved the track and the compilation project came together over a period of two years. Tara dealt with the Canadian arm of Summer's record company for permission to include 'Sometimes Like Butterflies' on the album.

The second single from 'Donna Summer' was the outstanding 'State Of Independence' which, reached no.41 in the US on the 2nd October 1982 and no.14 in the UK on the 20th November 1982. In Holland, 'State Of

Independence' was a no.1 single and stayed in the chart for nine weeks. The single peaked at no.4 in Belgium (five weeks), Poland at no.10 (six weeks) and reached no.10 in Ireland.

A slow track, 'The Woman In Me', debuted in the US chart on 18th December 1982 at no.78, finally reaching no.33. The beautifully seductive 'The Woman In Me' was not well received in the UK, only reaching no.62 on the 5th March 1983. However, it did better in Holland, climbing to no.8 and staying in the chart for seven weeks and entered the Top 20 in Belgium at no.18. 'The Woman In Me' was also released in a limited edition blue colour vinyl twelve inch with a picture label.

Summer's patriotic side showed up in one of the songs on the album. An encouragement to be strong and keep on trying to fulfil one's dream, the lyrics of 'Livin' In America' were co-written with Rod Temperton, David Foster and Steve Lukather:

'You're livin' in America. You're livin' in the home of the dream. Just make it what you want it to be . . .'

It was reported that neither Summer nor Jones were completely satisfied with the outcome of the 'Donna Summer' project.

The project was a critical test of Summer's ability to work with other major names in the business. Quincy Jones was extremely well-respected and also Summer's first producer since parting with Moroder and Bellotte. Both Summer and Jones had clear ideas of how they wanted things to go in the studio. In her 2003 autobiography, Summer said that it had been hard work in the studio with Jones. She was pregnant and as a result continuously tired and often feeling sick. Jones was a perfectionist and very persistent, insisting that everything was done again and again until it met his satisfaction.

Summer admitted in the December 1982 *NME* article 'From Sex Goddess To Bad Girl To American Superwoman' (Barney Hoskyns) that it was easier working with Giorgio Moroder and Pete Bellotte as they had developed together as a team from the 1970s. Making the transition to a new producer was very hard. She said she had to 'learn how to walk again' and to 'learn what to say' and 'what not to say'.

Summer told Hoskyns that Quincy Jones produced 'Donna Summer' 'with almost no help' from her. Summer noted that it was not her usual way of working, as she loves to get involved in her album productions. Summer claimed that it was more Jones' album than hers.

Whatever happened in the studio during the making of the record was ultimately worthwhile. The result was a successful album that consolidated Summer's shift away from the world of disco to that of pop-rock. 'Donna

Summer' abandoned the dance-pop-rock sounds that were introduced in 'The Wanderer'. 'Protection' was the only track that fitted this description and, good as it is, it seemed an uncomfortable fit on the R&B, jazz-flavoured pop album.

For many critics, the album was very 'middle-of-the-road', despite being produced by the legendary Quincy Jones. Even though he had selected the best tunes for the project, it still lacked soul. The only really soulful element of the project was Summer's voice. However, Quincy Jones is said to have thought that Summer's voice, although powerful and a great asset, was not as good an R&B voice as that of other female singers in the genre.

Collectors of Summer's work were thrilled that the project was also marketed as a limited edition picture LP. In September 1982 'Donna Summer' was awarded Gold status in the US.

The author of *The Rough Guide To Soul And R&B*, Peter Shapiro, says:

'With Summer singing the first two verses in a mock Puerto Rican accent to an electro-reggae lilt, 1982's "State Of Independence" worked from camp theatricality and kitsch exotica to the soaring emotion of reciprocated love and the orchestral grandeur of synthesized strings and gospel chorus. Like "I Feel Love", "State Of Independence" was a synth masterpiece that revelled in artifice.'

While Warner Brothers were releasing singles from 'Donna Summer', a new version of 'I Feel Love' remixed by Patrick Cowley was introduced to the UK record buying market on the 4th December 1982. This new version of 'I Feel Love' made it to no.21 in the UK. The full-length twelve inch version, fifteen minutes and forty-five seconds long, again became a dance floor hit five years after the original was released way back in 1977. It was also issued as an edited seven inch single. The remixed single was released before 'The Woman In Me' was marketed. With the success of the 1982 version of 'I Feel Love', Casablanca Records decided to re-issue Summer's first international hit, 'Love To Love You Baby', in 1983. The single surprisingly failed to make much of an impact. Perhaps if it had been given a new remix it might have been more successful.

Meanwhile, the up-tempo track 'Walk Hand In Hand', credited to B. Broderson, appeared in a compilation album 'Disco Round Vol. 2' in 1982, released in Germany, and 'Disco Stars' in 1983 which was marketed in Holland. The track was also featured in some bootleg copies of 'I'm A Rainbow'. It is not clear when it was recorded.

The following year, Michael Omartian produced 'She Works Hard For The Money', an enormous success for Summer. The project reached no.9 in the US (thirty-two weeks in the chart) and no.28 in the UK (five weeks).

In Zimbabwe it peaked at no.3, in South Africa it reached no.6, in Sweden and Norway it reached no.8 and no.12 respectively. In Japan, it peaked at no.27. This was Summer's first US Top 10 album since 1979's 'Bad Girls' and 'On The Radio: The Greatest Hits Volumes I & II'.

Donna Summer was thrilled, telling *Billboard* that Michael Omartian was a godsend. Summer said that Omartian was like Giorgio Moroder; mild tempered, incredibly creative and a perfectionist.

The album title was a tribute to the working woman. The tracks on 'She Works Hard For The Money' included more uplifting tunes than those on the 'Donna Summer' album. Fans and critics saw the album as a welcome and convincing return to form, with the album achieving Gold status in the US and Gold certification by the Canadian Recording Industry Association on the 1st September 1983.

'She Works Hard For The Money' was a song about strong, independent women, very much in control of their lives. It could almost have been Summer's answer to all of the doubters who questioned her professional survival, especially in view of the aborted double album and subsequent modest pop-rock efforts. 'She Works Hard For The Money' was inspired by a real-life experience. At a social event, Summer met Onetta Johnson, an attendant in the ladies' room. Summer recognised that for many people, it was a question of taking on any job in order to make ends meet and to support one's family, whether you like the job or not. Intimately caught in that moment, Summer created the concept of her hit song. Summer subsequently introduced Johnson to her fans – she featured on the back cover of the album. Johnson in actual fact (during the day) is a lab technician. In 2004 in response to a fan's query in *Attitude*, Summer said that she had not seen Johnson for at least fifteen years but she occasionally met members of Johnson's family by chance at her shows and sent her regards.

Uji Rashid, a popular singer and actor in Malaysia, was very much inspired by 'She Works Hard For The Money'. Although it's an up-tempo tune, the story is more about the hard realities of life. The Malaysian singer acknowledged Summer as a true star who really works hard for the money. In Rashid's own words:

'. . . the 1970s was an era where we started some new techniques in music. After the a-go-go in the 1960s, disco was intelligently blended with slow rock ballads. (Summer) was an "icon" and a strong woman . . . the song "She Works Hard For The Money" is a sign. Hey – stop, listen, and give it a thought!'

The single debuted in the US Top 40 on 18th June 1983, peaking at no.3 on the eleventh week. The single was in the *Billboard* chart for a total of twenty-one weeks. In the UK, the single peaked at no.25 on the 23rd July 1983 and stayed in the chart for eight weeks.

Summer's single releases have always been well received in Europe and this was no exception, reaching no.1 in Spain, no.3 in France, no.5 in Sweden, no.9 in Norway and no.10 in both Switzerland and Poland. In Australia, the single climbed to no.4 and in Canada it was a hit at no.5. The single was a no.11 hit in South Africa.

There are many strong pop melodies on 'She Works Hard For The Money'. 'Women' is a sassy, funky rhythm; a sound that had been missed by many fans. On 'People People' and 'Tokyo', Summer performed at her best. The sentimental track 'I Do Believe (I Fell In Love)' starts off deceptively low-key, slow and sensual but towards the end of the track it suddenly changes gear and becomes an up-tempo pop-rock number with Summer's multi-track vocals overlapping each other in a rising crescendo, before gradually fading out.

Summer also explored new musical territory by recording a reggae pop tune titled 'Unconditional Love' with British group Musical Youth. The track was a hit in the UK, climbing into the Top 20, but failed to make the Top 40 in the US. The single debuted in the US on 3rd September 1983 hitting no.43 (eight weeks in the chart). The reggae track peaked at no.14 in the UK after it entered the chart on the 24th September and stayed in the charts for thirteen weeks. The 'Unconditional Love' twelve inch UK single was also marketed in a limited edition that was packaged with a separate twelve inch single of 'Love To Love You Baby'. The single was a no.3 hit in Zimbabwe staying as long as sixteen weeks in the chart. It was a no.24 hit in New Zealand and it peaked at no.28 in both Ireland and Canada.

The ballad 'Love Has A Mind Of Its Own', sung as a duet with Matthew Ward, debuted at no.70 in the US on the 14th January 1984 but failed to enter the Top 100 in the UK. The last single from 'She Works Hard For The Money', 'Stop, Look And Listen', only managed to reach no.57 in the UK on the 28th January 1984. These two singles failed to make much of an impression anywhere.

In 1984, 'He's A Rebel' from the album won Best Inspirational Performance at the 26th Annual Grammy Awards, her first Grammy win since 1979. All the tracks on 'She Works Hard For The Money' were co-written except for 'I Do Believe (I Fell In Love)', credited solely to Summer.

'She Works Hard For The Money' was part of the final settlement Summer came to with her former record label, Casablanca (now Mercury Records). The agreement was to produce one original studio album, releasing her from her contract with the Casablanca label. Fortunately for Summer and her old label, 'She Works Hard For The Money' (Gold status by the Recording Industry Association of America) was the most successful project since Summer's disco era. The album was certified Gold in Canada on the 1st September 1983.

From an interview with US rock band Hypnogaja (vocals Jason 'ShyBoy', keyboard Mark Nubar Donikian, drum Adrian Barnardo, bass Bryan Farrar, guitar by Abe Parker):

'There are a couple of favourite albums floating around . . . for different reasons. "Four Seasons Of Love" is a stunning concept album, as conveyed through a four-song cycle – there's so much emotion in the tracks. It really captures what love can sound like. The "Once Upon A Time" album should really be turned into a Broadway musical – there's so much depth and style, and it's so visual. "Bad Girls" is the ultimate classic, right up there with Pink Floyd's "Dark Side Of The Moon", Fleetwood Mac's "Rumours" and Michael Jackson's "Thriller". Aside from the obvious smash hits, the album contains so many gems – "Lucky", "Our Love", "My Baby Understands" – all of which sound just as fresh today. There's also "I'm A Rainbow" (which sat in the vaults, unreleased for many years), a really great document mixing post-disco dance music, New Wave, rock and pop.'

Taken from 'She Works Hard For The Money', a page on Wikipedia (as of February 15th 2011):

'Many fans saw the album as a "return to form" for Summer – she was once again presented as a strong, powerful woman very much in control. During the 1970s, Summer's management had worked hard to portray her as a powerful, sexual fantasy figure to the point where they had become too involved in her personal life (which led to a period of depression for Summer before becoming a born again Christian and filing a lawsuit against her record label)'.

In her autobiography written with Marc Eliot, *Ordinary Girl: The Journey*, Donna Summer claimed that no one from her past or current label expected the album to be a hit and it caught them off guard. PolyGram was upset after seeing her chart success, knowing that they had agreed to free Summer from her contract. On the other hand, Geffen Records were stuck with their signing having a major hit with her past record label. Geffen Records felt that Summer should have kept this big hit for them and the label was eager for Summer and her team to repeat their success with their next project. Interestingly, the 1982 album 'Donna Summer' spent slightly longer in the *Billboard* chart than 'She Works Hard For The Money'.

Life after disco showed that Summer was a versatile survivor. Despite having one album shelved, her other productions were all at least moderately successful. Her songs continued to get airtime and she kept her place in the public consciousness. Rather than falling into some kind of post-disco obscurity, Summer evolved both her image and her music and gained new fans along the way. The release of her 1980s albums had fulfilled a wish that she had expressed back in a 1978 interview; she wanted to be an all-round entertainer and not just a sex symbol. Her wish had come true and she had entered the new decade no longer the Queen Of Disco, but as a successful pop-rock act instead.

8

There Goes The Diva

Summer held her popularity with music fans until it was alleged she criticised the gay community for the spread of AIDS in the early 1980s. This led to the 'mass burning' of her records and her popularity slumped amongst her gay fans. Perhaps the industry itself felt uncomfortable with the alleged comments.

This episode seriously damaged Donna Summer's career. She denied making the remarks in all her subsequent interviews. It was said in *The Advocate* (4th July 1989) that the 'rumour' had started with newspaper writer Jim Feldman in his 1983 review of Summer's Atlantic City concert in the *Village Voice*. In 1984, Summer issued a press release stating she was not anti-gay and her true feelings had been misinterpreted by a third party.

In an article 'Wrongly Punished', published in the *Gay Times* in November 1999, Richard Smith said that the rumour was spread after her show, by someone who was at the concert where the discussion had started. A 'debate' was had and a certain atmosphere developed. Summer is a famous singer and also a born again Christian, which might have resulted in certain tensions coming to the fore. This could be viewed as a classic case of envy and malicious gossip, which can happen to anyone in the public eye. Some press noted that the matter was made worse by Donna Summer's team because they shielded her from the bad press.

In defence of her team, Donna Summer noted in *Boyz UK* magazine in 1999 that:

'My manager had tried to keep me insulated, because they knew I was going through so much internal stuff, they didn't want me to do something crazy, but when I surfaced, that was when we went to the press ...'

This is not the only rumour she had been the subject of. In the 1970s, in an interview with Charles L. Sanders for *Ebony*, 'Donna Summer: Singer Talks About Her Loves, Her Child, That Rumor', Summer said it had also been suggested that she was a transvestite and later had a sex change:

'... I guess I'll have to live with it, because I've always heard that you can't trace a rumour and you can't kill a lie.'

Richard Smith wrote in 'Wrongly Punished' that Donna Summer said in 1987 she was not concerned by the anti-gay allegation. The reason for this laid-back approach was that Summer had been the subject of odd rumours before and she just assumed that this one would fade away like all the others. Rumours and gossip were an occupational hazard of being a star.

Indeed the 'Donna Summer being a man' story was first started by a writer for a gay publication in New York mentioned by *Ebony* magazine in Chicago, October 1977. However *Ebony* did not state which publication it was from. Interestingly, the stories went as far as Europe and Asia. But finally it stopped after a newspaper article dated 25th December 1976 stated that, after confirming it with Donna Summer's manager, there was obviously no truth to the rumour. A bizarre way to prove that Summer is a real woman!

Weirdly, in *Ebony* (Charles L. Sanders), the tittle-tattle was also backed with a 'garish picture' of Summer looking 'a little "hard," a bit masculine' on the album jacket 'I Remember Yesterday' (photo by Victor Skrebneski). Summer's front cover for *After Dark* magazine for the article 'Donna Summer: Queen Of Sex Rock' also 'caused further spreading of the rumour'!

Charles L. Sanders describes his interview with Summer at her home in 'Donna Summer: Singer Talks About Her Love, Her Child, That Rumor':

'Donna is a tall, heavy-hipped woman who moves with the elegance she learned as a part-time model in Europe, and as she bends to put an Edith Piaf record on the turntable and her low-cut silk dress reveals the marvellous ripeness of her breast and clings oh-so gently to the curves of her behind, it seems ridiculous that she is defending herself against the absurdity that she may not be a woman at all.'

It was such a bizarre rumour, and even more absurd that it needed to be quashed by a semi-official pronouncement! Obviously those who believed the 'tales' needed to have their eyes checked!

In *Off The Record: An Oral History Of Popular Music* by Joe Smith, he quotes Summer as saying that rumours she was actually a man came about because several transvestites at the time would sing 'Love To Love You Baby' in their acts.

Summer, in an interview with Simon Button in 2004 for *The Sunday Express*, again noted that the tales started because a transvestite singer used her name and song. After meeting the performer she said that he 'was pretty cute, actually – cuter than me!' The revolutionary sound and theme of 'Love To Love You Baby' made it very 'adult' entertainment.

Unfortunately however, the rumours regarding Donna Summer's alleged anti-gay remarks were never forgotten.

Back in 1989, during a concert in the UK, the AIDS activist group ACT-UP London asked Donna Summer to make a positive statement in support of the human rights of the HIV and gay communities. It was reported she turned down the invitation. It is very possible that the request was simply not passed on to the star, as it may not have been deemed important or relevant by her management. Agents and managers are employed to take much of the pressure off their star clients and they will, rightly or wrongly, filter a lot of the requests and demands 'received' by the star from fans, the media and other interested parties. So Summer may never have been aware of the request but unfortunately got blamed anyway! To make things worse the 'reported' refusal only served to confirm rumours of Summer's alleged previous remarks.

Paul Gambaccini maintains that the situation was not as serious for Summer as it may appear. Gambaccini acknowledged that allegedly Summer had made the remark; there were a couple of religious artists who certainly did make uninformed remarks about AIDS but they didn't get into sales trouble because the gay audience were not a large percentage of their fan base. The pain, suffering and loss of the community in the 1980s were profound. Donna Summer definitely lost most of her gay audience overnight but the type of material she recorded at that time did not really appeal to gay audiences. Gambaccini said if this situation had happened in 1978, the 'Bad Girls' album would not be as big as it was because a large part of her dance audience was gay. But, for example, 'State Of Independence' was more of a mass audience record, it does not require a gay fan base. What Donna Summer lost would be a percentage of first week sales to the fans who bought every one of her records. Gambaccini's point of view was that when the gay audience have a favourite they are very loyal, but there was a great sense of betrayal. Summer and other uninformed acts happened to be in a place far away from the situations and problems faced by many people and were liable to make comments that would affect them. For example, if Donna Summer had said that anybody who had unprotected sex was looking for trouble, she wouldn't realise how hurtful it would be to some of her fans. Being a religious girl, removed from such a lifestyle, Summer wouldn't have realised how many of her fans had unprotected sex on a regular basis. Gambaccini didn't believe Donna Summer had set out to hurt anybody. The remark, if she did indeed make it, just showed how far away her own lifestyle was from that of her audience.

In August 1991, *New York* magazine published an article reiterating the previous allegations. Donna Summer filed a libel suit claiming that the story was completely erroneous and that it had caused serious damage to her career. Summer said at a press conference on 1st October 1991 at a Los Angeles hotel:

'. . . I did not say it, I do not believe that. I would never say the things attributed to me in that article.'

This would once and for all settle the question in the eyes of the public and the media; Donna Summer would set the record straight. It was a tough moment for the star and her fans. Eventually the case was settled out of court. According to Summer in *Attitude*, December 1994, 'Donna Summer: What's She Like?' the artist expressed her hurt at the allegations and was concerned that people who read the article would take it at face value. Summer is aware that her work has been celebrated in gay clubs and on the gay scene and that many of her fans are gay. She was one of the first stars to have a considerable gay following, paving the way for singers such as Cher, Madonna, Kylie Minogue, Beyonce and Lady Gaga. The impact of a 'gay' following is probably exaggerated by the press. The cliché that gay men have better taste is not backed up by any evidence – and what is good taste? There might be a tendency for camp, glamorous female acts to have a gay following but a successful act will be successful with or without her gay audience. Donna Summer speaking in 2008 to Clay Cane for his 'The Queen Is Back' interview in *Pride Source*:

'From the beginning, my whole scene broke out in the gay clubs. I don't know if I would have a career if it hadn't been in some ways for the way "Love To Love You Baby" started off and everybody jumped on it. It was in the gay clubs the song took off – they really embraced the new sound. I have to give credit where credit is due.'

Some fans and media still have some reservations regarding the 'gay' comment. It is still a sensitive subject for many people who remember the difficulties of the time when the remarks were allegedly made. There was, and still remains, much ignorance surrounding HIV and AIDS and it is a condition that still brings with it political and social issues even in 'modern, liberal' democracies. It is still a condition associated with the gay community and drug users, in the West at least, although the majority of sufferers worldwide are heterosexual.

In 1994 Jody Watley's single 'When A Man Loves A Woman', written by her and Larry 'Rock' Campbell, was also released with different lyrics celebrating love in all its forms and even mentioned AIDS:

'When a man loves a woman he knows the reality of AIDS, he won't bring it home to you by some other love he's made'.

Donna Summer was familiar with the 'gay lifestyle' as early as the 1970s.

In 'Live And More', (1978) in an introduction to 'My Man Medley' she said:

'You know. I just want to say this. This is something I think you ladies will identify with... and maybe some of you men too...'.

In Asian countries the rumours did not receive much press coverage, almost certainly because the subject of homosexuality is taboo and freedom of speech and media expression are limited in such conservative, authoritarian societies. Although Asian countries have the same proportion of gay and lesbian people as any other society in the world, it is a life shrouded in secrecy. The media may not have noticed what Western Donna Summer fans must have felt at that time and so no backlash as a result of the alleged comments was seen. Her songs remained popular on radio stations and in the clubs, with stations playing whatever was popular in the West at that time.

From a Malaysian artist's perspective, Francissca Peter said the gay community loved Summer. While Summer's American and European fans freely expressed their anger at her alleged comments by burning her records, returning them to stores and boycotting her music, the 'Paper Dolls' in Malaysia (cross-dressing males performing drag queen shows) carried on performing to her songs and impersonating her, although as most of us are aware these tributes were not all necessarily by people who were themselves gay. Peter understood how Summer's fans in the West had felt, but she also thinks that there should not be hatred in the world of music.

In an interview in the *Windy City Times,* Summer said that it was understandable for the public to believe stories that had been published – but readers shouldn't believe everything they read or hear. Things are easily taken out of context and complete untruths can be spread as if they are facts. That has happened to Summer in many ways.

In an interview with Kevin Koffle for *The Advocate*, Summer admitted at that time she certainly did not have any idea about the illness. Summer would not wish AIDS on anyone – it was a horrifying condition. She felt that more needed to be done to combat the disease globally:

'I don't think they're doing enough for it ... I've lost a lot of friends who have died of AIDS ... I'm hurting as much as anyone else at the amount of people who are gone ... It is devastating.'

Summer told Koffle that some of her family members were gay as well as many of her friends and associates when AIDS was still unknown. Summer is not a person who passes judgement on an individual's personal life. She said she had enough things in her own life to 'clean up'!

In an article for *Boyz UK* by Howard Wilmot, Summer said that she had been close to gay people all her life. In a 1979 interview with *Penthouse*, Summer told how she even had a relationship with a man who later came out as gay and with whom she remained best friends. She always assumed that, because of her history, people would know such rumours to be false.

Summer still feels she cannot defend herself. She said in an interview with *The Advocate*, 1989 that the public think that she can say 'anything now', it won't make a difference. It continues to hurt Summer deeply. She says it is her strong belief in God and prayer that helps her to be strong and deal with the unfairness, setbacks and sadness that life sometimes brings.

As time moves on, it is only Summer and the few individuals who were there who know the truth about what was said, so we should let it be. Donna Summer has many times performed at HIV/AIDS charity functions.

In 'The Queen And Her Crayons: An Interview With Donna Summer' by Christian John Wikane for *PopMatters*, discussing the bad and sad memories in her life, Summer said that the very worst moments could not shared publicly. There are things that were too painful to talk about.

Some things are private matters and should remain so, even for the famous. Some members of the public and the gay community wanted Donna Summer to apologise but that would just be an admission that the allegation was true. Some people might choose to apologise even if they are innocent, as a means to close the matter and move on. But such an admission by a star in her position would have been extremely damaging both personally and professionally and would have compromised her integrity.

In 'Donna Summer: What's She Like?' (*Attitude*) in 1994, Summer said that the case was settled amicably with both parties satisfied with the outcome. A simple exchange of views in private had been exploded into something that had dogged Summer for years and now it was time to move on and forget. The allegation, although partially forgotten, is still often mentioned in the music press. The 'Pandora's Box' that was maliciously opened might never be completely put to rest!

The public and fans are nowadays generally uninterested or unaware of this old story and the young gay community probably don't take much notice of the subject, simply seeing Summer as an established international star. She began her career as an icon of the gay disco scene but now, years later, her music is just as likely to be heard on a mainstream radio station or in a 'straight' nightclub as in a gay club.

Returning to her recording work, Summer failed to repeat her previous successes with the 1984 project 'Cats Without Claws', produced by Michael Omartian. Donna Summer was again involved heavily in the creative side of the material. 'Maybe It's Over' is her own composition with other songs credited to her and Omartian. Exceptions include 'Supernatural Love' and 'I'm Free', credited to the producer and Bruce Sudano, 'There Goes My Baby' by Benjamin Nelson, Lover Patterson and George Treadwell and finally 'Forgive Me' by Reba Rambo and Dony McGuire.

The album was predominantly pop-dance with some good soulful sentimental tracks such as 'Oh Billy Please', 'Forgive Me' and 'Maybe It's Over'. The album made US no.40 and stayed in the album chart for seventeen weeks. It only reached no.69 in the UK, managing just two weeks in the charts.

The project did not receive the commercial reaction Summer and her fans had hoped for. Although it was unsuccessful by her standards, one of the tracks from the album, 'Forgive Me', won 'Best Inspirational Performance' at the 27th Grammy Awards and 'There Goes My Baby' was a fair success in the US.

The first single from the project, 'There Goes My Baby', was a cover of The Drifter's 1959 no.2 hit. Donna Summer in actual fact did not plan to record the song. In *The New York Times* article 'The Pop Life; Donna Summer Seen On Two Pop Music Videos' (26th September 1984) Summer shares how she came to cover 'There Goes My Baby':

'I was in the studio and it literally popped into my mind. My producer, Michael Omartian, started playing it on the piano, but I didn't really know the whole song, so I started as-libbing. Then I started getting the character of the women singing the song, like I knew who she was. She was somebody who really loved her family and would do anything to keep it together, and I knew that the reason they were breaking up wasn't lack of love. Once I knew the character, I had a direction for the song.'

Summer's single debuted in the *Billboard* chart at no.59 on the 11th August 1984 and climbed to no.21. The single only made it to no.99 in the UK on 1st September 1984. 'There Goes My Baby' included the track 'Face The Music', a song not included on the 'Cats Without Claws' album. Although a bonus for fans, this strategy still did not make the single a big success, especially in the UK. Having said that, 'There Goes My Baby' managed to stay in the US chart for fourteen weeks! In Sweden the single climbed to no.15, in Holland it peaked at no.31 and in Canada it reached no.22.

The follow-up single 'Supernatural Love' made it to no.75 on the 24th November 1984 (five weeks). It entered the *Billboard* dance chart at no.39, the lowest entry yet for a Summer track in the dance chart. 'Supernatural Love' was a flop in the UK, not even making the chart and the follow-up single 'Eyes' failed to make an impact, debuting at no.97 in the UK on 25th May 1985.

Contemporary music at the time when the 'Cats Without Claws' album was released, was dominated by the electro pop flavour of Prince's 'When Doves Cry', Frankie Goes To Hollywood's 'Relax', Cyndi Lauper's 'She Bop' and Laura Branigan with 'Self Control'. From the middle of 1984 to the middle of 1985 the charts has been conquered by the sounds of George Michael, Miami Sound Machine, Madonna and Chaka Khan. Summer's music, despite being high quality pop, seemed suddenly out of step with the prevailing sound.

It was a time of declining chart success for Summer. Fans loved the songs on 'Cats Without Claws' but acknowledged that the project did not have enough strong material to make it a hit. It was another experimental work from Summer and the team. Some fans felt that the album was not fun to listen to and that the arrangements were a bit bland and impersonal. Summer's vocals were excellent on the tracks, but it was a more mature sound that needed time to grow on the listener rather than instantly accessible pop.

The track 'No It's Not The Way' was an energetic rock-pop-dance tune. 'I'm Free' had a catchy calypso R&B flavour. 'Cats Without Claws' was lyrically creative with 'mysterious' sound effects adding another dimension. And finally the Grammy award-winning ballad 'Forgive Me', a beautiful, soulful, gospel flavoured tune ended the ten-track album on a high note.

'Cats Without Claws' received moderate reviews but according to the allmusic.com album review site, the project deserved a better critical reception. Great to know that 'Cats' does have claws! The album was a success in Sweden. After its entry on 14th September 1984, it peaked at no.10 on 28th September, remaining in the album chart for ten weeks. In Switzerland it peaked at no.4 (four weeks) and in Norway it reached no.15 (three weeks). Perhaps by Donna Summer's standards it might not have been a great success but neither was it a complete commercial failure.

Three years passed before Summer returned with the single 'Dinner With Gershwin', first entering the chart on the 22nd August 1987 at no.85, reaching US no.48. Summer's dinner party was over after eleven weeks. In the UK, the single debuted at no.84 and then fell out of the chart. However, 'Dinner With Gershwin' re-entered the chart on the 17th October 1987 and after seven weeks it peaked at no.13, staying for thirteen weeks. The single came with the track 'Tearin' Down The Walls' as a B-side, a song not included in any of her albums to date. Fans were pleased. A limited-edition twelve inch picture disc was also marketed with a new picture printed on the vinyl. 'Dinner With Gershwin' was also released for the fiftieth anniversary of George Gershwin's death (11th July 1937).

The single was a no.2 hit in France, peaked at no.13 in Ireland, no.34 in Holland and at no.39 in Canada. 'Dinner With Gershwin' is a mature-sounding song with clever lyrics. It is a song about great figures from the worlds of science and art and wanting to meet interesting people from the past, or is it suggesting that there aren't many great individuals left? Or maybe it was about unrequited love?

The 'All Systems Go' album, from which 'Dinner With Gershwin' was taken, was produced by Harold Faltermeyer with other producers used for different tracks, Peter Burnetta and Rick Chudacoff for 'Bad Reputation', Richard Perry for the hit 'Dinner With Gershwin' with associate producer Brenda Russell and Keith D. Nelson, Jeff Lams and Donna Summer herself producing the beautiful ballad 'Thinkin' Bout My Baby'.

The album revealed a new, mature Donna Summer in control of her vocals in 'Thinkin' Bout My Baby', 'Fascination', 'Love Shock' and 'Voices Cryin' Out', although still the album was not a huge success. 'All Systems Go' is a synthesis of sounds of the 1980s, synth-style pop-dance with soul and R&B touches, including both upbeat songs and ballads. But on first listening there are no stand-out melodies that immediately grab you. 'All Systems Go', 'Dinner With Gershwin' and 'Voices Cryin' Out' were the only three clearly catchy tunes. The album however is a mature and clever creation that will grow on the listener and be more appreciated with time.

From a review of 'All Systems Go' in the *Los Angeles Daily News*:

'Despite the delays, "All Systems Go" is a state-of-the-art pop album that reflects Miss Summer's studiousness. The singer co-wrote the bulk of the album. And although the disk features strong songs, it is Miss Summer's singing that impresses most.'

Ralph Novak wrote that Summer had to travel to West Germany to record 'All Systems Go' with Harold (Axel F.) Faltermeyer. Novak reviewed and graded the album an 'A' in *People* magazine on 26th October 1987. He discusses the tracks in the following quote:

'On ballads such as "Jeremy" or "Voices Cryin' Out" or ... "Only The Fool Survives", Summer gets to flex her considerable vocal power. Such dance tunes as the title track and "Bad Reputation", however, focus a lot more on bass figures and percussion surges than on Summer ... on "Dinner With Gershwin" ... Composer Brenda Russell came up with a clever concept ... Midway through the tune, though, she seems to give up on the idea, ending up by repeating her first verse ... That's not Summer's fault, of course, and the song is still fun. The same could be said of the album as a whole. Summer is a victim of her own talent in a way: a performer as good as she is generates high – perhaps unfairly high – expectations. Whoever said showbusiness was supposed to be fair?'

It was the first album by Summer that fell quickly off the *Billboard* album chart, peaking at no.122. The album managed to stay at least six weeks in the US but unfortunately failed to enter the UK chart. On a better note it reached no.27 in Italy and Sweden. 'All Systems Go' reached no.49 in Holland and even entered the Japanese album chart at no.69! But it is in the huge US market that artists hope to be successful, commercially at least.

The 'All Systems Go' single was not released in the US. The upbeat, young-sounding single, which was said to be Donna Summer's favourite track from the album, entered the UK chart on the 23rd January 1988 peaking at no.54 a week later. A second single release 'Only The Fool Survives', a ballad recorded with Mickey Thomas, failed to make an impact in the US, resulting in it being available as a promo disc only for music fans. The ballad was released in Japan.

It is a shame that the other songs from 'All Systems Go' were not as successful as 'Dinner With Gershwin', but it did at least get Summer into to the chart again, having been out of the limelight for some time.

Brenda Russell, in an interview for *PopMatters* for the article 'She's A Rainbow: A Tribute To Donna Summer' by Christian John Wikane, said when she sent the demo 'Dinner With Gershwin' to David Geffen for her own album, he 'flipped out over' the material. Geffen told Russell that the tune had to go to Summer, who had been 'off the scene for a little bit'. It did the trick and was a hit.

Russell, a fan of Donna Summer, added that she enjoyed working with her and was over the moon that she agreed to record 'Dinner With Gershwin'. She said that Summer did a great job with the song and praised her talent and voice. Unfortunately, 'Dinner With Gershwin' was not enough to make 'All Systems Go' a success. The record label was probably not impressed!

In 1987, Summer received an award for her long-term career achievements at the Diamond Awards Festival in Belgium. In the same year, the publication *British Hit Albums* showed that Summer had amassed a total of 159 weeks in the UK album charts. The publication listed all the acts that had spent 100 weeks or more in the charts between 8th November 1958 and 26th December 1987. Summer had the same number of weeks as Elvis Costello, Prince And The Revolution and Neil Young.

This period saw a marked decline in Summer's fortunes as a recording artist. Her albums had been on a rollercoaster; both fans and the industry seemed to forget her. Some of the material she proposed to the Geffen label was rejected and ultimately commercial disappointment with Summer's albums resulted in David Geffen dropping her from his label. The new sounds the label wanted from Summer had failed to impress the public. More importantly, rightly or wrongly, Summer did not bring any more money to the label. Summer acknowledged that her relationship with the company had not worked out for her.

Summer told Kevin Koffler in an interview for the article 'Not The Last Dance: Donna Speaks Out On Aids, Gays And Coming Out Of Exile' in *The Advocate*:

'It was one of those situations where they didn't have the confidence they needed to have in me. David Geffen desperately wanted to sign me as his first act, so he did ... I used to go to his house to write songs. I don't know at what point things started going awry, but they did.'

In the interview, Summer said that when she signed to the label there were 'promises' of film roles. But she said it just turned out to be 'blah, blah, blah', that David Geffen failed to deliver what he promised. Donna Summer knew then she had made a huge mistake.

In *The Encyclopedia Of Popular Music*, Colin Larkin writes that Geffen (a very successful music man) was a ruthless businessman, for whom friendship would always take second place to a successful deal. He learned this from Tom King's biography.

In *Ordinary Girl: The Journey*, Summer writes that her departure from the record label was amicable; her move to Geffen Records was not a successful one. The hit records she had with the Casablanca label could not be recreated by her and Geffen. But the split upset her. Summer was 'disillusioned' and 'depressed'. The performer who sang 'I want to have dinner with Gershwin' also wrote that she realised she didn't have that many real friends outside of her small circle of professional associates.

Perhaps, besides her loving family and truly close friends, Summer also longed to speak to the one person that understood her musically. The creative mind 'the ordinary girl' was seeking was Neil Bogart – the master-mind of Summer's Casablanca years. Sadly, he was no longer there for the star to confide in, having died in 1982. Donna Summer had always loved Bogart and acknowledged that, without him, she would never have achieved the fame and renown that she had.

From the 'Special Thanks To' notes on the album 'Donna Summer' (1982):

'In Memory Of Neil Bogart, who was instrumental in getting me to where I am today. He was a man who loved to live, and always had a goal. "Why head for a mountaintop when you're reaching for the sky?" He made the world believe … they could see right through his eyes. I will always love you!'

Paul Gambaccini sums up Summer's career in the 1980s:

'When she moved to Geffen, instead of the iconic leader of a movement she become a talented artist; one of many. Although the records are of good quality they have to be exceptionally good to become hits. Because there is no sense of follow-through any more … She's no less talented an individual but her recordings are not part of a recognisable sequence, not part of a genre. You can't be a "queen" of nothing. She's gone from being a Queen Of Disco to being a good singer. That's a whole different thing.'

Her songs from this era are still quite satisfactory for fans! Gambaccini was sure that some of her records would last. 'She Works Hard For The Money' was well received in the US, while 'State Of Independence' was more popular in the UK. Her last melody with Geffen 'Dinner With Gershwin' was very interesting but again too classy for the young music-buying market. Donna Summer just wound up being bigger than she ever thought she would be. Departing the world of disco, Donna Summer would adapt to the current music scene.

The media reported that the lack of success was the result of not producing 'signature' dance tunes. Others felt the failure to reproduce Summer's previous success was due to her criticism of the gay community. In the 1980s, as she found her new belief in God, Donna Summer said that she would not be performing 'Love To Love You Baby' again, because of the songs sexual imagery. These remarks upset some of her loyal fans and many of them later stopped supporting her. Also during an interview with BBC Radio 1 on 12th November 1994, when answering the DJ's question, she said in a low voice, that if given a choice, 'Love To Love You Baby' would not be included in 'Endless Summer: Donna Summer's Greatest Hits'. Ironically, Summer still sings 'Hot Stuff' and 'Bad Girls', both of which have sexual elements in the lyrics.

But 'Rumour Has It' that during the recording session for 'Love To Love You Baby' Summer had to 'Dim All The Lights' in the studio. Alone, without any other production team members except her producer present, Summer was only then able to create the atmosphere for the song. Giorgio Moroder sure was one lucky gentleman having first-hand experience with the 'raw' sound that came from that microphone. In fact, Donna Summer was shy and being in the dark allowed her to relax and concentrate on delivering the perfect performance. Giorgio Moroder said in the TV show *A & E Biography* that her voice in 'Love To Love You Baby' was a conceptual presentation for the melody.

Time passed by and in 1999 she performed 'Love To Love You Baby' as a rap and sang the track at a 2009 concert in Paris. A true star, Summer performed it with a mature, classily seductive vocal. Perhaps she had now mellowed and realised that the sexy elements of her songs are part of the entertainment of pop music and don't go against her own personal beliefs. Recording religious tracks such as 'I Believe In Jesus' in 1980 put off some of her non-religious fans. Many fans found the gospel sound uplifting, but if the lyrics were too overtly religious, many fans would hesitate to buy an album full of them. If Summer produced an entire album with an openly religious theme then that would be a different matter; fans would have the choice to take it or leave it altogether, depending on their sensibilities.

Paul Gambaccini explained that there is a huge market for Christian music in the US and even in those days, there were separate shops to buy it in. Religious albums sold in large volumes in religious bookshops. The general audience did not register these on their radar. Gambaccini took Cliff Richard as an example. He had his amazingly successful career but most music fans didn't realise that he also had an independent religious musical career. Richard occasionally toured singing religious music. He separated the two musical elements knowing that his pop fans would not be interested. The danger arrives when an artist releases religious material that is not in line with the pop market. Very rarely does a religious-flavoured song become a pop hit, although it can happen. Usually it would be from a massive hit record such as 'Oh Happy Day' or 'He's Got The Whole World In His Hands'. Paul Gambaccini also noted that Donna Summer sees herself as a well-rounded artist; she didn't box herself in as some of her fans did. Summer offered religion as part of her creativity, but the mass audience wasn't interested. Gambaccini explains that if Summer had tried to impose the religious material on a mainstream career, that would have been a source of resentment for fans.

Gloria Gaynor didn't think Summer's popularity had dwindled due to the fact that she had become religious. In fact, her religious feelings could contribute to her overall creativity. Gaynor believes everyone responds to religion in different ways. Some sections of the media and general public might feel that when religion becomes part of an artist's life, then that artist might become more judgemental and their creativity might be stifled by their new-found beliefs. Gaynor felt that the public would learn to accept artists with faith. Music fans understand that religion is a sensitive issue. It is also true to say the world of the music business and stardom might sit uncomfortably with the restraint and moral certainty associated with a person's religious beliefs.

Joel Whitburn said that even though Summer's hits had slowed down, she had moved to other areas of interesting musical styles. She crossed over into the R&B chart with the well-received 'Love Is In Control (Finger On The Trigger)' at no.4, 'She Works Hard For The Money' at no.1, 'Unconditional Love' at no.9 and 'Dinner With Gershwin' at no.10. However, the Queen Of Disco label dominated her image so strongly that her non-disco songs were not received as well by the public. Musical tastes had changed and, as Whitburn noted, many previously successful acts suffered mixed fortunes as time passed.

Summer's relative lack of chart success could also have been the result of a lack of media support, such as publicity, TV, radio airplay and magazine features.

The albums 'The Wanderer', 'Cats Without Claws' and 'All Systems Go' explored new musical directions. Some of the albums and singles may not have been hits in the US or in the UK, but they found success in other parts of the world. Her creativity had evolved in other directions, with less sensual or sexual elements to her lyrics. Summer told Jacob Dahlin in a TV interview for 'Jacobs Stege' in the late 1980s that success was now not as important to her as it had been at the start of her career; she was now more interested in developing herself as a person. On the contrary, the big record labels wanted successful income-generating records with lots of airplay, lots of sales and a big return on their investment.

Her songs were, by now, getting much less airtime; they didn't fit with the radio network's idea of what was popular and contemporary. She was still making music, but the public were increasingly unaware of her work. It was a tough time for Summer, professionally speaking. She was absent from the charts for long periods of time and she faded from public consciousness. Her fans dreamed of the day when their diva would return with more disco-inspired beats.

An American group, Shalamar, had several hits in the UK charts with their disco-dance tracks 'I Can Make You Feel Good' at no.7, 'A Night To Remember' at no.5 and 'There It Is' a no.5 hit, all in 1982 when Donna Summer and her team were experimenting with their sound. In 1984, Sister Sledge's 1979 hits re-entered the chart with 'Thinking Of You' (no.11), 'Lost In Music' (no.4) and 'We Are Family' (no.33). UK group The Real Thing's 1976 hit was revamped and entered the UK Top 5 in 1986 with 'You To Me Are Everything (The Decade Remix 76–86)'. Even Barry White had brief success with an old hit with 'Never Never Gonna Give You Up Remix' in 1988. Certainly these songs were remixed and face-lifted, but it demonstrated that the disco beat was still popular with the public.

From *Popular Music Since 1955: A Critical Guide To The Literature* by Paul Taylor (1985):

'In 1975 ... she was launched as the "Queen Of Disco" with a series of over-produced singles featuring a good deal of heavy breathing and not a little innuendo. After worldwide success, she now seems to have passed her peak but she is a creative writer and skilful recording artist and always likely to produce more hit records.'

Some critics have forgotten that there are hit songs by Donna Summer from after the disco era. Summer by this time had changed her musical direction. She chose not to sing or record certain kinds of song and insisted on performing a song about Jesus for 'The Wanderer'.

In *Turn The Beat Around: The Secret History Of Disco*, Peter Shapiro explains that Summer was no longer interested in portraying herself as 'the sex machine'. Her new religious beliefs and values now 'conflicted' with her past image. Summer moved from disco and 'decided to play it safe' with a more restrained pop sound. According to Shapiro, 'Moroder kept the electronic for himself'.

In the 1980s, Summer also had to compete with other young female singers at a time when the new club scene and *Billboard* Top 40 chart was dominated by hits such as Irene Cara's 1983 single 'Flashdance ... What A Feeling'. This was produced by Summer's former producer Giorgio Moroder, reached no.1 and stayed in the chart for twenty weeks. Madonna's 1984 no.1 dance single 'Like A Virgin' stayed in the chart for fourteen weeks. In the same year, 1970s diva Chaka Khan stayed in the charts for seventeen weeks with the R&B flavoured 'I Feel For You', which climbed to no.3, and Tina Turner celebrated her 'What's Love Got To Do With It', a no.1 pop success which stayed in the Top 40 for eighteen weeks. The younger singer Janet Jackson's 1986 no.4 smash hit 'What Have You Done For Me Lately' stayed in the *Billboard* Top 40 for thirteen weeks; Jody Watley's 1987 no.2 hit 'Looking For A New Love' stayed in the chart for fourteen weeks and Paula Abdul's 1988 no.1 dance hit 'Straight Up' was in the chart for sixteen weeks. Never the less, even though these acts were new names to young record-buying fans, Tina Turner, Chaka Khan and Jody Watley were not the new girls on the block. They had already established themselves as chart regulars. Turner, together with Ike Turner, first hit the charts in 1960 with 'A Fool In Love', Khan had a hit in 1974 as lead singer in the band Rufus, singing 'Tell Me Something Good' while Watley charted with Shalamar's 'A Night To Remember' in 1982. With new tunes, music videos and images suited to the mid 1980s they appeared as 'fresh faces' to young listeners!

In *Donna Summer: For The Record,* Craig Halstead said Summer turned down the offer to record 'Flashdance . . . What A Feeling'. On the website of *The Dennis Miller Radio Show,* the section 'Bumper Music' states that Donna Summer rejected another song that later become a hit – 'What's Love Got To Do With It'. Halstead quoted Summer in a 1999 interview as saying that she had the song for two years; she said that she would not have made 'What's Love Got To Do With It' sound like Tina Turner's record. She acknowledged that Turner's 'raspiness' and the sensitivity of the song made a perfect match.

Summer's fans' musical tastes have also evolved, taking in new acts and genres of music. New acts might focus more on their dance routines and appearance but Summer was there first, at the birth of the whole 'dance' genre. Donna Summer is a star that uses her voice, her very own freestyle dance movements and her persona with her audiences during her shows.

There are few acts that survive the test of decades, but Summer's songs remain popular, played by club DJs all over the world. Donna Summer keeps on coming back with new songs and remixes of classic dance tunes, all of which never fail to enter the *Billboard* dance chart.

9

Back On Track

In March 1989, Donna Summer was on the sidelines again. She began to work with the hit UK song writing team Stock, Aitken and Waterman.

'This Time I Know It's For Real' entered the chart on 25th February 1989, at no.42. The single later peaked at no.3 in the UK singles charts on the 25th March 1989 and went on to be an enormous hit around the globe. According to Donna Summer in a 1991 TV interview with Janet Langhart for *Talk Live*, she and Stock, Aitken and Waterman had a good time during their first session, with 'This Time I Know It's For Real' being the first song they composed for the project.

Pete Waterman kindly explained his first experience working with Summer:

'When you work with an artist as talented as Donna Summer, they know whether you're talented or you're not talented because they can spot it. She knows it's not about ... having hits. She knows that what you're writing are great songs. You've never met each other so you turn up like in a boxing match sparring, you're not quite sure what to expect ... you know that these people are really talented, this is a real pleasure and when you start to work together you know chemistry happens and then you just trust each other. And that's what Donna did ...'

The album 'Another Place And Time' was received well and kept her name in the minds of the record-buying public. With a run of fourteen weeks in the UK charts, 'This Time I Know It's For Real' remains Summer's longest charting single in the UK, certified Silver by the BPI on 1st March 1989. It proved to be Summer's last *Billboard* pop chart success in the US at the time of writing.

The single debuted in the *Billboard* Top 40 on the 20th May 1989 and later peaked at no.7 on 24th June 1989 with Gold certification on 11th July 1989. At its peak, 'This Time I Know It's For Real' was in the company of other hits from established stars and new acts such as Richard Marx at no.1 with 'Satisfied', New Kids On The Block at no.2 with 'I'll Be Loving You (Forever)' and Neneh Cherry's no.3 single 'Buffalo Stance'. Summer's single also shared the limelight with 'Baby Don't Forget My Number' by

Milli Vanilli at no.4, Fine Young Cannibals at no.5 with 'Good Times' and Bette Midler's huge hit 'Wind Beneath My Wings' at no.6.

The cheerful dance tune was a hit in Ireland, peaking at no.4. It climbed to no.2 in Belgium, no.5 in Holland and no.6 in Sweden and France. The single was a massive hit in Germany, spending three months in the charts, peaking at no.20. In Canada the single reached no.4, enjoying a seventeen-week chart stay and in Japan it got to no.12, staying in the chart for twenty weeks!

The album 'Another Place And Time' was released first in the UK as Summer did not have a US label. Following the album's success in the UK, it was finally released on Atlantic Records. However, by this time most of her American fans had already bought the imported album.

According to R&B: The Essential Album Guide 1998:

'... (the album) is bland and soulless, diluting Summer's powerful presence in the antiseptic arrangements that are the British production trio's stock-in-trade.'

Although the album did not get enthusiastic reviews from some critics, it was one of the most successful Summer albums of the 1980s and many fans were happy that she had teamed up with the 'hitmakers' Stock, Aitken and Waterman (SAW).

Paul Gambaccini said it was important for Donna Summer to work with SAW, as was collaborating with Giorgio Moroder. In his view, 'This Time I Know It's For Real' and the poppy album 'Another Place And Time' still sounds great to this day.

Donna Summer shared her experience working with SAW in an interview with Kevin Koffler for The Advocate. She claimed that SAW came the closest to reproducing the sound of Moroder, and that the album was a success, even if it had a very 1980s feel to it.

Summer's profile was again raised with a new audience of young music fans. The album had an attractively designed cover, from a concept by Summer and Lawrence Lawry, and her music videos for 'This Time I Know It's For Real' and 'Love's About To Change My Heart' presented Summer as a vibrant star.

'Another Place And Time' was her best-selling album with Warner Brothers in the 1980s, going Gold in the UK on 18th December 1989. It only made no.53 in US, spending twenty weeks in the chart in total, but reached no.17 in the UK (twenty-eight weeks). This achievement was a thrill for Summer, one that she had not had since 1979. The album was also a success in Sweden, peaking at no.16 (fourteen weeks). In France it reached no.26 (sixteen weeks).

In a 1990 article, 'Donna's Back At Her Best', for *Teleskop* magazine, Summer said she and her family spent six months in London while working on the album. She said:

'People's reaction to the new record has been really good . . . I'm surprised almost. I like it, but you never know what's going to happen until you get it out there.'

Working with the British team was a new experience for Summer. They worked very quickly on their projects and in Summer's personal analysis, the album was not balanced enough. Summer surely used to work quickly in the studio, 'Once Upon A Time' took 'four night sessions' and preparing the lyrics took just a few days. By the time of 'Bad Girls', Summer was more involved in the making of her recordings. By the time SAW came into the picture, the more mature Summer was working in a very different way from when she started in the 70s. She wished she could have had more time during the making of 'Another Place And Time', once saying that working on the album did little for her lyric writing and song composition. But she was also the first to realise how important it was in terms of a career move.

In an interview with Kevin Koffler in July 1989, Summer explained that all three of the producers worked on the songs, mutually agreeing on the writing and composition of the work. Summer left them to it because she wanted 'to go to a polo match'.

There are only three songs credited to Summer with the trio – 'This Time I Know It's For Real', 'Whatever Your Heart Desires' and 'Sentimental'. Pete Waterman saluted the fact that they had different ways of working with Donna Summer and she agreed that Waterman and his friends' work was fantastic. Waterman cheerfully recalls that Summer would leave them to fight for their creativity among themselves. Later the 'queen' would return to see who had won the creative battle.

A battle between the three creative forces was surely worthwhile! A hit record and some great compositions were the result! But it didn't come easy. Pete Waterman explained:

'. . . (it's) very difficult for most people to understand how passionate we were about pop songs. I mean, Donna worked with some very famous writers and producers. I don't think she ever worked with anybody as passionate as us. She wasn't used to people wanting to change the lyrics, or not accepting anything she wrote. I think she found it really strange that we cared about lyrics as passionately as we did. We laughed about it. But in the end she came around to our way of thinking. The way we worked was quite brutal so it was better if she went back to America for a while,

while we were sorting out all the basic stuff out. That's how it works.'

Waterman thought that Summer would be a bit cagey when she first heard the songs but she wasn't. They wanted her to add some ideas. However, after her return from the US, coming to the studio to listen to the tracks and read the lyrics, Summer loved the final work and agreed that she didn't need to touch their masterpiece compositions! Waterman claimed she was one of the greatest singers there was and it was unbelievable she was so happy with the results, hence he felt privileged to have worked with someone that both he and his team idolised. When asked if the star was punctual for work, Waterman laughs and recalls:

'No. Never, never no ... Donna Summer works on Donna Summer time. The first thing she tells you when you're going to work together ... you know you have to throw away your wrist watch. And that's when she turns up; when she's ready for work. You accepted that, the brief of working with her. Very much on the fact that when she's ready, you got to be ready! And if you're not there, well, you missed the moment.'

It was a great experience for Pete Waterman. The team did not simply wait all day for Donna Summer to arrive in the studio; they knew roughly when she would arrive: late afternoon to early evening. That suited the team very well. They would work on the compositions during the day.

Mike Stock discussed his time working with her in an article titled 'Endless Summer' by Fred Bronson for *Billboard*. He said Summer liked their sound and they produced the entire album in just three weeks. Stock recalled that she was a consummate artist, brilliant to work with, who could pick up and run with any song.

The album not surprisingly also comes complete with hit singles such as 'I Don't Wanna Get Hurt' which climbed to no.7 in the UK charts on 3rd June 1989. It did even better in Ireland, peaking at no.3; it reached no.4 in France and in Belgium the single made no.6. Unfortunately, the single was not released in the US.

Ironically, even though she loved 'I Don't Wanna Get Hurt', Donna Summer said in an interview with *Attitude* in 2004 that she felt 'out of her depth' singing it, adding that the lyrics and concept of the track were not appropriate for a woman of her age. According to Pete Waterman the song was a favourite of Summer's daughter, and she managed to convince her mother to record it. Waterman said that Summer was always worried about her age during the making of the songs for 'Another Place And Time'.

Donna Summer had already established her own image as a disco diva in the 1970s and then with more experimental New Wave, pop-dance-rock sounds in the 1980s. The Stock-Aitken-Waterman trademark sound was strongly associated with easy, lightweight pop acts, described as 'disposable' by some critics, such as Kylie Minogue, Rick Astley and Jason Donavon. Donna Summer perhaps felt uncomfortable being grouped together with such 'production line' acts.

Her producer Pete Waterman tried to put her at ease by telling her:

'Look, Shakespeare wrote about death. He didn't die to experience it. You know, you're an actor, you can sing these songs.'

The next single from 'Another Place And Time', 'Love's About To Change My Heart', stalled at no.89 in the US, but climbed to a higher position in the dance chart. US dance music lovers had a change of heart for 'Love's About To Change My Heart', pushing the track all the way to no.3 in the *Billboard* dance chart. In the UK it entered the chart on the 26th August 1989 and was at no.20 a week later. In Ireland it was a hit at no.11. Finally, the single 'When Love Takes Over You' stalled at no.72 in UK on the 25th November 1989 and was not released in the US. It is rumoured that the poor chart performance of 'When Love Takes Over You' resulted in the title track 'In Another Place And Time' remaining unreleased. However 'In Another Place And Time' was popular in Japan, hitting no.22 in the charts. In Australia it peaked at no.24.

The Stock, Aitken and Waterman team got on very well with Donna Summer. Pete Waterman said that after 'Another Place And Time', he and Summer continued to work on their creative ideas together. Waterman explained his team was very serious about their music and that working with Donna Summer's record company was very difficult because they didn't seem to grasp the way they wanted to do business. Pete Waterman shared his encounter here in his own words:

'By the time we did Donna Summer, she was so unrecouped with the record company. They just wanted to give us a fee and we didn't want the fee. We wanted a normal royalty. To them that was a nonsense because they said "Well, we don't do Donna Summer royalties". We said "Well sorry, we do!" We're not interested in a couple of hundred thousand dollars upfront.'

As creative individuals who were very passionate about music, the team didn't work primarily for money. Stock, Aitken and Waterman wanted a stake in their creations and there was a lot of friction between them and the record company. Pete Waterman at one point told Summer's record label that he would take the album back to the studio, erase Summer's vocals from all the tracks and return the money that the label had paid for the musicians. Simon Cowell, not well known at that time, had offered to purchase three of the compositions from the project, offering a lot more money than Waterman and his team had charged the record company.

Pete Waterman could not recall precisely which tracks. Cowell used to hang out with them at the time and when he heard 'This Time I Know It's For Real' before it was finished, he went crazy! Perhaps that was one of the tracks that he offered to purchase. But the friction between Waterman's team and Summer's label carried on. It was actually Ahmet Ertugen, 'bless his soul', that stepped in and rescued the project. Ertugen, having heard and loved the album, went back to the record company and told them that if they did not want 'Another Place And Time' then he would buy it himself. Ertugen rang Pete Waterman and explained that he would release the album unchanged and he would pay the team the royalties. That is how 'Another Place And Time' came to be released – hooray!

It was reported that Stock, Aitken and Waterman would produce a second album with Donna Summer but continuing problems with the relationship between Summer's record company and the team meant that it never happened. The team simply couldn't deal with the record company. One song, 'Happenin' All Over Again', written by SAW, was said to be originally composed for the next Summer album but was recorded by Lonnie Gordon. The single was released in January 1990 and was a smash hit both in the UK, reaching no.4 in the UK singles charts, and also around Europe. Summer, in her autobiography, said that she had a great time working with the team and was pleased to be part of the mass-production that created so many hits. The album was a fun, easy-going pop product and did not pretend to be a work of deep artistic integrity.

Every Summer fan will have their own ideas about which albums and tracks are the most thrilling. When asked about his favourite, Pete Waterman had no doubts:

'. . . you know when you worked with somebody, that's the album you love . . . you were there when the artist was singing your songs. When you were in the studio, of course she's singing only for you! We worked with someone we idolised. She's singing our songs and that's the greatest! You can't get better than that if you are a record producer and a writer.'

It must have been a privilege for anybody to hear Donna Summer in the studio singing just for them – for most fans it could only happen in their dreams!

Summer believes that SAW were much better than the public gave them credit for. SAW's goal was to create a new Motown. The team wanted to discover new, fresh talent and develop their potential. Summer was the 'exception' at that time, being an established artist.

Talking about her SAW endeavour, Summer told *The Advocate* in 1989 that the public's reaction to 'Another Place And Time' was 'really good'. She was surprised with the outcome and loved it. Summer was also pleased to be with her new US record label, Atlantic.

Fan Tim Letteer recalled that he loved 'Another Place And Time' because it went back to Summer's roots and brought her back to the top of the charts again, rounding off the 1980s for his favourite star. Most fans love 'Another Place And Time' and all of the tracks are highly regarded, unlike some of her previous projects.

There were several compilation albums released during this period of her recording career in the 1980s and 1990s. 'The Summer Collection (Greatest Hits)' was issued in 1985; a special twelve inch of all Summer's single releases from 'Another Place And Time' was released in Japan in 1989 entitled '12 inchers'; in Europe, 'The Best Of Donna Summer' was released in 1990.

'The Best Of Donna Summer', released on 12th November 1990, reached no.24 in the UK and was in the album chart for nine weeks, helped by the release of several new single remixes. 'State Of Independence (New Bass Mix)' was released to promote the album and peaked at no.45 on the 24th November 1990. Following the album's popularity and the rerelease of Summer's 1982 hit 'State Of Independence', a brand new remixed version of 'Breakaway', a track from 'Another Place And Time', was released. The single made the Top 100 on 12th January 1991, peaking at no.49. 'The Best Of Donna Summer' was the most successful of the various compilations from this time, being certified Gold in the UK by the BPI on the 18th December 1990.

This all showed that Donna Summer was still a musical force to be reckoned with. A successful dance album introduced her to new, younger fans, the compilations reminded music lovers of the wealth of earlier material available and remixes breathed new life into some old favourites.

10

Colours On The Canvas

By 1989, Summer was dedicating her time to another talent; painting. Summer exhibited her paintings and lithographs in Beverly Hills, selling seventy-five pieces, some of which were reported to have fetched over $38,000.

Promotional information from the Circle Fine Art Corporation tells us:

'I just paint what comes out. I have no theme generally. I start off with a blank canvas, and I just start putting colours on, and when I see the colours move into position, I begin to make a painting.'

Driven By The Music, Lady M, Hard For The Money and *Starman* were some of the titles of her artwork. During an interview with Oprah Winfrey in July 1999, Summer said that the masterpiece *Starman* was one of her favourites. It has spiritual overtones and questions man's appreciation of the natural resources given by God.

Jack Soloman, Chairman and Founder of Circle Fine Art Corporation, describes Donna Summer's work:

'Donna Summer's art is music for the eyes. When you view her paintings, drawings and lithographs, you sense the same energy and harmony that permeates her music. She has been a painter for fifteen years, but it is only now, with this exhibition, that her visual art becomes accessible to the public.'

The Corporation was delighted to exclusively represent Donna Summer's paintings, gouaches, watercolours and limited edition original graphics at that time. Summer's exhibitions took place mainly in the US, meaning the international public could view her paintings only through the Internet or on T-shirt prints purchased at her concerts in the 1990s.

In an interview about the art that she finds most moving, Donna Summer said she loves a particular painting by one of the world's most celebrated artists – Van Gogh. She feels a close connection with Van Gogh's *Sunflowers* and said in *The Independent Review*, 2004:

'... because I believe God used those flowers to point out something to me when I was first starting out in music. In front of my window there were all these sunflowers. One day, I went outside to look at them and there was one that was much larger than the others – the flower was about a foot in diameter. And I really felt that was God saying to me: "That's you . . . that's what I'm going to do with your life." Ever since, I've had an attachment to sunflowers.'

In the article 'Donna Summer: Too Hot To Handle' by Craig McLean for *The Telegraph*, Summer said that some of her paintings were influenced by Picasso, Gustav Klimt and Ernst Fuchs.

Klimt's work mainly depicts female figures whereas the art of Ernst Fuchs is more contemporary and surreal. He focuses on the human figure, often accompanied by animals. Colourful paintings with deep tones, Ernst Fuchs work has spiritual overtones.

Summer's work is clearly not in the same league as Klimt and Fuchs but she can certainly paint. Her work has attracted media attention. Her paintings such as *Chiquita*, *Hard For The Money* and *Jazz Man* used vibrant colours, reds, blues and yellows, where as *Wounded Heart* uses moody abstract splashes of deep colour. Another work titled *Faces Of Rio* presents an architectural, abstract landscape, suggesting a joyful yet calm scene. A series of abstract drawings with titles such as *Driven By The Music, Driven By The Music: Spring Affair, Driven By The Music: Summer Fever, Driven By The Music: Autumn Changes* and finally *Driven By The Music: Winter Melody* used the various colour palettes of the seasons. The titles were taken from her 1970s 'Four Seasons Of Love' album on which Summer was at her most sultry. The artwork is attractive and brought a smile to my face. Each image revealed sexy, steamy eyes with kissable lips.

Donna Summer said in an interview for *A & E Biography* in 1995 that she enjoyed painting so much, she went 'wild' with her creativity on canvas and painted for two to three weeks continuously. The star once said that it is important to get the 'essence' of what she felt on the canvas. Some critics may question her artistic authenticity, but her fame as a musician might influence other people's appreciation of her work. They are less likely to be dispassionate and objective.

By the twenty-first century, her official website had taken the opportunity to trade Summer's merchandise. The Internet online shopping service enabled the public to purchase Summer's recordings, prints of paintings and tour books before it closed in early 2000s.

Although modest commercial success as a painter was welcome, Summer did not set out planning to sell her art. She did not take her painting work seriously until a persistent friend, Ceil Kasha, decided to relax after a concert by doing her needlecraft. While Kasha sewed, Donna Summer painted.

Kasha was impressed with Summer's work and the rest is history. In an interview promoting her record 'VH1 Presents: Live & More Encore!' Summer observed that many recording artists paint. She thinks the reason for this may be that painting is a solitary act and the most important critic is oneself. It is also a way of unwinding and being creative in a quiet, calm way.

No doubt some of her fans will have been able to afford her original art work. Others, with more modest means, will have been able to get their hands on her paintings in the form of lithograph prints. One fan was lucky to have the artist herself give advice about her work. Wes Miller, a fan, told me in his own words (17th May 2009):

"In 2003 I had the opportunity to attend a gallery event with the art of Donna Summer. Featured were the *'Driven By The Music – Four Seasons'* edition. I wanted one for my bedroom but I couldn't decide which one to select – so I asked Donna to make the selection for me. She looked me over then selected *'Winter Melody'*. I asked her how she made her decision. She said it was based on what I was wearing and the colour of my eyes. When the lithograph arrived at my home I took it to the bedroom and was shocked!! *'Winter Melody'* features a streak of turquoise and red lips. WOW – my bedroom is turquoise with a red accent wall. The litho was perfect for my bedroom!!! Thank you Donna for your inspired design suggestion. Maybe Nik should come and inspect to verify it is a good choice!!".

In 'Donna Summer: Too Hot To Handle', Craig McLean says:

'Donna Summer is fairly well regarded as an artist, it seems. She was part of a Steven Spielberg-sponsored exhibition of American artists in China.'

Summer's career as a painter began with a few small pieces. Summer told Craig McLean that, at dinner party hosted by Sylvester Stallone, she saw some big canvases created by the Hollywood star. It was this that inspired her to produce her own paintings on a larger scale. Summer's art introduced her fans and the public to another side of her. Summer continues to produce colourful, expressive canvases, creating yet another creative chapter in her life.

11

New Identity And The Melody Goes On

Enjoying success with her art, Summer continued working on her music and in 1991 released the album 'Mistaken Identity'. The album, produced and arranged by Keith Diamond, developed more R&B as a well as dance-pop influences.

Summer displays a more mature vocal style along with accomplished songs such as 'Get Ethnic', 'Body Talk', 'What Is It You Want', 'Cry Of A Waking Heart' and 'When Love Cries', with Summer moving into other areas of self-expression. The album was aimed at a wide range of music fans and developed different types of music, including high energy dance and urban R&B. The only typical dance floor standards were 'Work That Magic', 'Say A Little Prayer' and 'Fred Astaire'.

Interestingly, on the UK limited-edition album release, the 'Work That Magic (ISA Full Length Remix)' replaced the original track and on the German limited version 'When Love Cries Remix' replaced the original. The US 'Mistaken Identity' album contained the original of both tracks.

In the US, 'When Love Cries' entered the *Billboard* chart on 17th August 1991 at no.92. Ten new singles entered the chart that week, including Summer's song. The highest new entry was by Karyn White with 'Romantic' at no.52, with 'Get Off' by Prince And The N.P.G. at no.66. The top three positions were dominated by Bryan Adams' no.1 hit '(Everything I Do) I Do It For You', Amy Grant's 'Every Heart Beat' at no.2 and 'It Ain't Over 'Till It's Over' by Lenny Kravitz at no.3.

Other strong singles in the chart at the time included Roxette with 'Fading Like A Flower (Every Time You Leave)', Paula Abdul's 'The Promise Of A New Day', Boyz II Men with 'Motownphilly' and Color Me Badd's 'Mi Amor'. The beautiful R&B melody 'When Love Cries' climbed to no.77 in its second week and spent five weeks in the pop chart; not enough to qualify it as a hit, though it fared better in the *Billboard* R&B chart, rising to no.18.

'When Love Cries' was also released in some European and Asian countries, reaching no.43 in the Japanese music chart in October 1991, but it did not receive a UK release. The song had a much more urban feel than the upbeat dance sound normally associated with Donna Summer. The vocal was similar in style to some of her 1970s recordings, with a slightly low whispering sound, making use of her full vocal abilities. Summer's voice in 'When Love Cries' was a sexy, fresh and up-to-date presentation. The single also has Summer 'rapping'; following the popular trend at that time. The extended versions of the single, 'When Love Cries (Summertime Remix)' and 'When Love Cries (12″ Mix)', were delightful without losing the essence of the original recording.

In the UK, a much more typical Summer tune was released titled 'Work That Magic'. The single only made it to no.74 on the 30th November 1991 – not great news for Summer fans. The track is catchy but didn't have the pop 'oomph' of 'This Time I Know It's For Real' to propel it up the charts. The single remix 'Work That Magic (Extended ISA Remix)' is a good dance floor tune, with the 'Work That Magic (Capricorn ISA Remix)' more of a classy, spacey, ambient sound for chilling out. Fans may know the UK album version 'Work That Magic (ISA Full Length Remix)' from the dance floors of the 1990s. The single was a hit in Zimbabwe entering the chart on the 22nd February, 1992 climbing to no.3 and staying in the charts for four weeks.

Due to a lack of promotion and failure to market either the singles or album, the public did not buy the records in the numbers that had been expected. The release failed to enter the *Billboard* 200 album charts in the US or the UK charts but it did reach no.97 in the *Billboard* R&B album chart.

'Mistaken Identity' was vastly and unfairly underrated. The album was one of Summer's most important projects, demonstrating her talent and versatility as a recording artist. It was a statement that should have been acknowledged. Perhaps the media and some music fans were confused by the major transition to this new sound and were not ready for the 'new' Donna Summer. For example, there was no continuity or consistency of her image. Summer was responsible for the cover-art concept and presented herself with blond hair and coloured contact lenses. Summer, on the cover of 'Mistaken Identity', dyed her hair bright blond as a political statement to highlight what she saw as stereotyping of people with dark skin who chose a certain 'look'. Coloured contact lenses were a new invention which went well with the cover image concept. The new image was only shown elsewhere on her publicity photographs and the cover of the press pack for the album. Most of her media interviews and TV appearances had Summer with black hair. The 'Work That Magic' video presented Summer with beautiful silky dark hair, yet she was blond once again on her Japanese tour!

In a 'Talk Live' TV interview Summer says colouring her hair created a problem due to the high volume of hair dye that needed to be applied and she subsequently went back to her natural colour. Historically black stars had coloured their hair blond or used blond wigs including Etta James and Dinah Washington. Summer's 1991 'Mistaken Identity' album cover illustrated the theme of the project perfectly.

Summer composed and co-wrote ten songs on the album with just 'Heaven's Just A Whisper Away' and 'Cry Of A Waking Heart' written entirely by others. The urban-edged song 'Get Ethnic' provided social commentary on the tendency of some people to identify more with other ethnic groups than their own, denying their own nature. The song said it was all right to be proud of who you are!

The title track was a political comment on the infamous episode where Los Angeles police officers repeatedly beat Rodney Glen King on the 2nd March 1991 while cameras filmed the whole event. In an interview with Janet Langhart for the show *Talk Live*, Summer described an incident in Los Angeles where she was driving one night and was stopped by a patrol car.

To her surprise, the policemen instructed her via loudspeaker to get out of her car, as if she had committed some terrible crime. Shocked, confused and pregnant in her 'white station wagon Mercedes Benz', Summer said they had stopped her for just 'turning around'. The incident highlighted the casual and habitual racial discrimination that still occurs in the US to millions of Americans. The officers became models of politeness when they realised they had stopped Donna Summer by saying 'excuse me'.

She also touched on political issues in the sentimental gospel-tinged 'Let There Be Peace'. The song could have been influenced by the first Gulf War, which lasted from 2nd August 1990 to 28th February 1991, authorised by the UN and led by the US and the UK. Just over a decade later, the song could equally be a comment on the second Gulf War. 'Let There Be Peace' is a song that is always relevant in a world perpetually at war.

Other sentimental tunes were 'Heaven's Just A Whisper Away' and 'Friends Unknown'. The ballad 'Friends Unknown' was dedicated to her loyal fans. The crucial part of the 'friendship' is the evolution of their musical relationship; her fans support her work and in return she brings joy to her 'Friends Unknown' with her thrilling melodies. Donna Summer delights her audience with a diverse range of musical styles and ideas in 'Mistaken Identity', with both politics and love the focus of her musings.

However, after the success of the pop-dance dominated album 'Another Place And Time', fans wanted more of the up-tempo, Euro-dance sound that had brought Donna Summer back into the charts. The shift in style was a bit of a let down for them. It was not too long ago that she had huge hits around the world and 'Mistaken Identity' seemed to close the door on a successful chapter in her career.

The situation might not have been helped by unwanted headlines. The *New York Times* claimed on 25th August 1991 that one track had been dropped from the final selection for 'Mistaken Identity' because it would have served as an apology for the comments Summer had allegedly made about the gay community back in the early 1980s. The song, a beautiful ballad, with the working title 'We're Gonna Make it' or 'We're Gonna Win', was written by close collaborator Paul Jabara. Bob Esty shares his information about the track:

'In 1990, I recorded a demo of a two-song medley called 'We're Gonna Win / One World' at Donna Summer's ranch in Chatsworth, California. Donna's voice was so moving and stirring, just at the time when Europe was opening up, and the AIDS crisis was overwhelming the world. I played all the instruments in my computer, and we used friends who volunteered to sing as a choir. Paul Jabara and Jay Asher co-wrote the first song and I co-wrote 'One World' with Paul. The track was never finished, and it was never released. I don't know why, because it was very timely. Donna sang the piece with all the sincerity and strength she could give. Just two "takes"!! I'm so happy that I recorded her, and have the track to listen to. When Paul died in 1992, I never saw Donna again.'

The track was melodic and lyrically touching but a bootleg copy proves that the track would have not fitted with the concept of the album, being recorded a year before the making of 'Mistaken Identity'. In addition 'If I Could Live Our Love' was also rumoured to have been rejected from the album. The *New York Times* article affected sales of the album, as did a lack of promotion and support from the media. Summer sued the publication to clear her name.

The album, which showcased Summer in a variety of vocal styles, passed by largely unnoticed by the public. Summer, in an interview with *Ebony* magazine, said that she could sing in a 'variety of styles' that included 'Love To Love You Baby' disco, ballads, light opera, musical comedies and church hymns. She had successfully proven that. On the 1991 album it was the turn of high energy 'urban' sounds.

In a press release for 'Once Upon A Time', her record company Casablanca said:

'The phenomenal response from fans the world over reflects that her music touches a special place in people that transcends language. For fans everywhere, the message is clear: Take a little Summer with you.'

'Mistaken Identity' was actually Donna Summer's very first commercially unsuccessful full-length studio release in the US. But the project is a must-have for every passionate fan wanting to hear the evolution of Donna Summer. It wasn't for want of quality writing or production on the album but more a lack of aggressive and coordinated promotion that resulted in the album failing to gain the affection of the record-buying public.

It has been a long while since Summer has produced a 'concept' album, the last were 'Once Upon A Time', 'Bad Girls' and 'On The Radio: Greatest Hits Volumes I & II'. Despite this, she was at no.42 for The Top 100 Artists 1955–1991, in *The Billboard Book Of USA Top 40 Hits*.

In 1992, the single 'Carry On' by Giorgio Moroder featuring Donna Summer was released in Germany for Giorgio Moroder's album 'Forever Dancing'. The collaboration took over a decade and again the single achieved minimal exposure in the media. But fans were thrilled to hear the new recording. On March 18th 1992, Donna Summer's name was added to the 'Hollywood Walk Of Fame' in honour of her popularity. The Los Angeles Mayor, Tom Bradley, declared that date as 'Donna Summer Day'. Summer performed 'Friends Unknown' as a thank you to over 600 fans that came to celebrate the event. In 1993, Summer was at no.29 for the Top All-Time Singles Artist In The US and no.60 in the UK. The result was based on peak position and weeks in the Top 10 and the Top 20. These results were compiled from *The Warner Guide To UK & US Hit Singles* (1994).

In 1992, the UK public was once more presented with a disco sound with the stamp of Donna Summer. Again, 1970s music was in demand, perhaps due to the success of the Abba tribute single 'Abba-Esque EP' by Erasure that shot to the top of the UK chart on 13th June 1992, (twelve weeks). Several classics were rereleased successfully. Abba's old hit 'Dancing Queen' entered the Top 20 on 5th September 1992. Boney M's single 'Boney M Megamix' reached no.7 in December 1992 and celebrated nine weeks of chart success. The 1970s disco revival music continued into 1993. Sister Sledge re-entered the UK chart with 'We Are Family (Remix)', reaching no.5 in January 1993 (eight weeks). 'We Are Family' managed to enter the chart in three different decades; 1979 Top 10, 1984 Top 40 and 1993 Top 5. They had success with two other remixes, 'Lost In Music (Remix)' and 'Thinking Of You (Remix)' which both reached the UK Top 20 and were taken from the album 'The Very Best Of Sister Sledge 1973–1993'. 'Brown Girl In The Ring (Remix)' by Boney M entered the UK Top 40 in April

1993. In June, the gigantic disco song 'I Will Survive (Remix)' by Gloria Gaynor entered the UK chart at no.5, and stayed in the chart for ten weeks. However, many fans asked themselves where was the ultimate track by the ultimate Queen Of Disco? But there was no sign of any new remix.

At the end of 1993 PolyGram, celebrating Summer's success in the music business and perhaps taking advantage of the renewed interest in disco, released 'The Donna Summer Anthology' album. It featured her collection of hits from 1975 to 1992.

Compiling songs for the project certainly brought back a lot of memories for Summer. After listening to the tracks that were to be selected for the album, she realised how much work she and her team had produced. It was like reliving her musical life; both revealing and moving.

Unusually, PolyGram did not re-issue or remix any of Summer's past hit singles to promote the project. When 'The Donna Summer Anthology' was released, most of Summer's previous albums were still available in store and a single release would have helped to promote them. In France, 'I Feel Love' was released as a single to promote the greatest hits package. It featured, strangely, the 'I Feel Love' mix from 'On The Radio: Greatest Hits Volumes I & II'. The Patrick Cowley mega-edit version was also included.

'The Donna Summer Anthology' was certified Gold in France by SNEP in May 1994. This project was important for mainstream music fans to evaluate Summer's evolution in musical terms. Such a good package generated good reviews from popular publications:

'The Diana Ross of disco, Summer was one of the few divas who didn't seem a total producer's pet, blazing a new path in electropop . . .' 3 Stars/Good (*Rolling Stone*, 1993)

'Summer's oeuvre is far more diverse than is commonly acknowledged . . . (the collection) sounds surprisingly up-to-the-minute. If you ever proclaimed "disco sucks", suck on this and you may change your mind . . .' Rating: A (*Entertainment Weekly*, 1993)

'. . . it's remarkable how many classics can be found among these thirty-four tracks . . .' 4 Stars/Excellent (*Q Magazine*, 1994)

However, the album did not include singles produced for the European and Asian markets, such as 'I Remember Yesterday', 'Down, Deep Inside', 'Protection', 'People People' and 'Dinner With Gershwin'. Yet the project included the unreleased single 'Friends Unknown' and the unfamiliar German single release of Giorgio Moroder's 'Forever Dancing' that featured Summer on 'Carry On'.

Even though some tracks are not included, 'The Donna Summer

Anthology' is a fabulous package. The project also featured the promotional single version of 'MacArthur Park', which is rare on any of her compilations, and twelve inch versions of 'Hot Stuff' and 'Bad Girls'. Besides the standard single versions or radio edit versions, the album also featured the original album versions for some tracks, unlike most compilation projects which usually featured radio edits only.

Summer also signed to her previous record label. This was a great arrangement as all of her back catalogue was now under the same label. PolyGram celebrated Summer's return to the fold by remastering and re-issuing her entire back catalogue. In 1994, Donna Summer celebrated her twentieth anniversary in the music business. On 3rd September 1994 *Billboard* ran a special feature for the Queen Of Disco in honour of her achievements. The feature also promoted forthcoming releases of her work including a Christmas album, a greatest hits album with two new tracks and the legendary unreleased album 'I'm A Rainbow'. Many other parties also contributed congratulations to the star on her anniversary.

This period was one of relative obscurity for Summer. Listening to her songs was no longer seen as fashionable by the young record-buying public. Still, Donna Summer continued to move ahead with her evolution, and continued working in the studio recording songs. October 1994 saw the birth of the 'Christmas Spirit' album, produced by Michael Omartian, which she recorded with the Nashville Symphony Orchestra.

Summer told *Billboard* magazine that she had always longed to release a Christmas album and was very pleased with the outcome of the recording. She loved the Christmas albums by Nat King Cole and Barbra Streisand. Having listened to them extensively, she largely succeeded in her task and her album is the equal of those two festive perennials. Summer, remembering her time working in the studio recording the Christmas album, told Craig Rosen in 'On Nashville, Christmas, Barbra And Image-Breaking' for *Billboard*:

'I absolutely adored playing with the Nashville Symphony Orchestra. When they first started playing "White Christmas" tears just welled up in my eyes and I had to leave the room, because it sounded so beautiful . . . It was just a wonderful feeling, and I think that comes across on the record.'

The album was available only in the US and Japan. The tunes were mainly ballads and Christmas standards. Donna Summer recorded a few new songs for the album including 'Christmas Is Here' (D. Summer, M. Ormatian and S. Omartian), 'Lamb Of God' (D. Summer and M. Ormatian) and 'Christmas Spirit' (D. Summer, B. Sudano and M. Omartian). Summer's Gospel background can be heard in the track 'Lamb Of God'.

This was a more sedate and mature Summer. Each of the songs has a different feel, with Summer injecting her own style into the tracks, all of which come together to form a coherent and logical whole.

The songs 'White Christmas', 'O Come All Ye Faithful', and a 'Christmas Medley' (comprising 'What Child Is This'/'Do You Hear What I Hear'/'Joy To The World'), were all beautifully crafted. There are a lot of fine compositions in the album but the stand-out track is arguably 'Breath Of Heaven', originally recorded by Amy Grant. The spiritual depth of Summer's voice can be heard in this track, showing soul, joy and pain at the same time. It is a track to give you goosebumps and is sure to make you shed a tear!

In an interview with Christian John Wikane, 'The Queen And Her Crayons: An Interview With Donna Summer', Summer said that she listened a lot to Amy Grant's 'Breath Of Heaven' and the song had helped her to cope with the loss of her younger sister Amy.

'Christmas Spirit' was a beautiful holiday album. Fan and creator of the unauthorised Summer tribute site donna-tribute.com, Cathy Hawkins, says that she listens to the album in all seasons – to clear her head and for consolation.

Unfortunately, the UK public was not aware of the album's re-release in 1999 and the lack of creative direction for the jacket design makes the cover look dated. The album went unnoticed around the world. In 2005, the album was re-issued by Universal Music under the title '20th Century Masters – The Best Of Donna Summer: The Christmas Collection'.

Her follow-up to 'Christmas Spirit' was 'Endless Summer: Donna Summer's Greatest Hits', another compilation. This greatest hits project was also available on home video. The album was promoted well by Poly-Gram with TV features, radio interviews and TV advertisements. In 2006, Peter Shapiro, the author of *The Rough Guide To Soul And R&B* commented that 'Endless Summer: Donna Summer's Greatest Hits' proved 'she was the undisputed Queen Of Disco'. Shapiro declared that Donna Summer 'undoubtedly deserves a place in the soul pantheon'.

The project featured two new songs; 'Melody Of Love (Wanna Be Loved)' and 'Any Way At All'. 'Melody Of Love (Wanna Be Loved)' created by Summer, D. Cole, R. Clivilles and J. Carrano, was a mix of disco and house. This track was to take Summer back where she belonged and aimed to introduce her to a new club scene.

Many UK DJs obtained the single promo pack and the 'Melody Of Love (Wanna Be Loved) Mijangos Powertools Trip #1' remix version, designed for clubbers, was a dancefloor success. Summer's vocal was recognisable by the clubbers only when the DJs announced it was her new track! The high energy beat of the remix was taken from Summer's new single and took fans by surprise. The song reached no.21 in UK on the 12th November 1994 and stayed in the chart for three weeks. After a three-year absence from the UK chart, the entry position showed that Summer could still 'Work That Magic'!

Summer enjoyed making 'Melody Of Love (Wanna Be Loved)' saying it was not the best she had ever written, but was a joyful, upbeat and 'happy' song. The tune starts with a slow introduction and moves up-tempo at the middle. Most of Summer's songs follow this pattern, which has become her signature style ever since she recorded 'Last Dance'. The single 'Melody Of Love (Wanna Be Loved)' was competing with twenty other new UK entries including Chris Rea's 'You Can Go Your Own Way', The Saw Doctors' 'Small Bit Of Love', Salt-N-Pepa's 'None Of Your Business', REM's 'Bang And Blame', The Beautiful South's 'One Last Love Song' and Warren G's 'This DJ'. Although 'Melody Of Love (Wanna Be Loved)' failed in the US pop chart, it was the *Billboard* no.1 dance single for 1995.

'Endless Summer: Donna Summer's Greatest Hits' entered the UK album chart at no.37 and only lasted two weeks. It also failed to make much of an impact in the US, though it did reach no.10 in New Zealand.

A ballad composed by Summer, her husband Bruce Sudano and E. Silver, 'Any Way At All', released only in US, was another chart let-down. It is a pattern in the charts that Summer is better received with up-tempo dance standards. At this time her songs did better in Europe than in the US. Interestingly, the B-side of 'Any Way At All' included the track 'Donna Summer Medley': 'Dim All The Lights'/'Hot Stuff'/'Bad Girls'/ 'Last Dance'. The medley was remixed smoothly but has not appeared on any of Summer's greatest hits packages at the time of writing. The music video featured in the greatest hits VHS package.

'Endless Summer: Donna Summer's Greatest Hits' contained different tracks in the US, the UK and France, with each version containing those singles that were the biggest hits in each respective country. In January 1997 the project was awarded Gold in France by SNEP. The French version omitted the new up-tempo recording 'Melody Of Love (Wanna Be Loved)' and the beautiful ballad 'Anyway At All'.

She has recorded many fine ballads over the years, a few examples being 'A Man Like You' (1977, 'Once Upon A Time'), 'Sometimes Like Butter-flies' (1982 B-side of 'Love Is In Control' seven inch single), 'I Do Believe (I Fell In Love)' (1983, 'She Works Hard For The Money') and 'Breath Of Heaven' (1994, 'Christmas Spirit'). However, dance tunes are what Summer is known for in the media. Music fans, the media and recording acts have their own views on why Summer has not been as successful with her ballads.

Gloria Gaynor comments:

'That's generally the fault of a record company – if it isn't broke, don't fix it. If you're doing well in that area, they feel the public wouldn't accept you doing anything else. They think that's who you are ... you know ... they made you and they want you to remain what they made you because they are afraid to take a chance going in a different direction.'

Gaynor also suggested that maybe people in the recording companies fear for their jobs – a flop album that arose from their suggestions might result in the bosses giving them the sack. Award-winning Malaysian singer Francissca Peter observed that the media and music fans see Donna Summer as an up-tempo artist making great disco songs, and the marketing is designed to sell this image; no other tunes need to be pushed to propel Summer's popularity!

Currently in the music industry the 'accountants' seem to run the show. This state of affairs has had a negative impact on the way new artists are nurtured and developed. The 'suits' are not creative people and do not understand the creative process. All they understand is the bottom line – money and profit. The phrases 'taking a chance' and 'trying something new' are not in their vocabulary! There are, however, still some labels that allow the process of developing new artists to be driven by the 'creatives' in the company, not just the 'suits'.

The media forgets that Donna Summer can sing great ballads. If her ballads had been publicised as much as the dance tunes, then they would almost surely have been more popular. Summer definitely preferred slow numbers but her rise to stardom with high energy songs defined her in the eyes of the business and music fans. In 1998, Giorgio Moroder told *Sound On Sound* magazine that the American star originally did not want to record dance music and was not too keen on disco numbers! From the beginning of their recording sessions, Moroder knew Donna Summer was a great singer with an exceptional voice. But when her first disco single took off, Moroder realised they 'had a bit of a problem'. In reality, sentimental melodies and musical tunes were more of Summer's style. Summer said once to *Blues & Soul* magazine that her previous record label wanted fast, high energy numbers and was not too keen on her producing ballads. Using her creative mind, Summer combined both ideas in songs that started off slow and gradually moved to a more up-tempo beat.

Summer's slow tunes and lyrics are versatile – happy, sad, even painful. In fact, her biggest hit songs are about pain and loss. She noted in her autobiography *Ordinary Girl: The Journey* that hits such as 'Last Dance', 'Bad Girls', 'On The Radio', 'No More Tears (Enough Is Enough)' and 'She Works Hard For The Money', are 'about pain', the grief of lost love, unrequited love and an expression of the struggle to survive in life. The arrangement of these songs is often upbeat and they are good to dance to in clubs or even at home! It is this combination of happy music and sad lyrics that appeals to the true fan.

To date, her compilations do not include many of her ballads. Still, in 1999 Universal Records released Classic Donna Summer – The Universal Masters Collection which featured the ballads 'Full Of Emptiness', 'Winter Melody', 'Can't We Just Sit Down (And Talk It Over)', 'My Baby Understands', 'Don't Cry For Me Argentina' and 'I Do Believe (I Fell In Love)', a very rare opportunity for fans to have all these songs in one place. Note that the 2009 'Classic Donna Summer' release featured the same tracks as the 'Classic Donna Summer – The Universal Masters Collection'.

In an interview with Capital Radio UK promoting 'Endless Summer: Donna Summer's Greatest Hits', she was asked whether she still listened or performed to her old songs with pleasure. She explained that sometimes she didn't want to hear a certain song because she just got tired of it, not in a bad way, but there were many other songs to listen to. She also explained that when she performed those tracks, she enjoyed the response her audiences got from the songs. Each song would mean something different to people listening; different memories of people, places and times gone by.

Even though the 1994 'Endless Summer: Donna Summer's Greatest Hits' showcased two new tracks, there were no new plans for PolyGram to release a new full-length album.

Summer, although still in demand, was busy with family life by this time and major releases became few and far between. Most of her fans only heard of their 'diva' through singles, remix projects and studio tribute compilation albums. Nevertheless, Summer still maintained her status in the music world.

In 1996 *The Canadian Singles Chart Book 1975–1996* placed the late Whitney Houston at no.18, Donna Summer at no.17 and Lionel Richie at no.16 for the Top Singles Artist 1975–1996. In the section Artist Achievements (most weeks on the chart by artists) in Canada, Bruce Springsteen was positioned at no.17 with 231 weeks, Donna Summer at no.18 with 229 weeks and Michael Bolton, with 222 weeks, at no.19. In the Canadian Top Artist By Decade – Top Artist Of The 1970s (1975–1979), The Bee Gees took the crown at no.1 with 3235 points, Donna Summer was at no.2 with 2140 points followed by Paul McCartney and Wings at no.3 with 1978 points.

The points were calculated by adding the top singles peak position, weeks in the Top 10 and total weeks in the chart.

In July 1998, Summer exceeded 298 weeks for hit singles in the UK. By 1999 in the UK alone, Donna Summer was at no.28, for having the most weeks in the charts. She also scored at no.18 for Most Hit Singles by an artist with The Bee Gees (no.16) and Shakin' Stevens (no.17).

By the end of the 1990s and early 2000s, Summer's greatest hits compilations projects continued and became more popular.

At the end of September 2003, a compilation featuring two new tracks 'That's The Way' and 'Dream-A-Lot's Theme (I Will Live For Love)' for the album 'The Journey: The Very Best Of Donna Summer', was released in the US by Universal Music Company. One of the tracks was composed by Summer's long-term creative partner Giorgio Moroder. They had taken a while to record a song together simply because of a lack of time and opportunity.

In 'Donna Summer: The Empress Herself', Summer told Rusty Trunk in an interview for annecarlini.com:

'Well, I wasn't planning on recording with Giorgio as I was on Sony and I had been in the throes of the past two or three years of writing the book and writing other songs. I was writing the book and working with all these different artists and writers just trying to come up with the right sound for me now as a kind of a new thing and a new direction. And we had some cool songs that we'd written, but they weren't recorded yet and we didn't have producers lined up to produce those songs. So, Giorgio was available and he told me he had this song that he'd written for somebody else, but that he wanted to play for me. I thought it was cool ... that song is "That's The Way" ... and so we all had a family reunion out there. And then I had a song that I had written for a children's musical, which was the other song that he recorded for me.'

Although fans were thrilled to hear new work by Summer, some were unsure about the thinking behind the making of 'Dream-A-Lot's Theme (I Will Live For Love)', and also questioned why, with such a great CV, Summer even recorded the track 'That's The Way' by Giorgio Moroder and Keith Forsey. Moroder's magic had faded a little; he was no longer ahead of the pack.

Paul Gambaccini gives us an expert view on Moroder and Summer's 2003 recording:

'There are times ... when someone is pop music and pop music is that person and Giorgio Moroder was where pop music happened to be for a time and then it was over. It didn't mean he was bad but it meant that he didn't have anything to offer that he hadn't already offered. So things sounded kind of stale whereas once they been revolutionary. So by the time 2004 comes around ... I mean we are a quarter of a century away from his historic height and most producers haven't lasted that long. The magic goes just because the market moves somewhere where they are not interested. I mean clearly, in an era of rap, he had no interest in rap, and he certainly wasn't into any of the rock genre at that period ... anything that he would do with Donna would just be an echo.'

In Gambaccini's opinion, chart music is a young person's game. Anyone can record a great record regardless of age. However, as many fans acknowledge, older and established acts still continue to win Grammy Awards. But hit single status is generally for younger and newer artists. Neither Summer or Moroder were young anymore. Dance music is consumed in a different way. The icons of dance will be the people visually both novel and sexy. At this point Donna Summer was not going to be either to a sixteen year old.

Moroder is still highly respected as a composer and Summer is unquestionably a good singer. Giorgio Moroder, in an interview for *A & E Biography*, said that Donna Summer was the best female act he ever worked with. Perhaps Summer and Moroder had gone beyond making hit songs. It was now more about a good melody and a fun tune to record when it came to Moroder's compositions.

While promoting the album 'The Journey: The Very Best Of Donna Summer', Summer said she heard 'That's The Way' and instantly loved it. In her opinion the song sounded cool and had a young feel to it. In actual fact, 'That's The Way' was meant for Gwen Stefani, vocalist in the group No Doubt. Initially Moroder was not keen for Summer to record the song but after seeing the affection Summer had for the melody, and after checking that no one had recorded the song yet, Moroder let Donna Summer 'try' his piece of music. Summer said it took her four takes to get 'That's The Way' to perfection and was one of the most difficult songs she had recorded (at that time). Summer said that the young singer who sang the first demo made the song sound 'really cool'.

Both tracks, 'That's The Way' and 'Dream-A-Lot's Theme (I Will Live For Love)' in 'The Journey: The Very Best Of Donna Summer' were not to the standard that Summer's fans hoped for. The album reached no.111 in the US stayed in the album chart for four weeks.

As for British fans, they had to wait until the New Year for the release of 'The Journey: The Very Best Of Donna Summer'. Finally the UK music public were able to buy the album, the new songs 'That's The Way' and

'Dream-A-Lot's Theme (I Will Live For Love)' only being available on the limited edition release bonus CD. The remix of 'That's The Way' was only available as a promotional CD by Almighty Records on their 'Almighty Showreel 2005'.

The album, released in summer 2004, was promoted well in the UK and was at no.6 in the album charts for six weeks. It was a great success in the UK even though some fans bought the imported US version quite a few months earlier!

Summer was interviewed on *This Morning*, a popular UK morning TV talk show, and the album was advertised on TV. She also made an appearance at HMV store in Oxford Street on the 16th June 2004 for an album and book signing. It was a good opportunity for fans in the UK to see her close-up; some took advantage of this and brought their collections of Summer items to be signed!

This is the old fashioned way to promote a new release, but as noted in *Louis Walsh's Fast Track To Fame*, although it's hard work and time consuming, this method rarely fails. At the album and book signing session, fans also managed to take a few photos of their much-loved star! Summer, ever the professional, obliged with wonderful smiles for all her fans, although camera flashes were not allowed.

Dagmar, a professional photographer who has taken many of Summer's official and unofficial photos, said that Summer is a natural in front of the camera. Dagmar explained that during the early musical production days she never had to get Summer to pose. Sometimes she would put Summer and others in a place or a situation and then the pose would develop naturally.

The US and UK greatest hits releases were complimented with the autobiography *Ordinary Girl: The Journey* written with Marc Eliot. The book received mixed reviews from fans. Summer's albums had more prominence in the UK charts, compared to the US. 'The Journey: The Very Best Of Donna Summer' was also welcomed in Norway, reaching no.27 and spending three weeks in the album chart.

UK fans were delighted to hear that 'The Journey: The Very Best Of Donna Summer' released Monday 14th June 2004 had been certified Gold by the BPI on June 28th 2004.

By 2004 it was documented in *The Complete Book Of The British Charts: Singles And Albums* (written by Neil Warwick, Jon Kutner and Tony Brown in 2004) that Donna Summer was at no.93 for The Top 100 Chart Acts Of All Time based on chart performance of singles, albums and EP releases. Summer also achieved the no.17 position with thirty-nine hits for the Most

Hit Singles; there were 30 artists listed in the category. From the list, Tom Jones was at no.16 with forty-one hits whilst The Bee Gees were at no.18 with thirty-eight.

There are a lot of Summer compilations and as noted, 'The Donna Summer Anthology' (1993) and 'Donna Summer Gold' (2005) are the best ways to appreciate her musical history to date. 'Donna Summer Gold' is an updated version of 'The Donna Summer Anthology'. The 2005 'gold' compilation album included 'Dinner With Gershwin', 'Love's About To Change My Heart' and 'Melody Of Love (Wanna Be Loved)' and featured a new recording 'Dream-A-Lot's Theme (I Will Live For Love)' and 'You're So Beautiful'.

However, some tracks from 'The Donna Summer Anthology' are not included on 'Donna Summer Gold', part of a series of compilation projects from various artists by Universal Music Company.

In addition, mainstream music fans should get hold of 'On The Radio: Greatest Hits Volumes I & II' (1979), a non-stop compilation. Some hits in this album have been edited to a shorter playtime. 'The Dance Collection' (1987), gives fans the opportunity to enjoy a selection of Summer's finest 1970s twelve inches in one package. 'The Ultimate Collection' (2003) includes some original twelve inch versions, original album or single versions as well as the early European singles 'The Hostage' and 'Lady Of The Night'. The album also contains two live recordings from the 1978 album release 'Live And More' and the remixes 'I Feel Love '95' and 'State Of Independence '96'. The long version of 'Je T'aime (Moi Non Plus)', originally featured in the soundtrack to the movie *Thank God It's Friday*, is also included. Another compilation album deserving consideration is 'The Journey: The Very Best Of Donna Summer' (2003 US and 2004 UK) released as a limited edition CD including a second bonus disc featuring some of her classic twelve inches and current remixes. If rare extended versions and DJ remixes of Summer's tracks such as 'Highway Runner', 'Dinner With Gershwin', 'I Don't Wanna Get Hurt' and 'She Works Hard For The Money' were included then the limited edition project would be even more desirable.

The Head of Press and PR (HMV and Fopp), Gennaro Castaldo said, that demand for her work keeps ticking over, including for albums such as 'She Works Hard For The Money', but realistically it is mainly channelled into her various hits compilations, including recent re-mastered and re-issued albums. Castaldo says in 2012:

'That's probably more a question to put to Donna's labels, who pretty much determine these things. Ultimately labels will say that they are merely responding to demand, while, of course, these days the trend is towards digital albums, so that's how a new generation of fans will be able to enjoy her wonderful music.'

Castaldo also said that Donna Summer enjoyed huge amounts of radio airplay and promo in the 1970s, which was bound to be reflected in media interest and demand from fans for her songs.

Malaysian singer Francissca Peter said:

'I believe that Donna Summer has been blessed because dance music will always be dance music and will be needed in the market ... her music is still very much alive ... "Bad Girls", "Hot Stuff", "She Works Hard For The Money" and "Last Dance". I think her dance music will always be appreciated ... her greatest hits ... have been remixed into dance house music ...'.

Peter went on to explain that Summer was still very much respected as the Queen Of Disco. Summer's sound is very pop, commercial but yet soulful, her style of singing crossing over to all cultures and languages.

Although her songs were ever-present on the playlists of club DJs, the periods between releasing new albums became increasingly longer. Not having chart success did not mean that the songs or singer were not worthy, but it did affect the market for the albums and Donna Summer's popularity and image in the minds of the public.

'Different Love' fan Mark Tara said in an interview:

'I think every creative person has their own time when they can tap into a *River* of creativity that the masses can relate to. However long that river-ride lasts I don't think anyone can know. In the 70s the songwriting team of Summer / Moroder / Bellotte was a train that could not be stopped. Everything they created turned to gold. Donna did have a couple of smash hit singles in the 80s. 'This Time I Know It's For Real' and the iconic 'She Works Hard For The Money' the latter would became part of pop culture's lexicon. How many times have you said or thought "She works hard for the money". . . genius! By the 90s the heat of the Summer sun had cooled and the record 'Mistaken Identity' heralded that cooling. The 90s and into the 2000s we saw sporadic singles and a multitude of Greatest Hits packages. When an artist starts becoming successful it's usually the time of greatest creativity. Why? Because they have drive. They want to see how far they can go. Over time that drive gives way to either a more driven artist – case in point Madonna – or an artist that feels the ever-growing pressure of success to be too much and they become reluctant to grow and evolve – in other words musical death. Harsh but true. In this business of show the key to success is to stay relevant.'

Music fans need to remember that, as acknowledged by Russell Sanjek in *American Popular Music and Its Business: The First Four Hundred Years From 1900–1984 Vol. III*:

'Donna Summer had established herself as the queen not only of disco but of pop, soul and rock, the second black woman to achieve superstardom, after Diana Ross blazed the way.'

Fans are naturally selfish, wanting more and more from their idol, and they might feel that their star would be sad as a result of the slow down in her career. But Summer has mentioned before in an interview that she is relieved to be away from the limelight. Fans miss the thrill of expectation whenever a new release is announced, but at the same time listening to all the greatest hits will do the job! Summer has recorded many different types of songs, some she will love and some she might rather forget!

In an interview 'Donna Summer: The Empress Herself' with Rusty Truck in 2004 for annecarlini.com, she said that there were songs written with more heavy lyrics and some for a lighter feel. The simpler 'poppy' songs were not really her favourite anymore but she just had to put aside her personal preferences and make tunes for all her audience, no matter how difficult it was.

During the mid to late 1990s and early 2000s, fans could have easily worried that their idol was slowly withdrawing from the music scene. Should they have worried about their star's state of mind? Was Summer sad about her declining chart success? The answer was almost certainly no! Summer was certainly pulling back from the business, but this was to concentrate on the other aspects of her life and her family. She had been a highly successful pop star for over twenty years and it was time to take a little break, to relax and take stock of her life and career.

This was not the 'end' of Donna Summer. She continued to release singles and perform live but fans would just have to wait for the next studio album. The wait would surely be worth it.

12

The Thrill Of A Live Show

Summer continues to sing and write songs and participates in large charity events. She performs at Pride events, live radio sessions, TV shows and fundraisers and fans enjoy her studio productions and back catalogues. Devotees are still thrilled by her live performances.

Earlier in her career, Summer co-hosted and performed on the *American Bandstand* TV programme. Dick Clark, American Bandstand TV host and popular media personality, said that Summer was interested in taking part and fitted perfectly into the 'disco special' themed show aired on 27th May 1978. Summer said she had a great time filming, which is obvious when watching the finished product. Clark also mentioned in the 1995 TV programme *A & E Biography* that Summer had made history because she was the only musical artist to host the programme at that time. To compliment his appraisal of Donna Summer, Dick Clark also mentioned that there were no limits when it came to Summer's creativity. From her humble beginnings in musical theatre she rose to performing in Las Vegas.

During the first week of January 1979, Summer was one of the singers to record 'A Gift Of Song – The Music For UNICEF Concert' album, to celebrate the International Year Of The Children Of The World. The venue was at the General Assembly Hall of the United Nations in New York. She sang 'Mimi's Song' and donated the royalties of the song to UNICEF. Paul Gambaccini believed Donna Summer's performance (a tribute to her daughter) was very professional, showcasing Summer's versatility and emotional depth.

The concert aimed to raise money to provide food, healthcare, shelter and education for children in a hundred developing countries around the world. The concert was broadcast in seventy countries. Shel Kagan wrote in the article 'Rock & Roll At The Summit: Superstars Of Rock Give A Concert For UNICEF', that home spectators did not get to see Donna Summer's duet with Olivia Newton-John and some other acts due to half of the programme being cut. The producer-director Marty Pasetta had only ninety minutes of TV time and said it was cruel to eliminate those fantastic moments. Among other acts involved were Rita Coolidge, Kris Kristof-ferson, Olivia Newton-John and Rod Stewart. The concert also featured the late John Denver, the late Andy Gibb, Abba, The Bee Gees and Earth, Wind & Fire.

Another awesome moment for Summer's devotees and perhaps for the 'diva' herself was on the 25th January 1982, when Summer performed a tribute to Stevie Wonder with selected popular acts at the 9th Annual American Music Awards. She performed with the jazz legend Ella Fitzgerald and other famous names including Lionel Ritchie, Ray Parker Jr, Quincy Jones and Sheena Easton (to name five acts). They performed 'You Are The Sunshine Of My Life' and 'Isn't He Lovely', a play on Wonder's track 'Isn't She Lovely'. The performance was to celebrate the 'Award Of Merit' for Stevie Wonder. Summer said in a 1999 interview during the rehearsal for her solo VH1 TV show, that she always cherished working with other stars. As for Ella Fitzgerald, Summer noted that she performed and had been in the same venue on several occasions with the lady she regarded a 'legend'.

In 1994, Capital Radio announced that Donna Summer was ready to tour again. Fans were delighted to hear that the diva was certainly ready to 'rumble', according to an excited Summer statement. The desire to perform live in front of an audience will always be at the heart of an entertainer's motivation.

During promotion for the tour for her 1994 'Endless Summer: Donna Summer's Greatest Hits' album, Summer decided to do a live studio session with BBC Radio which aired on the 18th November. Summer was accompanied by a guitar solo, played by Bruce Sudano. Radio One listeners had the exclusive privilege to hear 'So This Is Lonely' a country cut that had never been performed in the UK. Summer also sang a medley of 'On The Radio'/'Bad Girls' as well as her third and final song, the ballad 'Any Way At All' (new material) from the greatest hits album.

1995 saw the return of Summer to the road with successful concerts in the US and Brazil. From a 1995 review in the Los Angeles Times of her sell-out headlining show at the Universal Amphitheatre in Los Angeles by Robert Hilburn:

'Donna Summer's name was a powerful magnet on the marquee in the late 1970s, when she turned out some of the most appealing and well-crafted dance minded records of the era. But is there still an audience for the one time "Queen Of Disco" at a time when pop music is still dominated by grunge and hip hop? Absolutely.'

She toured Europe in 1996; her concert in the UK was held in The Royal Albert Hall. It was a tour for 'Endless Summer: Donna Summer's

Above left: Photo session for 'On The Radio: Greatest Hits Volumes I & II' in Los Angeles, 16th May 1978. *(Harry Langdon / Getty Images)*

Above right: A more laid-back pose, 15th May 1987. *(Rex Features)*

Below: Donna Summer with Musical Youth during the filming of the 'Unconditional Love' video in London, 1983. *(Andre Csillag / Rex Features)*

Above: A talented artist, Summer presents 'Hard For The Money' and 'Starman' at her art exhibition at the Javits Center, New York. *(Time & Life Pictures / Getty Images)*

Below: Donna Summer headlines the Heineken Festival Holland in Rotterdam, April 2001. *(Vicken Couligian)*

Above: Chaka Khan, Donna Summer and Gloria Estefan at the Lunt Fontanne, December 1996. *(Richard Cokery, NY Daily News Archive / Getty Images)*

Below left: At the Royal Albert Hall, London. *(Brian Rasic / Rex Features)*

Below right: Donna Summer with a new look at the American Kiss Radio Station Charity Concert, Boston, 15th May 1999. *(Rex Features)*

Above: Attending Archbishop Desmond Tutu's 75th birthday event, at the Tribeca Grill, New York, 24th October 2006. *(Startraks Photo / Rex Features)*

Below: Summer at the filming of the TV programme *Discomania*. *(ITV / Rex Features)*

Above left: Donna Summer with Tony Bennett at a 50th birthday event for Jerry Inzerillo. *(Startraks Photo / Rex Features)*

Above right: Summer as a guest judge for the *Platinum Hit* TV show 'Dance Floor Royalty' in 2011, episode 102. *(NBCUPHOTOBANK / Rex Features)*

Below: With Westlife, at the filming of the TV programme *Discomania*. *(ITV / Rex Features)*

The 'Mistaken Identity' album image. *(Araldo Di Crollalanza / Rex Features)*

Donna Summer performing her hits at the Royal Albert Hall,
London, on 25th March 1996. *(Nik A Ramli)*

GRANADA Celebrates

Discomania

Hosted by Donna Summer

on

Friday 11th June 2004

DOORS OPEN 6.45pm
DOORS CLOSE 7.15pm
Strictly no admittance after 7.15pm
FINISH 10.00pm approx.

at

THE LONDON TELEVISION CENTRE
UPPER GROUND, LONDON SE1 9LT

**Strictly no admittance to anyone
under the age of 16**

Come dressed ready for the Disco!

ADMIT ONE Nº   2352

Top: Summer with fans.

Left: Images from the 'I Got Your Love' tribute video produced by Stor Dubiné Productions, 2003. *(Stor Dubiné)*

Above: 'Discomania' TV programme ticket.

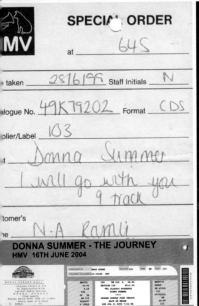

DONNA SUMMER - THE JOURNEY
HMV 16TH JUNE 2004

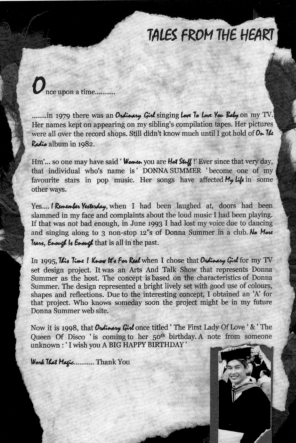

TALES FROM THE HEART

*O*nce upon a time...........

........in 1979 there was an *Ordinary Girl* singing *Love To Love You Baby* on my TV. Her names kept on appearing on my sibling's compilation tapes. Her pictures were all over the record shops. Still didn't know much until I got hold of *On The Radio* album in 1982.

Hm'... so one may have said ' *Women* you are *Hot Stuff* !' Ever since that very day, that individual who's name is ' DONNA SUMMER 'become one of my favourite stars in pop music. Her songs have affected *My Life* in some other ways.

Yes.... *I Remember Yesterday*, when I had been laughed at, doors had been slammed in my face and complaints about the loud music I had been playing. If that was not bad enough, in June 1993 I had lost my voice due to dancing and singing along to 3 non-stop 12"s of Donna Summer in a club. *No More Tears, Enough Is Enough* that is all in the past.

In 1995, *This Time I Know It's For Real* when I chose that *Ordinary Girl* for my TV set design project. It was an Arts And Talk Show that represents Donna Summer as the host. The concept is based on the characteristics of Donna Summer. The design represented a bright lively set with good use of colours, shapes and reflections. Due to the interesting concept, I obtained an 'A' for that project. Who knows someday soon the project might be in my future Donna Summer web site.

Now it is 1998, that *Ordinary Girl* once titled ' The First Lady Of Love ' & ' The Queen Of Disco ' is coming to her 50th birthday. A note from someone unknown : ' I wish you A BIG HAPPY BIRTHDAY '

Work That Magic........... Thank You

Top: Summer captured on stage by fans.

Right: 'Tales From The Heart', written on 12th November 1998 or Donna Summer's 50th birthday scrapbook. (*Nik A Ramli*)

Summer on stage, 15th June 1977. *(Rex Features)*

Greatest Hits', two years after the album was released. The long-awaited concert on the 25th March 1996 was an opportunity for fans to see Donna Summer live again.

As reviewed in 'Slipped Disco – Donna Summer May Have Slowed Her Pace, But The Beat Goes On' (Barbara Ellen, 1996):

'Tonight she does not fail to disappoint, belting out the classics from her impressive oeuvre using all three of her ranges – bellow, louder bellow and even-louder bellow. This is why we love Summer – she is unashamedly the most melodramatic, angst-ridden chanteuse on the block ... Entertainment is one thing, tonight is quite another. Summer even performs the fragile "Don't Cry For Me Argentina" like the good people of Buenos Aires might be listening in.'

It was indubitably a night to remember for fans. For some younger fans it was the first time to experience their 'idol' live in action. Comments from fans suggest an explosive, magical and mystical moment; a once-in-a-lifetime event – that was certainly my fruitful experience!

Summer also shared the loss of her mother through the gospel song 'Amazing Grace'. It was a touching moment. To lighten the atmosphere, Summer treated fans to a moment of comedy with some funny tales and introducing the next number in a little 'girly' voice.

The story begins in New York City. The girl (sitting at the dressing table) feels depressed in her luxury penthouse suite. Looking into the mirror, loving herself 'as all girls do' (Summer interjects to the amusement of the audience), the girl goes and puts her hand in her coat pocket and suddenly finds $20,000. That makes her feel happy and she decides to shop. While shopping, she meets an Italian guy and gives him that 'sort of look'. Summer moves her hips seductively, fluttering her beautiful eyelids to the audience. He asked her out, days pass, months pass and then he asked if he could move in with her. Summer looks 'shocked' making the audience laugh. The sketch continues a week later when the boyfriend's Ferrari gets towed away. When he asks her if he can borrow $50,000, the girl's mother advises:

'Girl, when a guy starts asking you for money ... well ... honey ... ENOUGH IS ENOUGH'!

As the audience screamed with joy, Donna Summer sang 'No More Tears (Enough Is Enough)' with her sister Mary Gaines Bernard. This moment was a fantastic example of Summer's musical theatre background and comical story telling ability.

Speaking to Dr. Wendy Henderson, a friend of mine, about her experience of the show she said:

'Summer's performance at the Royal Albert Hall was very magnetic and certainly had the audience on their feet for most of the time; a very enjoyable evening!'

That night the audience let go of any inhibitions, and got up on their feet to dance to Summer's 'Hot Stuff' melodies. Things got hotter with 'Bad Girls' as the diva changed costume with a beautiful red outfit that maximised her feminine curves.

After years of performing, Summer continues her charity shows and in 1997 she performed with Chaka Khan and Gloria Estefan in 'Three Divas On Broadway'. The event was at the Lunt-Fontanne Theatre in Manhattan and was broadcast on radio. A total of $20,000 was donated to each of the divas' favourite charities. One of her most important appearances came on the 16th March 1998 at Carnegie Hall, New York, for an AIDS charity concert. As reviewed by Larry Flick in *Billboard* magazine in the article 'A Benefit For The Gay Men's Health Crisis':

'The performance proved to reverberate in the minds and hearts of those who plunked down a sizeable chunk of chance ($50–$500) to experience Summer in an unusual, deservedly dignified setting. Although the show was organised as a fundraiser to benefit the Gay Men's Health Crisis (GMHC), it ultimately served as a shrewdly-timed precursor to what could easily be a triumphant career renaissance for the artist.'

From 1997 to 1999, Summer's performances were confined mainly to the US. In June 1999 the VH1 TV network, which featured acts such as the late Whitney Houston and Chaka Khan, invited Summer to perform on their annual 'Divas' live show called simply *VH1 Presents: Donna Summer Live & More Encore!*. At that time she was the only act to have a solo show.

Cathy Hawkins, creator of donna-tribute.com, said it was a night to remember:

'I was there. It was quite a night. First of all ... we found out that the only way to get tickets was to win them. You couldn't just go ... and buy them ... the show itself ... wow. It opened with "MacArthur Park"... the crowd goes nuts ... when Donna came out.'

It was a memorable moment for Summer's devoted fans. Hawkins says that Donna Summer enjoyed being there and was overwhelmed by her fans' response. Other observers commented on the quality of her sound.

While promoting the album, Summer made an appearance in a UK club called G.A.Y. at the Astoria Theatre, now at Heaven. Many established and new acts including Sheena Easton, Kylie Minogue, Lady Gaga and the late Amy Winehouse have performed in the club. However it is not only the 'ladies' that have performed there. Other acts to have done so include J C Chasez, Pet Shop Boys and Boyzone. McFly, an English pop group, grabbed attention when they stripped naked on stage during their show. Donna Summer was one of those stars that excited and thrilled G.A.Y. – The Queen Of Disco still rocks! In the book *Louis Walsh's Fast Track To Fame*, Walsh notes that the club is very particular about who performs at their venue.

Summer was also featured on *The Today Show* (1999), a popular American morning talk show. She performed three tracks 'MacArthur Park', 'I Will Go With You (Con Te Partiro)' and 'Last Dance'. The live version of 'I Will Go With You (Con Te Partiro)' appeared in the US on 'Live From The Today Show: The Best Of The Summer Concert Series' album in 2000.

Dagmar, a photographer and a friend of Summer since the *Hair* days, said that she had never seen Summer suffering from stage fright. Dagmar has always loved Summer's concerts, especially when Summer makes comments every now and then when seeing familiar faces in the audience. Summer mentioned in an interview for *VH1 Divas 2000: A Tribute To Diana Ross* (invited personally by the singer) that she was nervous of the unexpected, for example slipping on the floor while performing.

In a review of the event published in *Variety* on 17th April 2000, David Sprague said:

'Donna Summer, however, struck a fine balance between sexiness and sincerity: she stood out as the only performer who didn't lose momentum between set changes, maintaining the same heat on her own "Bad Girls" as on a cover of "Reflections".'

In a biography of Diana Ross, J. Randy Taraborrelli wrote that the VH1 television network finally decided to end the *Divas* series because it had become too difficult to book female acts. The series began production in 1998 and ended in 2004 (returning in 2009).

In 2004, the *Discomania* TV special hosted by Donna Summer with Neil Fox, was aired in the UK on ITV, partly to promote the album 'The Journey: The Very Best Of Donna Summer'. Summer told Karen Hockney in the *Daily Mirror* that the 1970s was a great time for her career and that she loved London and could never refuse an invite. Summer said that the fashion and music of that era was full of colours and 'about having fun and doing things differently.'

It was an experience for British fans as they were asked to dress in smart jeans, glittery tops, boob tubes and bright colours. Some younger fans took the opportunity to shop for the 1970s look while older fans relived their youth. Many fans travelled all the way from Europe for the show. Other featured guests included Rachel Stevens, Girls Aloud and Kool And The Gang, to name but a few. Summer did a great job as the host with Neil

Fox. She performed live to 'The Donna Summer Eternity Megamix' medley of 'Hot Stuff' and 'Bad Girls'. For the performance, Summer dressed in a long leather jacket and leather trousers complemented with a beautiful corset. She was accompanied with four male dancers dressed as policemen and four 'bad girl' female dancers! The audience were thrilled; they danced and sang along to the chorus and clapped their hands all through her routine! Young audiences saw the 1970s diva at her best! Summer also performed 'MacArthur Park'. Recorded at the London Television Centre in June that year, the programme featured a new version of 'No More Tears (Enough Is Enough)' recorded by Donna Summer with popular Irish male group Westlife. The performance was shown at the finale of *Discomania*.

Peter Stegaard, a music producer who had seen Summer performing live, said:

'I saw her shortly after the release of 'I Got Your Love' in Universal City here in LA – she's incredible live as well as in the studio. She is a true artist and seems to forget everything around her when she sings ... she really goes into performance mode like no one else I've ever worked with.'

Summer has never stopped touring. On the 11th April 2005 she joined big names such as John Legend, Alicia Keys, Joss Stone, Rod Stewart and Rob Thomas for the show 'Save The Music: A Concert To Benefit The VH1 Save The Music Foundation', which took place in New York's Beacon Theatre.

When 'Crayons' was released in 2008, she was busy travelling in the US. On the 22nd August 2008 *The Orange County Register*, reviewing 'An Evening With Donna Summer' at the Hollywood Bowl in Los Angeles, noted that during the first half of the show Summer focused more on material from the album, including the ballad 'Sand On My Feet' and the reggae-infused 'Crayons' before going back to her biggest former hits. The review says:

'...."She Works Hard For The Money" got the dancing into high gear again. Then "Bad Girls", with its catchy chorus, flowed straight into "Hot Stuff", performed here in a faster, harder-rocking style. Just as "The Queen Is Back" served as the perfect opener, there was never any doubt what would wrap up the night, and from the opening chords of "Last Dance", a huge cheer went up and nearly everyone in this audience of more than 14,000 rose to their feet.'

Bryan Cooper, a big Donna Summer fan, said he had always enjoyed her music and owned some cassettes (rare these days) and LPs from the 1980s, the era he felt most connected to. Cooper said the audiences kept on dancing and shouting 'WE LOVE YOU' to their icon. He was amazed by Summer's energy, her voice and the vibes she gave off to the fans that night. Cooper added he was waiting for his favourite track to be sung, 'This Time I Know It's For Real' but to his surprise and disappointment the 1989 hit was not included that night. He was still thrilled to be part of the whole experience.

Jeff Walsh wrote about Summer's Paramount show as being full of costume changes, backing singers and a stage decorated with 'hot male dancers' who danced routines around Summer. He noted that her voice was great and the 'new album is surprisingly well put together'. Here is an extract from the review of Summer's Paramount Theatre, Oakland, show, published on 7th September 2008 in *Oasis* magazine:

'. . . amazing how many songs you know of Summer's until she keeps playing big hit after big hit . . . Summer's music has always been very producer-driven, in that you can tell which tracks are from the late 1970s, which are from the early 1980s, and her newest tunes follow that pattern, too. They are all "2008 Dance Floor-Ready", although she does explore different high-RPM rhythms, such as reggae.'

Donna Summer continued her 'Crayons' tour in Europe. Her Paris show was on 7th July 2009 and she performed later in Germany, but not in the UK. Eddie Sorell, who travelled from Sweden, observed that Summer's music appealed across differing age groups, the youngest probably around fifteen years old to some lively octogenarians! Sorell recalled her tribute to Michael Jackson with the song 'Smile' and the ever popular Piaf classic 'La Vie En Rose' and, of course, 'Love To Love You Baby'. Summer had developed a seductive elegant style for her 'sensual love song'.

In an article in *The Telegraph* titled 'Donna Summer; Too Hot To Handle' by Craig McLean, Summer discusses the song 'Love To Love You Baby':

'If I were to do that song like I did it in the old days, the fire department would have to be at that show. Seriously.'

Why not? Surely a visit from the fire brigade would be a huge thrill and would be welcomed by her audience, male and female!

During an interview with McLean, Summer described an interesting moment about performing 'Love To Love You Baby' on stage, describing a time when she was trapped in a trailer surrounded by 5,000 Italian men! Following a performance of the song in Italy, the emotion of it all got too much for the audience, who chased a hastily-retreating young Summer back to her trailer which they began to rock back and forth!

She said the 'Love To Love You Baby' track is not the type of melody that can just be thrown out there.

Other than touring, Donna Summer continues with her charity events.

It was reported that she raised two million dollars at 'An Enduring Vision 2009', the benefit for the Elton John Aids Foundation, where she performed 'On The Radio', 'Smile' and 'Last Dance'.

A true admirer, Joseph Solis celebrated his '30th Fan Anniversary' in 2011. 'On The Radio: Greatest Hits Volumes I & II' was a Christmas reward after 'hounding' his parents to buy it for him. Solis's first concert was in 1981, 'The Wanderer Tour' at Providence, Rhode Island on July 25th. He says:

'I've seen Donna live well over thirty times. My most memorable concert was in 1986 in Atlantic City. I met her for the very first time. It was an amazing experience to say the least!'

In 'Photos: David Foster And His Friends At Mandalay Bay Events Center' by Don Chareunsy for the lasvegasweekly.com (2nd October 2011):

'Super-producer David Foster was front and center in the spotlight for his multi-artist concert . . . in a change of pace, Foster was a headliner along side his successful collaborators ... Tom Donoghue was on duty for a super-sized Vegas De Luxe photo gallery and also served as reporter. "Mandalay Bay rockin' last night. David Foster & Friends captured the crowd completely for nearly three hours. Kenny Loggins, Charice and Ruben Studdard were unbelievable, and Donna Summer stole the show."'

As a singer Summer felt 'blessed' to be doing something that she loves so much: to sing and provide joy to her fans and to get gratification for it beyond her wildest dreams. In any show each audience will experience the thrilling ambience in their own way. To be in a concert hall sharing the same excitement as they come into contact with other fans. They become captivated and transported on a voyage that only lasts a short time. Feeling the pride of the crowd, they sing with their idol, forgetting their real lives.

Fans that missed Summer in concert were able to view the 1983 video and laser disc release *A Hot Summer Night*, recorded live at the Pacific Amphitheatre, Los Angeles.

The video included performances of 'Unconditional Love', 'Don't Cry For Me Argentina' and 'She Works Hard For The Money' accompanied by an imaginative theatre design. Summer's opening act, 'MacArthur Park', was an impressive introduction to the show. Her loyal fans, especially in Europe, are hungry to see more of Donna Summer. A more mature Summer in concert can be admired in the 1999 DVD and video release of *VH1 Presents: Live & More Encore!*. These two videos are the only official live concerts that have been released at the time of writing.

13

Glory Of The Past

There have been many remixes of Summer's previous smash hits. In 1982 the seminal disco track 'I Feel Love' was remixed to a length of fifteen minutes. This first official single remix by Patrick Cowley reached no.21 and spent ten weeks in the UK charts. Sadly, Cowley died before his masterpiece even entered the chart on December 4th 1982. The twelve inch remake by the late disco and Hi-NRG dance music composer has deservedly become a collector's item.

Nick Johnstone wrote that the original 'I Feel Love' was the first crossover hit by Donna Summer.

Both the original and remixed versions influenced the UK charts in the 1990s with Europop, Eurodisco and techno sounds emanating from acts such as Culture Beat, Haddaway, Modern Talking, CC Catch and 2 Unlimited. Congratulations to Giorgio Moroder, Donna Summer and Pete Bellotte for the birth of 'I Feel Love' and also to Patrick Cowley's remake of the song.

A new version of the 1982 hit 'State Of Independence' was released for 'The Best Of Donna Summer' album in 1990. The 'N.R.G. Mix' for the track gave a 'jungle sound' that was once popular on the club and DJ scene, but has now faded away. The single enjoyed chart status for three weeks. It entered at no.78 on the 10th November 1990 and peaked at no.45 by 24th November 1990. Her follow up was 'Breakaway (Remix)' which featured a rap section. On 19th January 1991 the remix peaked at no.49, staying in the chart for four weeks. The single was taken from the same compilation, and both of these singles made it to the chart in the UK. July 1995 marked the return to chart success when a brand new version of 'I Feel Love' was marketed. 'I Feel Love '95' entered the charts and reached no.8 on 9th September 1995 in the first week of its release in the UK, spending five weeks in the chart. Her last Top 10 hit in the UK was way back in 1989 with 'I Don't Wanna Get Hurt' which reached no.7. Hipsters Rollo and Sister Bliss approached Donna Summer for the eighteenth anniversary to rerecord 'I Feel Love'. The new version of the single 'I Feel Love '95' entered the French chart at no.33 and stayed in the charts for six weeks.

145

There are many mixes of 'I Feel Love' but the 1995 facelift was the one that thrilled Summer. Although at first she was cagey about the proposal, she insisted on recording a new vocal for the track. The full length 'Rollo/Sister Bliss Monster Mix' available in the double twelve inch promotional is to die for! A killer 'Master At Work Mix' runs to a total of eleven minutes thirty-three seconds and was officially released in France. It was a tremendous idea to record a new vocal as it brought a new expressiveness that can be heard in the 'I Feel Love Master At Work 86th St. Mix', bringing the song to a new arena. The vocal no longer resembles more of a 'backing' track than an 'orthodox lead line' as Brian Eno once said when commenting on the 1977 UK no.1 hit single! The new recording showcased Donna Summer's blossoming mature vocal rather than the soft, sexy voice heard on the 1977 track.

In the article 'Giorgio Moroder At Future Music' (1996), the producer was asked if he had heard any of the remixes of 'I Feel Love'. Moroder replied:

'I heard several versions of it. Some were good; one particular mix I liked a lot. If they change the chords, usually it's not for the better. But in this particular case the guy changed one particular chord and I thought, "Wow, I should have done that!" So that was quite good.'

Back in June 1977, Caroline Coon wrote in *Melody Maker*:

'With her producers, she's created an atmosphere of futuristic space-drama and old world romance. Her voice adds the earth dimension to sounds that would otherwise beat heartlessly. Already a disco hit. Should cross over into the pop chart.'

An author of thousands of popular music reviews, Chuck Eddy said in his publication *The Accidental Evolution Of Rock 'N' Roll* about the initial 'I Feel Love':

'There's actually two synthesizer figures that are represented – one like a giant spinning helium Slinky spring and the other one passes in and out. The singing feels like helium, too. And the big spring encircles the inner perimeter of whatever room you're listening to it in, a circle within a square, and you feel every time the shapes intersect, because the pitch changes for a split-second. Or maybe the shapes don't really intersect; maybe the spring just skims the surface of the walls, ceiling, and floor and keeps right on moving. And sunlight keeps peeping in and out of the clouds, through your window and into the room, getting lost then reappearing.'

In 2004, the original 'I Feel Love' was ranked by *Rolling Stone* at no.411 on their list of the 500 Greatest Songs Of All Time. The review for the song noted that Giorgo Moroder and Donna Summer claimed tomorrow in the name of disco. In the same year a remix titled 'I Feel Love 2004' featured in the 'Almighty Showreel 2004' CD. In 2005 a new remix called 'I Feel Love (Almighty Mix)' featured in 'We Love Disco' released by Almighty Records. In July 2011 in an article called 'James Brown's Sex Machine Is Top Of The Dance Floor Tunes' for walesonline.co.uk, 'I Feel Love' was at no.5 for The Top Floor Fillers survey. Over 2000 people participated in the survey at an event at Long Marston Airfield, Stratford-Upon-Avon, conducted by electronic music festival GlobalGathering.

David Bowie told David Sheppard the story of Brian Eno's disco evangelism; that Brian Eno, formerly of Roxy Music, said that he had heard the sound of the future when he first listened to 'I Feel Love', and commented that the song was going to change the sound of club music for the next fifteen years. His prediction was right!

In *On Some Faraway Beach: The Life And Times Of Brian Eno,* David Sheppard explains that the futuristic sound of 'I Feel Love' was accidentally created when Giorgio Moroder unintentionally was 'flicking on his synthesizer's arpeggiator switch'. Eno's love for the 'tomorrow' sound of Summer's recording was later revived by Summer's cover of Vangelis and Jon Anderson's 'State Of Independence', released in 1982.

Continuing the success of 'I Feel Love '95', in March 1996 a new remix of 'State Of Independence' was released. The single was released on the date of Donna Summer's Royal Albert Hall concert in London. 'State Of Independence '96' reached no.13 on the 6th April 1996 in the UK, and spent five weeks in the charts. The single also featured the late Dr. Martin Luther King's voice in respect for the memory of his African-American Civil Rights Movement. In *Donna Summer: For The Record,* Craig Halstead wrote that Eddie Gordon was thrilled to have the approval of Quincy Jones and Summer to include Dr. Martin Luther King's speech. It featured in the 'New Radio Millennium Mix'.

The new version of 'State Of Independence', released in 1996 in memory of Dr. Martin Luther King, included extracts of his speech 'Some Things We Must Do':

'Yes if you can't be a pine on top of the hill, be a shrub in the valley, but be the best little shrub on the side of the hill – be a bush if you can't be a tree. If you can't be a highway be a trail. If you can't be the sun, be a star. It isn't by size that you win or fail – be the best at whatever you are.'

The remixes of the single brought 'State Of Independence' to the dance market. A 'Creation Mix' featured lyrics by Stevie Wonder, (written for the 1982 release) opening the song before Summer's vocal kicked in. Wonder added these lyrics:

'Just as all creation is one with the universe, may we too be one with each other.'

In an email titled 'The State Of Independence Remix: Info Right From The Source', sent to one of Summer's previous tribute sites, the DJ Alejandro Guerrieri shared the making of the 'State Of Independence '96' (DJ Dero Mix):

'. . . We first listened to the three versions we knew . . . Donna Summer's . . . Jon & Vangelis'. . . and Moodswing's . . . We carefully listened to the way the choir was arranged in Donna's and Moodswing's versions. We first decided to use a tempo of about 130 bpm and did a primitive drum background and bass line to work over.'

The information provided by Guerrieri was very technical. Summer's vocal was sampled in a sampler arrangement with 32 Mb RAM. Her voice was later divided into small fragments, due to the tempo needing to be increased a great deal for their version. The result however sounded unnatural. The team wanted to preserve the dynamic of the original tune. It was hard work, their ears being the main tool to judge the sound of the new remix. Also the original choir in 'State Of Independence' was not available so the team were 'forced' to sample it from a CD. Guerrieri said that as it is in stereo, it would be remarkable to use a Centre Channel Eliminator to focus on the vocals he needed. He ran SAW Plu's CCE (whatever that might be) over the initial choir and the idea worked!

Guerrieri explained his technical achievement on 'State Of Independence '96':

'It took fifteen minutes . . . to equalize the result to get a pretty fair choir, without the rest of the band that played behind on the CD! At this time DJ Dero suggested a few great improvements in the structure of the remix (that's one of his strongest points). We added some sorted and filtered keyboards, a lot of "Batucadas" (a style of samba), and did the "slow-down" part, the hip hop. Four days after we started, the mix was done!'

DJ Dero's 'State Of Independence '96' was received enthusiastically by fans, the new version being bundled with five great remixes. Although these remixes were successful in the UK, Summer's US record management did not take the opportunity to release 'I Feel Love '95' and 'State Of Independence '96' in US. This may have been a chance for Summer to repeat her US chart success after being absent for so long. However 'I Feel Love '95' did reach no.9 in the US dance chart.

In 1997, this time credited to Donna Summer and Giorgio Moroder, 'Carry On', a tune unfamiliar to the public, was remixed and released in Belgium, Australia and the US. 'Carry On '97' was a hit in the *Billboard*

148

dance charts and when NARAS (The National Academy of Recording Arts & Sciences, Inc., known variously as The Recording Academy or NARAS) created a new Grammy award category for Best Dance Recording, Summer won in 1998. She was the first winner in that category. Donna Summer was convinced that she did not stand a chance of winning a fifth award; the achievement caught Summer completely off guard. It was a great acknowledgement from the music industry for both Summer and Moroder. Two people that played a huge part in the development and popularisation of disco – now evolved into dance.

The award success in June 1998 afforded a chance to release the remix of 'Carry On' in the UK. A review of the single, printed in *The Guardian* in the UK on June 27th 1998, was received with disbelief by avid followers of Donna Summer. The article was more of a personal attack; 'Donna Summer And Giorgio Moroder: Carry On (Almighty)'. Someone called Ben Marshall penned a vicious and personal diatribe against Summer, reviving old discredited rumours, which was clearly more about his personal feelings about Summer than any objective, professional critique. It was rounded off with a rather childish obscenity. One hates to think how Mr. Marshall would react to any really serious issues!

It was not a very professional analysis, neither constructive nor insightful. Fans were surprised by its bitter and vitriolic tone. Some fans took the opportunity to express their discontent by publishing their riposte – Ben Marshall's article was out of all proportion! It was clear the journalist had not done his homework when reviewing an established artist who has made many different types of records as well as contributing to charitable causes past and present. Or, maybe, high expectations of the dance diva were not met so, 'upset' and 'frustrated', he got carried away with his review? Maybe he got out of the wrong side of bed that morning!

Everyone's entitled to their opinion. Unfortunately, Summer had been absent from the music market in the UK for a while and the 'media' only remembered her with the remakes of past hits – 1995 'I Feel Love' and 1996 'State Of Independence'. Music fans and the media wanted a new, fresh sound from the original disco diva Donna Summer! The responses to *The Guardian* were competently crafted by Donna Summer fans, but the strength of emotion caused by the review was not acknowledged by the publication.

The single was still played in clubs and featured in a few high-profile dance compilation albums, as well as being released in stores. It also featured briefly in a scene of the hit UK TV series *Queer As Folk*. The lack of promotion and radio play meant the single 'Carry On '98' did not take off in the UK. The new remix single debuted at no.65 in UK on the 17th July 1998.

The revamped 'Carry On' that had gone 'twice' into the surgery studio was worth every penny! The 1997 reworking of 'Outta Control' as well as 'Mr. Jack & Frank Degrees' was fantastic, with the 1998 revamped 'Euro Mix' and 'Diddy's Hard For The Money Mix' sounding fresh and up-tempo. These remixes did not ruin the original composition by Giorgio Moroder but simply made it sound fresh and modern.

Summer's songs have provided popular source material for remixing by DJs. They have been reworked by successful and popular teams, such as Masters At Work. Groove Armada produced an unreleased 'Love 2 Groove Ya Baby', a sample from 'Love To Love You Baby'. Summer, interviewed by *Electronic Beats* in 2009, said that the electronic music scene had come full circle. Successive generations will add new interpretations to existing music, e.g. 'I Feel Love'. Technology creates infinite possibilities of producing new sounds.

Summer's songs, often updated and remixed, have also been included in the soundtracks to many movies over the years. Back in 1977, 'Prelude To Love/Could It Be Magic' and 'Try Me, I Know We Can Make It' featured in *Looking For Mr. Goodbar*. She has also recorded songs specifically for films. These include 'Down, Deep Inside' for the 1977 *The Deep* and the following year she recorded 'Last Dance', 'With Your Love' and a cover 'Je T'aime (Moi Non Plus)' for *Thank God It's Friday*. 'On The Radio' was recorded for *Foxes* in 1980. Some of Summer's unreleased material has also featured, such as 'Highway Runner' which was used in *Fast Times At Ridgemont High* in 1982 and 'Romeo' for *Flashdance* in 1983.

Donna Summer's songs continue to be used in film, with the anthemic 'She Works Hard For The Money' used in 1995 in the comedy *Birdcage* featuring Robin Williams, Nathan Lane, Gene Hackman and Dianne Wires. Summer returned to the studio in 1996 to record 'Ordinary Miracle' for *Let It Be* and in the same year 'Whenever There Is Love', a duet with Bruce Roberts, was released from the movie *Daylight*. In 1997 Summer was back in the public eye when 'Hot Stuff' was featured as one of the main tracks in the British blockbuster *The Full Monty*. Due to the success of the film, 'Hot Stuff' got on to the regular playlists of UK radio stations and clubs.

'Hot Stuff' was so popular that during a 1998 UK press event for Prince Charles' fiftieth birthday, the Prince of Wales helped recreate the scene from *The Full Monty* in which the four main characters overhear the song while waiting in line at the unemployment office. While attending a Full

Monty party at the Langseft Foundation in Sheffield to showcase the work of the Prince's Trust, Prince Charles joined one of the actors from the film, Hugo Speer who plays Lunchbox, in performing some of the 'Hot Stuff' routine. Charles is quoted in a BBC online article 'The Full Monarchy' as saying:

'I've even been given a bit of choreography on how to do things in the queue.'

The publicity helped to raise Summer's profile. Loyal fans hoped for a new remix of 'Hot Stuff' after its appearance in *The Full Monty* but it was not forthcoming. The 'Bad Girls' album, where 'Hot Stuff' was taken from, became popular and the film soundtrack was a no.1 in the UK, staying in the chart for forty-three weeks! Gennaro Costaldo, Head of Press and PR (HMV and Fopp) says the success of the soundtrack album absolutely brought fame to Summer's 'Bad Girls' and her other records. If music fans are given an opportunity to discover them then Summer's records will be in demand. (Not from the actual sales data but as an estimate for Summer sales) Costaldo says:

'. . . it received a huge amount of exposure, and I recall it helped to boost interest in her music again – with a rise in sales of her hits albums. Today if that had happened you would have seen a spike in downloads. It just needs a spark – such as her songs to be featured on *Glee* or *The X-Factor*, or perhaps for her music to be featured in a TV ad campaign, for demand to surge again.'

In 1998, 'Bad Girls' featured in the film *Picture Perfect* and also in a comedy starring Steve Martin and Goldie Hawn, *Out Of Towners*, in 1999. In 2000, while Donna Summer was contracted to Epic Records, a new track 'Dream-catcher', composed by herself and Michael Hanna, was recorded for the movie *Naturally Native*. A sentimental tune 'The Power Of One' was released for the animated film *Pokemon 2000: The Power Of One*.

A full-length edit of 'Last Dance' appeared in *Charlie's Angels: Full Throttle* in 2003. 'Hot Stuff' again featured in a soundtrack, this time for the comedy *Eurotrip* in 2004.

Donna Summer's songs have featured in many TV plays, shows, series, dramas and video games. In the 1970s, the BBC banned Donna Summer's 'Love To Love You Baby' because of the provocative moaning. This resulted in the 1977 BBC play *Abigail's Party* using a cover version of the song by Clare Torry.

In 1993, 'Love To Love You Baby' was chosen for a TV drama, inspired by Armistead Maupins' 'Tales Of The City'. The release of this hit series and its soundtrack in 1993 proved that there was a huge demand for the

1970s sound. The album featured twenty classic tunes from that era, including songs by Gloria Gaynor, The Bee Gees, Labelle and of course, Donna Summer.

In the late 1990s, the introduction to 'Love To Love You Baby' was featured on Channel 4's hit show *TFI Friday*, during Chris Evans' 'Baby Left Baby Right' section, when a baby was placed upright on a cushion and the guest was asked to guess which way the child would fall. In a 1998 episode of the American animated series *South Park* titled *Roger Ebert Should Lay Off The Fatty Foods* (season two, episode eleven), the song 'She Works Hard For The Money' was sung by Cartman in an audition for a Cheesy Poofs commercial!

In 1999 'Love To Love You Baby' was featured in the hit comedy series *Friends*. In the same year 'This Time I Know It's For Real' was used in *Ally McBeal*. In 2001, 'Last Dance', performed by a guest vocalist, was used in the same series. Another US comedy series, *Will & Grace,* featured the chorus of 'No More Tears (Enough Is Enough)' sung live by Grace Adler (played by Debra Messing) with Tim Bagley playing Larry in the 2001 episode *An Old Fashioned Piano Party*. In season five, 2003, the episode *Sex, Losers And Videotape,* Grace Adler sings 'Love To Love You Baby' twice. Also 'Hot Stuff' and 'Bad Girls' appeared in season three of *Sex And The City*, in the episode *Where There's Smoke . . .*, and in 2003 'I Got Your Love', a new recording by Summer, featured in the same series in the episode *The Post-It Always Sticks Twice,* even before the song was released in the shops. This was the very first time that a new track by Donna Summer had been featured in a TV series before being released.

In 2003 'Hot Stuff' featured prominently in an episode of the UK mystery series *Jonathan Creek,* in the episode *Angel Hair,* where the track was sung by Caroline Carver playing a pop star named Sally Ellen Oakley. In 2006, Summer's 1983 hit 'She Works Hard For The Money' was featured on the pilot of *Ugly Betty.* 'Last Dance' appeared in an early scene in the drama *An Englishman In New York* in 2009, first aired on ITV1 in the UK.

There are so many of examples of Summer's songs being featured in the media that it is impossible to list them all. In October 2011 'Hot Stuff' featured in *Dance Central 2*, a video game for the Xbox 360 Kinect.

The rock band Hypnogaja, who won an award for their cover of the Summer song 'On The Radio', commented that:

'Film and television and video games tend to use music that's got a visual, dramatic side to it. If it's one thing we have in common with Donna Summer, it's a sense of theatricality!'

The dance music singer and Summer fan Inanna said that the songs stir the public's emotions and that is what the music business is all about. Donna Summer's music is very effective at this; this is one of the things that make her unique.

Mark Nubar Donikian from Hypnogaja said in an interview:

'Donna Summer has always been an original – as well as an innovator. We were recently watching the film *Frost/Nixon*, set in 1977. For one of the only source cues in the movie, they used 'I Feel Love' in a club scene. It was such a powerful moment because it conveyed just how futuristic that song sounded back then when it first came out – and how it still sounds so fresh and interesting today. She's an artist who's always had a unique point of view, and one that's been able to transcend genres and stand the test of time – a true inspiration for all of us who endeavour to have a career in music'.

The continued presence of Summer's songs in various media has helped to introduce her work to new generations of music lovers. When asked in an interview for her thoughts on the renewed popularity of disco and house music and its effect on public interest in her own work, the star explained to Johannes Bonke in 'Talking To The Prima Donna' for *Electronic Beats* magazine:

'It's extremely exciting . . . it just shows you that music never dies, it finds its own life over and over again . . .'

Can music change the world? This question was posed to Summer by *Electronic Beats*. She replied that it can change the world and it can change the way people think; music as sound therapy. Summer pointed out that when played to different people, classical music will elicit different reactions, including feelings of peacefulness, whereas if one wants to get stimulated, then rock 'n' roll songs will do the trick!

Fans seemed to agree, one explaining that Summer's tunes have comforted him during times of loss and through the ups and downs of his life's journey. He posted that 'Forgive Me' reassured his soul during a time of sadness and grief and 'This Time I Know It's For Real' gave him strength when he felt powerless. 'Bad Girls' and 'Hot Stuff' gave him 'raunchy' inspiration!

Gloria Gaynor agrees that lyrics can be powerful motivators. 'I Will Survive' is reputed to have prevented at least one person from committing suicide. One young woman told Gaynor that while suffering depression, she listened by chance to a version of 'I Will Survive' with slightly different lyrics. 'It took all the strength I had not to fall apart' had been modified by Gaynor to 'Only the Lord could give me strength not to fall apart'. This had given her the power to carry on. Gaynor found it hard to put into words how wonderful she felt to have known that her song been used that way.

One fan had battled all her life with her weight and had been a subject of fun since she was young. Depressed and ashamed of her appearance, when teased by a group of boys she took the advice of her uncle and fought back, pushing one of the boys – he fell flat on the ground.

After this they left her alone! Now able to laugh at the situation, she recalled the Donna Summer song 'If You Got It, Flaunt It' which she found by chance in the 1980s in her parents' record collection. The words to 'If You Got It, Flaunt It' by Donna Summer, Giorgio Moroder and Pete Bellotte:

'Baby if you got it, You have got to flaunt it now ... All you catty creatures I got my better features too. So step aside you leeches, I can teach a trick or two.'

'If You Got It, Flaunt It' gave this fan strength and helped her to 'move on'. She is grateful to Summer for those lyrics. Gloria Gaynor mirrored these feelings when she said that music added meaning and purpose to one's life. Summer told *Electronic Beats* that music changes the way you are. Music fans agree that songs can provide a meaning to life, whatever era the songs have come from. They can provide inspiration, make you feel at ease or transport you to a dream world!

The author Philip Ball noted in his *The Music Instinct: How Music Works And Why We Can't Do Without It* (2010):

'... it's true that music can, in the appropriate context, both heighten and quell emotions, and both for better and worse. But we should be sceptical of the idea that a sequence of notes has an intrinsic power to pervert or purify. Music alone can't make us do good or bad things.'

In the 'Law And Order' section of *The Telegraph*, an article tilted 'Donna Summer Fan Has Speakers Confiscated' reported that a fan played 'Love To Love You Baby' and 'other Donna Summer hits' at maximum volume until the small hours, which understandably upset the neighbours. The music played until the 'walls shook with the vibrations' and she was heard to accompany on 'bongo drums'! Unfortunately for her, she was found guilty.

This does not mean that music could not deliver messages and suggestions. Philip Ball suggests that music can be used to make explicit 'programmatic statements'.

In the *Daily Express*, an article by John Twomey and David Pildith, 'Gun PC "Used Song Titles" In His Evidence At Mark Saunders Inquest', noted that a policeman had been 'allegedly planting' titles from popular songs in 'his evidence'. It was noted that one of the phrases used by the officer was 'Enough is enough; the title of a Donna Summer song'. After the officer 'denied inserting' song titles at the inquest 'the matter was left to rest'.

'She Works Hard For The Money' was performed by 'about twenty Australian Services Union (ASU) members' at a demonstration to support the 'equal pay for social and community sector workers' promised by the Victoria Liberal Party in their pre-election campaign. The headline 'Union Flash Mob Rallies Outside Prahran MP's Office' by Nicole Cridland for the *Stonnington Leader* on 25th July 2011, said that the song was used:

'. . . as part of a larger push for equal pay that had already gained support from the Federal Government as well as other State Labour governments.'

Philip Ball writes in *The Music Instinct: How Music Works And Why We Can't Do Without It* that:

'because context can create and transform meaning, composers can't hope to anticipate or control the way their music will be used . . .'

So the sounds of the 1970s, 1980s, 1990s and even current hits will keep on making a comeback, constantly being 'recycled'. Donna Summer's past and present hits will be part of the experience of many future generations of young music lovers. Her new fans will increase sales of her back catalogue. Her music has become part of the soundtrack of people's lives.

Her melodies, featured in so many films, captured the atmosphere of the moment. Working in the studio is equally important. Though some of her new recordings have featured on the screen, her fans are constantly hungry for new material showcasing that fabulous voice.

Donna Summer never stops; she keeps working, recording solo or collaborating with other acts, established and new.

14

Singing Along

Donna Summer continued her studio work throughout the 1970s to the present day. Back in the late 1970s and early 1980s, she made lots of guest appearances on various albums and she continues to contribute vocals to various projects.

In the early 1970s, on Three Dog Night's 'Hard Labor' album (1974), Summer was not credited for her backup vocals in 'Sure As I'm Sittin' Here', 'Put Out The Light', 'I'd Be So Happy' and 'Play Something Sweet'.

Summer performed on Gene Simmons' self-titled album (1978) 'Burning Up With Fever'. Summer's contributed vocal for Gene Simmons' song brought out the rock soul in her. The project explored her ability to travel in another direction from her natural pop territory. She also appeared in Brooklyn Dreams' self-titled album (1977) in 'Old Fashioned Girl'.

In *Ordinary Girl: The Journey* Summer explains how she came to record with the group. The Brooklyn Dreams recorded background vocals for her 1977 hit album 'I Remember Yesterday'. She later returned the favour on their track 'Old Fashioned Girl'.

She also contributed vocals to their version of 'Heaven Knows', on the album 'Sleepless Nights' (1979). This version was as good as the performance on the Donna Summer 'Live And More' album. 'Heaven Knows', the Donna Summer version, was the only Top 10 hit the group had in the US. Fans of Brooklyn Dreams and Summer will be thrilled to know that a previously unreleased 'Heaven Knows' twelve inch Disco Mix was included in the 'Sleepless Nights' 2010 re-release. It was a great version that should have been released at the time.

Subsequent to the work on the Brooklyn Dreams 1979 album, Summer continued her collaboration with tracks like 'A Lover In The Night' and 'Never Let Them Go' featured on the album 'Never Let Them Go' (1980).

Summer and Sudano's relationship started out as purely professional. Summer always wanted to write more songs after her international hit in 1975. She had written a couple of hits, but she wanted to learn more. In *Ordinary Girl: The Journey* Summer says she was thrilled to find that Bruce

Sudano was actually a music composer. She realised that perhaps Sudano could point her in the right direction. As she explained in her autobiography, after 'Love To Love You Baby' she was keen to write more songs, but even though she learnt from her producer the 'form and structure' of music-making, she regretted her inability to read music or play an instrument. Bruce Sudano presented an opportunity for her to learn. An experienced musician Sudano, co-founder of Brooklyn Dreams, previously gained fame with the group Alive 'N' Kickin' with 'Tighter, Tighter' in 1970 (Billboard no.7). To gain experience and learn more, Summer was open to working with several acts and most of her collaborations were with acts from her label 'Casablanca'.

She appeared on Paul Jabara's album 'Shut Out' (1977) in 'Shut Out' as well as 'The Third Album' (1979) in 'Foggy Day/Never Lose Your Sense Of Humor'. These tracks were tuneful but not the best disco songs that have been recorded. The singles did not get much interest in the charts in the US or UK. 'Foggy Day/Never Lose Your Sense Of Humor' written by Paul Jabara, Donna Summer and Greg Manthieson has been released only once on CD format – 'Paul Jabara's Greatest Hits ... And Misses' in 1989. It has never featured in any of Donna Summer's compilation albums to date!

Bob Esty, who was hired by Giorgio Moroder to arrange and conduct Summer's 'Once Upon A Time' album in Munich, says:

'In 1977, I wrote 'Shut Out' with Paul Jabara (for his album by the same name) that featured Donna Summer singing as herself'.

Esty continue to work with the team and in his own words:

'Paul Jabara wrote 'Last Dance' and I wrote the hook and the bridge. I arranged and conducted it and co-produced it with Giorgio Moroder. In 1978 I produced The Brooklyn Dreams and Donna would hang out on the sessions with her husband-to-be, Bruce Sudano. After that, I co-wrote many songs with Paul Jabara for Donna, and she always did the demos, but never recorded them.'

Summer continued her studio work and recorded 'No More Tears (Enough Is Enough)' with Barbra Streisand. The song appeared both in Summer's 'On The Radio: Greatest Hits Volumes I & II' and Ms Streisand's album 'Wet' in 1979. The song proved a great success and, interestingly, was created by Paul Jabara with Bruce Roberts.

She also participated in Bruce Sudano's 'Pretender' (1980) for the title track, and Musical Youth's 'Different Style' (1983) as a backing vocalist on 'Incommunicado'. Summer featured the group in 'Unconditional Love', taken from 'She Works Hard For The Money'.

Besides recording on disc, Summer also appeared in Frank Sinatra's video single 'LA Is My Lady' in 1983 wearing her popular waitress uniform from the album photo shoot of 'She Works Hard For The Money'. In 1987 Donna Summer was invited to participate in the documentary VHS release *The Power Of Faith – The Planet Is Alive: A Portrait Of Pope John Paul II*. Her participation included writing and recording the theme song 'Planet Is Alive', which featured in a music video in the documentary. Continuing this trend for guest appearances, Donna Summer participated in the 'Earthrise – The Rainforest' album (1989) and appeared on a single 'Spirit Of The Forest' designed to raise ecological awareness. This single was recorded with other popular names including Olivia Newton-John, Ringo Starr, Sam Brown, Joni Mitchell, Mick Fleetwood, Kate Bush and Belinda Carlisle.

Donna Summer continued to collaborate with other artists throughout 1996. She had not given up, even though the hits had slowed down. She collaborated with Liza Minnelli on the single 'Does He Love You?' from the album 'Gently'. The track was originally released in 1993 as a country song, by Reba McEntire and Linda Davis. Summer and Minnelli both cleverly stamp the remake with their own signature. The track garnered good reviews from *Billboard* but didn't receive much airplay in the US. Donna Summer had a 'really intimate time' with Liza Minnelli during the 'Does He Love You?' sessions, as she told Fort Laundale in 'Donna Summer Exclusive Interview: Bringing Her Summer Tour To Hard Rock Live On August 18' for *All Voice* publication. She also noted that they got 'as crazy' as they 'can get' and that it was a great experience to have 'that level of intimacy with other people'. Liza Minnelli credited Summer as the best in what she does and one 'extraordinary talent' and thanked Summer for her 'generosity'. Minnelli wrote in her 'special thanks' notes for 'Gently' about Summer:

'Thank you for the love, the faith, the long talks, and your willingness to show your own pain by creating a character . . .'

In the same year, Summer worked on the 1996 Olympic album 'One Voice' with Nanci Griffith and Raul Malo in 'From A Distance', an odd vocal combination. Summer's voice was at its best but fans were not overly thrilled with the song.

A soundtrack single 'Whenever There Is Love' was taken from the film *Daylight*, featuring a duet with Bruce Roberts. The single reached no.109 on the *Billboard* chart. The single was beautifully produced and the pair used their voices to their best ability. Not surprisingly, the German release of the single featured 'Whenever There Is Love (Club Mix)'. It's a great remix which fans will love dancing to. Despite her previous achievements, in 1996

'Whenever There Is Love', composed and written by Bruce Roberts and Sam Roman, was nominated for the Golden Raspberry Award for 'Worst Original Song' from a movie. The Golden Raspberry (Razzie) Awards is an annual award ceremony held in Los Angeles to 'honour' the years 'worst' films. Founded by American copywriter and publicist John J.B. Wilson in 1981, the event precedes the famous 'Oscars' Academy Award ceremony. 'Whenever There Is Love' was nominated not as a result of any failings of Summer and Roberts, or even the movie theme itself, but because the movie *Daylight* was a disaster.

Around this time, Summer had a very low profile, not having released a major pop album since 1991 with 'Mistaken Identity' (she had released a Christmas album in 1994). However, in *British Hit Singles: 11th Edition*, she was placed at no.17 out of ninety acts in the Most Hits category. The calculations are based on original recordings or concerts but not including any remixes, re-issues and re-entries. All double-sided hits, double singles, EPs and albums only counted as one hit each time.

Later, in 1999, Donna Summer recorded 'My Prayer For You' written by herself and Nathan DiGesare for a low-profile contemporary Christian collection album 'Sing Me To Sleep Mommy'. It consisted of a beautifully recorded, simple and easy melody. Summer delivers an introduction with a talk to her child in the song before the actual singing. Summer had already used this device in a few of the songs on the 'Mistaken Identity' album.

In 2000, Summer recorded 'Dreamcatcher', a beautiful yet unexpected song written by Summer and M. Hanna. Her song fitted in nicely with the Native American music that featured for the film *Naturally Native* soundtrack and in the same year she collaborated with a gospel singer, Darwin Hobbs, in 'When I Look Up', a contemporary Christian concept song for his 'Vertical' album.

Besides new materials, Donna Summer also revisited one of her no.1 hit singles, not in the studio but as a live piece. 'No More Tears (Enough Is Enough)', a live performance track, was recorded with Tina Arena, an Australian singer, for the VH1 Presents: Live & More Encore! album in 1999. An immaculate performance gives the melody a new personality.

Back in 2000, Summer continued recording for the original cast musical album 'Child Of The Promise' on tracks titled 'When The Dream Never Dies', and 'I Can Not Be Silent', a duet with Crystal Lewis, both tracks not disappointing and keeping to her typical style. The album was a Broadway-flavoured work representing the complete story of the birth of Christ like never before. In the same year 'Take Heart', soulful material written by Bruce Sudano and Nathan DiGesare which showcased Summer's mature vocal, was recorded for 'The Mercy Project' album. Summer ended the year with a Christmas song – a cheerful pop tune nicely titled 'Rosie Christmas' written by Summer, D. Rich and G. Lorenzo for Rosie O'Donnell's album 'Another Rosie Christmas'.

A new studio collaboration for 1979 hit 'No More Tears (Enough Is Enough)' was recorded with Westlife for the 'Discomania' various artists project in 2004, released only in the UK. 'The Donna Summer Eternity Megamix', a selection of her 1970s hits, was remixed for 'Discomania'. The album was well received, peaking at no.7 and remaining in the chart for six weeks.

In the summer of 2005, Donna Summer participated with various artists on a tribute project 'Songs From The Neighborhood: The Music Of Mister Rogers' a winning album at the 48th Grammy Awards. Summer recorded 'Are You Brave?' with her own interpretations of Rogers' song and 'Thank You For Being You', singing it with two acts from the album. Although a relatively low-profile project, the album received positive critical reviews and won several prizes including the Family Approval Award from the Dove Foundation, the Creative Child Award by *Creative Child* magazine, Parents' Choice from the Parent's Choice Foundation and the 2006 Notable Child Recording by the ALSC (Association for Library Service to Children).

Summer worked with jazz saxophonist Dave Koz on the track 'A Whole New World' for the 'Dave Koz At The Movies' album in 2007. The album was put together as a tribute to classic movie themes and is filled with spectacular guest vocal tracks from Anita Baker, Vanessa Williams, India Arie and Barry Manilow, to name a few. Fans of smooth jazz appreciated the release and the project introduced Summer to a wider audience. It was a bonus that the project was a success in the contemporary jazz album charts. However, Summer's 1982 jazz influenced 'Lush Life' sounded more classy.

Unfortunately, these later collaborations somehow failed to propel Summer's career and her by now low profile in the music business meant the majority of music fans were not aware of the work she had been doing.

Devotees know that Summer continues her work on stage and in the studio. Her featuring as a guest is just an introduction or a warm up for her up and coming venture! By 2012 O'Mega Red, an award winning artist for 'Urban Music Awards Rap Artist Of The Year (2006–2007)' featured Donna Summer in his 'Angel' single. Excited followers always welcome her guest feature work, however this is not Summer's song. Still, 'Angel' is not something that has been created within a short period of time. On the 15th April 2012, O'Mega Red shared his story of 'Angel' and how he came to feature Summer:

'I worked with Donna in the past, but we never released any music. This was five years in the making, she is family. She always said that I was a talented writer and musician and when the time came I wrote something undeniable she would record a song with me … she kept her promise. 'Angel' is a true story based on members in our family. She fell in love with the record, the melodies and writing I composed. She also had a lot of input to the direction and subject matter of the song which brought it over the top'.

The story of 'Angel' is in the lyrics. The single received the acclaim it deserved: O'Mega Red's 'Angel' has been nominated for the 'Hollywood Music In Media Awards 2012'.

In terms of collaboration, although her work with Brooklyn Dreams on 'Heaven Knows', Barbra Streisand on 'No More Tears (Enough Is Enough)' and 'Unconditional Love' featuring Musical Youth are the stand-out tracks, the other projects provided Summer with the opportunity to expand her experience and elevate her musical creativity to another level. She recorded gospel-flavoured music, emotional tunes and also brought her own musical style to the various tribute projects. All this helped to introduce her to new audiences. Even though some tracks may lean towards sentimentality, the various club remixes helped to bring Summer back to her roots in pop-dance music. Although her fans would prefer to have a brand new solo album to listen to, they were happy enough to hear Summer's voice on these various new individual projects rather than old remixes.

15

Back To The Roots

Her 1990s collaborative recordings were mostly ballads. Still, Donna Summer had not forgotten her popular roots in the music business. Summer recorded 'La Vie En Rose' which featured on the 'Edif Piaf Tribute' album in 1994. This single was released only in France.

According to a review for *Billboard* on 7th September 1994:

'. . . the song suits Summer's own distinctive phrasing nicely as the tune rises above a chugging jack/funk groove. Diehards will be in heaven, while everyone else will take this lovely single as a reminder of a talent that has been away from the pop mainstream for way too long.'

The 'Edif Piaf Tribute' album featured well known contemporaries such as Corey Hart, Pat Benatar, Ann Wilson and Leon Russell. The album did not feature newer acts who might have appealed to a younger audience. This might have been a deliberate decision by the producer, perhaps to better capture the essence of Piaf by using more experienced and mature acts, and it worked. The song was a hit in Japan, climbing to no.18 and spending thirteen weeks in the chart! Summer's French and Japanese fans were thrilled with her interpretations of Piaf's 1946 hit.

In 1996, Summer recorded 'Ordinary Miracle' for the soundtrack to the movie. 'Let It Be Me'. An official statement by Summer's management from the 21st April 1996 read:

'The song "Ordinary Miracle" was recorded for a movie soundtrack. The film, tentatively titled "Let It Be Me" has yet to be released. In fact, the film's distributor was bought out by another studio and because of that, the movie is on hold. "Ordinary Miracle" is a wonderful song. The track was produced by Narada Michael Walden. Unfortunately we will have to wait until the movie is released before a soundtrack album or single are available.'

Although at the time fans were excited by the news, the single and the soundtrack album remained unreleased. The movie was released straight to video, partly due to a lack of interest and also as a result of its small budget. Summer's 'Ordinary Miracle' can be heard during the end credits and the film has been shown on television in the US and in the UK. 'Ordinary Miracle' was a great pop-dance tune, similar in style to 'Melody Of Love (Wanna Be Loved)'. The song has been copied to tape and CD by fans desperate to have a recording. The first few seconds of the song are distorted by the last scene in the movie but for desperate fans, it's as close as they will get to a playable tune.

In late 1996, Donna Summer joined a cast of fellow superstars in an ABC network special celebrating the 25th Anniversary of Disney World. Later, Summer recorded the theme from *The Hunchback Of Notre Dame* film 'Someday' for the Disney children's 'Mouse House Disney's Dance Mixes' album in 1996. A new remix appeared in 'Disney's Greatest Pop Hits' album in 1998. The original 'Someday' track was recorded by All-4-One in the US and Eternal in the UK, for *The Hunchback Of Notre Dame* soundtrack.

Continuing her studio work, she recorded the track 'Love On And On' for the movie *54*, but it was not released. The song became popular in clubs and was available as a 'white label'. Fans eagerly anticipated its release and it became a hot topic of discussion among avid followers; they may not have been able to buy it but the song was played by DJs across the US. A popular online music service, initially designed to sell music only to professional DJs, did feature 'Love On And On' in a 'one year anniversary' monthly CD in September 1998. The CD was limited to a thousand copies. It was talked about between fans and was stated on the Internet that Summer was not pleased with '*54*' after the screening of the film, and she withdrew the song from the movie. Still the unfinished version was leaked and played by one popular radio station in New York City, KTU. The popularity of 'Love On And On' along with exciting listeners made the song no.1 on KTU's request chart! Still, Summer was not happy to hear that the unfinished work had been leaked, and furthermore made it to airplay. However, in 1999 'Love On And On' was included in the US version of 'I Will Go With You (Con Te Partiro)' single part 1 & 2, released in a Hex Hector remix version. This could have been done to limit the circulation of unofficial copies. Fans were not too pleased with the Hex Hector remix of 'Love On And On', simply because they loved the original, unreleased version.

The tracks 'Someday', 'Ordinary Miracle' and 'Love On And On', although catchy, were still not considered to be up to the usual standard of Summer's best dance tunes.

In summer 2000, 'The Power Of One', a beautiful ballad, appeared in *Pokemon 2000 The Movie: The Power Of One* soundtrack. The maxi-single presented the ballad remixed into raw dance tracks. 'The Power Of One (Tommy Musto Vocal Mix)' gave the tune a pop-dance-funk feel.

In 2002, another upbeat dance number was introduced to Summer devotees. Fans of dance floor grooves were in heaven at long last! The 'You're So Beautiful' dance remix could be heard in clubs in the US and the UK, but the hype and excitement felt by fans was not shared by Summer herself! In an article by Michael Paoletta in *Billboard*, the star acknowledged she was unhappy that the unfinished song appeared in clubs and online. Following the publication of the article in 2003, the president of Universal Music, Bruce Resnikoff, said they could not 'stop the leak' and so now they took advantage of the underground hype! 'You're So Beautiful (The Ultimate Club Mix)' subsequently featured in the US limited edition 'The Journey: The Very Best Of Donna Summer', 2003 (bonus CD) and 'You're So Beautiful' edit on 'Donna Summer Gold', 2005. The beautiful, romantic lyrics were composed by Summer, Tony Moran and Nathan DiGesare. The seductive Tony Moran and Glenn Friscia mixes are available only on promo issues. The track climbed to no.2 in the *Billboard* dance chart and it also peaked at no.8 in France for one week according to an on-line music chart information (sort.info).

Donna Summer continues to thrill her fans with one off recording projects. She recorded a theme for a children's musical 'Dream-A-Lot's (I Will Live For Love)', which also featured in the US release of 'The Journey: The Very Best Of Donna Summer' album in 2003. The song was composed by Donna Summer and Nathan DiGesare and was not universally appreciated, being described by some fans as being a vulgar sound suitable for the Eurovision Song Contest. The promotional single did receive some success, climbing to no.20 in the *Billboard* dance chart in 2004.

A new track, 'I Got Your Love', was first introduced in *Sex And The City* and was available in 2005 as a digital download and later in the shops as a single in the US. The single didn't climb into the US pop chart but reached no.4 in the *Billboard* dance chart. However, even though the song didn't get much airplay, 'I Got Your Love' entered the Top 20 *Billboard* sales chart! It was a privilege to be able to get information about the track from the original radio edit producer himself. In January 2010 Peter Stengaard said:

'I had met Bruce Roberts who also wrote "Enough Is Enough" and is a good friend of Donna's and he played me a little thing they had done together. The melody and lyrics were basically there and he asked me if I would like to try to work up a track for it. I was honoured to, of course, and they liked it! So we took it step by step and I finally ended up recording Donna in London and mixed the record in Nashville.'

Stengaard was not only the original radio edit producer and mixer for 'I Got Your Love' but he also played all the instruments including drum/synth programming etc. The track took a couple of months to be completed according to Stengaard, because they needed to prepare before getting Summer to record her vocal, then preparing for the final mix and other typical studio recording processes. Studio work would often take a long time. In his own studio, he could work faster but at the time 'I Got Your Love' was in the making, Stengaard was in the process of moving to Los Angeles from Copenhagen and all the necessary 'gear' was spread between continents! Peter Stengaard says he loved her songs not only because of his respect for Summer as an artist, but also her musical style.

'. . . I'm a huge fan of the old synth-driven stuff! Right up my alley – I met Giorgio Moroder at a party in Hollywood and he had heard "I Got Your Love" and loved it . . . made me feel like I was kinda cool for a minute.'

Back in the studio, Donna Summer also contributed to the 'So Amazing: An All-Star Tribute To Luther Vandross' album in 2005, recording an up-tempo version of 'Power Of Love', a cover as good as the original with Summer giving it a fresh new sound. The promo release single remixes represented the old school extended melody style – not overpowered by dance beats. The project featured many new popular acts such as Usher, Mary J. Blige and Beyonce, not forgetting music royalty Aretha Franklin and Elton John. The project helped to introduce Summer to the fans of younger acts participating in the album. The album debuted at no.4 on the *Billboard* 200, achieving the same position on the *Billboard* Top Internet Album chart and also charted at no.1 on the US Top R&B/hip hop and *Billboard* Top Compilation Album Chart, apparently selling 104,000 copies in its opening week.

Despite releasing covers and new material, the public still associate Summer most strongly with her classic hit 'Love To Love You Baby', arguably the most famous record of her career.

Would Donna Summer have achieved the same fame if she started her career with the song today? Gloria Gaynor has no doubts that she would. As for Inanna, a young dance recording act and fan, she agrees but doesn't think it could recapture the magic it had then. As a result of changes in music fashion, a good new remixed version could easily give it another breakthrough. Mark Nubar Donikian, from the rock band Hypnogaja, agrees Summer's mega hit would absolutely have the same impact today but would be produced differently. He said Donna Summer, Giorgio Moroder and Pete Bellotte created a new style of music production that influenced and inspired many artists, writers and producers. If they were just starting out, they'd be taking the same innovative approach. Keyboard player Donikian and lead singer Jason 'ShyBoy' Arnold from Hypnogaja said:

'Talent is talent. Whether she started in 1976 or 2010, Donna Summer would still be a very successful recording artist. The only thing that's changed is the industry itself. The 1970s were a whole different time, when the artists needed a record company and a whole machine to make stuff happen. Today, Donna Summer would've been discovered somewhere on YouTube.'

With the song's melody and her looks and youth, Summer was almost guaranteed to be a success. But Joel Whitburn, a *Billboard* expert, suggests that if Summer were to start her career with that song now, it wouldn't work at her age. At the time 'Love To Love You Baby' was released, its like had never been heard before. During the last thirty years, almost every look and sound has been explored making it is incredibly difficult to come out with such an innovative new style. According to Whitburn, Summer had her day and her fun!

Gloria Gaynor, Inanna, the musicians of Hypnogaja and Joel Whitburn agree that Summer would have the same impact if she was to start her career today with 'Love To Love You Baby' as she did in the 1970s, if she were the same age as she was when she originally released the song. However 'Love To Love You Baby' would probably not have quite the same impact and would certainly not provoke the controversy it did back in the 1970s. Music has evolved to the point that some acts are now known more for their image or behaviour than for their songs. In this sense, the whole idea of 'Donna Summer' in her heyday would be successful nowadays.

Summer's name is still 'Hot Stuff' as a result of all the great work she and her team have given to the music world. Young musicians like Inanna and Hypnogaja and many others remember Donna Summer's hits.

Inanna, who adores 'Love To Love You Baby', 'Heaven Knows' and 'Bad Girls', recalls Summer's early stardom:

'I remember the 1970s as a child and Donna Summer was constantly played on the radio, she took disco music to whole new level . . . especially with "Love To Love You" . . .'.

As for a new listening generation in their twenties and thirties, they probably remember Summer for her dance anthems 'She Works Hard For The Money' and 'This Time I Know It's For Real', which were huge global successes in the 1980s, not forgetting 'I Feel Love', a huge hit in 1977 and still in vogue to the present day.

Joel Whitburn, an expert in the US charts and producer of over 150 CD compilations with Rhino Records, during an interview with Whitburn with 'I Feel Love' playing in the background, said that all eight Donna Summer songs in his iPod have been given five star status! Whitburn clearly adores 'Love To Love You Baby', 'Last Dance', 'I Feel Love', 'Hot Stuff', 'No More Tears (Enough Is Enough)', 'State Of Independence', 'She Works Hard For The Money' and 'I Will Go With You (Con Te Partiro)'.

Although a majority of mainstream music fans recognise Summer only for her dance material, she has recorded, written and sung a wide range of music. Folky in one of her earlier singles 'So Said The Man' (1971), sexy in the gigantic hit 'Love To Love You Baby' (1975) and slow in 'Winter Melody' (1976). She sang Broadway in 'My Man Medley' (1978), rough in 'Leave Me Alone' (1981), even sophisticated jazz in 'Lush Life' (1982). Summer also sang Caribbean style in 'Unconditional Love' (1983), as well as country in 'So This Is Lonely' (1994) and world music with 'Tant Qu'il Y Aura De L'Amour', or 'Whenever There Is Love', recorded in French for the single release in France in 1996. 'I Will Go With You (Con Te Partiro)' was recorded in Italian, available on part two of the US single released in 1999. Donna Summer further broadened her musical horizon with a different style of music in her 2008 'Crayons' album, by recording a blues track titled 'Slide Over Backwards' and contemporary reggae in 'Crayons', featuring Ziggy Marley.

The songs mentioned above reflect Summer's evolution as a singer. She was, and still is, exploring different types of music. Dance music producer Tim Letteer says:

'The 1970s of course was disco, but it was so much more. It was the beginning of modern dance/electronic music. I think she helped define the word "Diva". The 1980s became more pop and experimental. She tried lots of things. It was a very strange time. I still bought every album and enjoyed them, but my tastes had changed ... I got more into New Wave and rock. She returned to dance at the beginning of the 1990s and in 00s ... She started the continuous mix and it has become the norm with DJ compilations.'

The industry and music lovers believe that Donna Summer has not been credited enough for her singing ability, even at the beginning in her heyday. Summer worked really hard to be heard by the industry, being a woman in a 'man's world'. Expressing her creative side as she wanted it to be heard had taken a lot of effort and strength.

Now there is no argument that the music industry and music fans have discovered what Donna Summer is capable of. Summer's work will continue to be an inspiration and influence to her fans and the music industry across the world.

16

Inspiration, Influence And The Tribute

In her earlier glory days, the US Electronics Industries Association used Summer to promote their products. 'Love To Love You Baby' played throughout the advert for their consumer information programme and Donna Summer recorded an opening introduction to promote the corporation. The EP commercial 'Donna Summer Sings For The Electronic Industries Association' contained five segments on the A-side. The first sixty seconds of advertising went as follows:

'Hi! This is Donna Summer for the Electronics Industries Association. Be sure you're getting the best in high fidelity that I can give. With today's variety of high fidelity audio equipment on the market, a good hi-fi system doesn't have to be complex or expensive. There's a components systems that's just right for you. Shop around, compare prices and sounds and if you have questions, don't be afraid to ask. Between you and me, and your radio dealer we can get it together with high fidelity.'

Many of her hits have been used in TV adverts. 'Hot Stuff' was adapted for a TV commercial in Australia advertising the 'Four 'N Twenty Pie' in 1981 to persuade hungry viewers to buy a particular 'hot' pie. 'Hot Stuff' was also featured in a DiGiorno Pizza advert. From www.inthe80s.com:

'A man in the kitchen is eating DiGiorno Stuffed Crust Pizza, sings along with the radio (with changed lyrics). The woman comes and tells him, "Don't tell me that pizza delivery guy saw you like that" and the man says, "It's Not Delivery. It's DiGiorno"!'

'Hot Stuff' was also used for a Capital One credit card advert in the UK. In the mid 1990s 'She Works Hard For The Money' was featured in a campaign by the Canadian department store Zellers. The same song had been rerecorded by Summer for a McDonald's commercial with a new lyric written for the chorus. As noted on www.inthe90s.com, the song was changed to:

'You get more for your money cause McDonald's treats you right'!

In an interview in 1994, Summer was asked if she had personal favourites from her back catalogue. She had different favourites depending on various criteria. For instance, 'She Works Hard For The Money' was the best song when it came to earning royalties. The song had been featured in several TV advertisements.

Using the right song for a TV commercial can be key to gaining wider success for a product. Established brands often use popular songs to sell a 'lifestyle'. Some companies use the original track and singer or might make a cover using a different act. Some songs and even vocals have been reconstructed to sound as close as possible to the original. This situation arises because many companies don't want their songs to be used in commercial adverts. British former girl group Honeyz recorded 'Love To Love You Baby' for a UK Diet Coke advert in 2000. The song remains unreleased but is available as a promo. Big brands such as Coca-Cola and Pepsi often use big name acts to promote their goods, but this time they chose to use a cover version by a contemporary act instead of the original.

Donna Summer's original songs are still used in advertisements. In *Donna Summer: Her Life And Music*, Josiah Howard writes that Summer collected a 'handsome fee' for allowing 'Love To Love You Baby' to be featured in a national TV advertisement campaign for Mercedes Benz automobiles.

However, Summer turned down a proposal to use 'Love To Love You Baby' for a high-profile jeans advertisement. In 1995 Levi's hoped to use the song for a scene where a sultry young lady (who is actually a transvestite) catches a cab, a scene which suited the song perfectly. TV producer, Philippa Crane, said in a Channel 4 programme *TV Adverts' Greatest Hits*, that the record label reported to the agency that their proposal was declined by Summer. The track 'Turn On, Tune In, Cop Out' by Freak Power was used instead and entered at no.3 in the UK singles chart in 1995. Music fans were disappointed and surprised by Summer's reaction. This was an opportunity to raise her profile in the UK at a time when Summer's star seemed to be fading. 'Love To Love You Baby' could have re-entered the British chart at a high position in time to celebrate the twentieth anniversary of its international release! Clearly it's Summer's right to decide not to have her music associated with a particular image or product. This can be seen as principled or naive. The ability of an advert to boost the sales of a cleverly-placed tune should not be underestimated. Many old hits have received a second run of success on the back of good marketing.

In 2009, Gucci used a new remix of 'I Feel Love' in their 'Flora' perfume advert, filmed by Chris Cunningham. It was reported that in 2008 Cunningham paid a visit to Nashville to work with Summer on a brand new vocal and he also produced and arranged the new version of the song. Remixed to suit the storyboard of the Gucci advert, this new version took the song to another horizon in pop music. But the main concept was all from the original composition. Kee Chang in *Anthem* on the 15th April 2009:

'Shot beautifully on location and accompanied by a reworking of Donna Summer's classic tune, "I Feel Love", Gucci and Cunningham score big.'

To her fans' delight in September 2011 Summer's 'Love To Love You Baby', with its new sound, was used in a 'Loverdose' perfume advert for Diesel. The new recording delivered a sensual, mature sound and the backing track sounded current. Summer delivered her original essence without fail. At 60-something Summer brought her classic song into the digital world. Relating it to the world of interior design 'Love To Love You Baby' 2011 version is a contemporary living space that combines luxury and practicality. The wall treatment of claret with textured cream wallpaper complements the classy leather upholstery. The hard edges of the interior are softened with silky soft accessories. The echoing chorus of Donna Summer's voice in multiple tracks are the lighting, mirrors and glass objects that create the illusions of space. It's current with 1970s touches!

During the middle of the 1970s, disco had become a major part of popular culture. Diana Ross was thrilled to see her no.1 single 'Love Hangover' (1976) stay in the *Billboard* Top 40 chart for thirteen weeks. Rod Stewart had a no.1 with 'Da Ya Think I'm Sexy?' (1978) (eighteen weeks) and Barry Manilow's 'Copacabana (At The Copa)' (1978) (nine weeks). Cher with 'Take Me Home' (1979) stayed in the chart for eleven weeks. Many acts tried to join the trend that had made Donna Summer a star. Let's not forget the easy listening 'diva' Barbra Streisand's duet with Summer in 'No More Tears (Enough Is Enough), a huge hit which stayed in the 1979 *Billboard* Top 40 for thirteen weeks!

Although it was a popular phenomenon in the 1970s, there are many critics of disco. In his 1985 book *Popular Music Since 1955*, Paul Taylor writes:

'The style is notable for its lack of emotion, the use of repetitive rhythms and, more recently, the use of synthesizers. It is often dismissed as the most manufactured of all pop music. Its leading artists include Donna Summer, The Bee Gees and Boney M as well as many American and British groups who simply changed their soul styles to comply with the trend.'

Others considered themselves as disco's originators. Craig Werner, in his book *A Change Is Gonna Come* (2006) notes that James Brown 'the funk founder' marketed himself as the original disco man. Even jazz legend Herb Alpert recorded up-tempo dance flavoured songs for his 1979 album 'Rise', which shot to no.1, taking advantage of the vogue for dance music during that period. *'Legends' Herb Alpert: Tijuana Brass And Other Delights* was aired on BBC4 on 17th September 2010.

Originally an underground movement, disco had now become so popular that it began to be criticised for becoming bland and irrelevant. The book *American Records* by Chuck Miller (2001) suggests that disco's currency had been so degraded and trivialised that it was now suitable for children's tunes.

The releases that triggered this comment were the albums 'Sesame Street Fever' and 'Mickey Mouse Disco'. One disco diva who it could be said gained success on the back of Summer's 'I Feel Love' was the artiste Sylvester. The 'love' rhythm that caught Sylvester's attention was actually a 'homemade' remix by Patrick Cowley. From *The Faber Book Of Pop* by Jon Savage and Hanif Kureishi:

'Cowley had kept his song writing and synthesizer experiments secret until his homemade remix of Donna Summer's "I Feel Love" became the local rage. Impressed, Sylvester asked Cowley if he wouldn't mind making similar synth additions to what was a ballad, "You Make Me Feel (Mighty Real)", and another up-tempo cut "Dance (Disco Heat)".'

Cowley agreed and, with inspiration drawn from Summer's 'I Feel Love', 'You Make Me Feel (Mighty Real)' and 'Dance (Disco Heat)' were Top 40 hits and propelled Sylvester's album 'Step II' to Gold status.

In the UK, the music industry claimed Tina Charles as their no.1 disco diva. She was a long way from really competing with Summer on the international market – both stars had been 'packaged' by their record company in very different ways. Both disco queens had one thing in common – a no.1 hit in the UK. Miss Charles had one no.1 hit single with 'I Love To Love (But My Baby Loves To Dance)' in 1976. The single was successful, staying in the UK chart for twelve weeks. Charles's take on the disco queen was 'decent', the opposite of Donna Summer at that time – raunchy! Charles has always been credited for her high vocal energy. Her chart popularity only lasted for two years. During this period, she scored seven singles in the Top 40. Her last hit in the UK was 'I'll Go Where Your Music Takes Me', reaching no.27 in 1978. Between 1976 and 1978, Charles's songs enjoyed sixty weeks in the chart. Summer's songs on the other hand enjoyed one hundred and six weeks in the UK charts. Music fans throughout Europe and Asia still remember Tina Charles with 'Dance Little Lady Dance', one of her Top 10 hits in 1976. A remix of her 1976 no.1 hit single entered the UK chart at no.67 in 1986. Charles is still active in the music business.

The BBC have acknowledged Summer's talent by claiming that Jade Ewen, the UK Eurovision Song Contest competitor in 2009, was one of the finest vocalists the UK had produced, having the 'eternal cool' of Donna Summer.

Colin Larkin writes about US act Ultra Nate in *The Virgin Encyclopedia Of Nineties Music*:

'Reminiscent of . . . Donna Summer, Ultra Nate has all the correct stylings down to a tee, measuring jazz, funk and gospel within her compass. All are made distinctive by her slightly unconventional and highly arresting vocal phrasing.'

Summer's influence can be seen in other songs, old and new, that have drawn inspiration from her music. In *1000 Songs To Change Your Life (Time Out Guides)* Peter Shapiro comments on the single 'Love In C Minor' by Cerrone, noting that it sounded like an up-tempo, saucy version of 'Love To Love You Baby'. Karyn White, singer of 'Super Women' and 'Romantic' is supposed to have wanted her 1994 song 'Hungah' to have 'the same aura' as that of 'Love To Love You Baby'.

There are endless examples of Summer's influence on the world of pop music. In 1980 Malaysian artist Noor Kumalasari recorded a song titled 'Aku Dan Dunia Seni', translated as 'I And The World Of Entertainment'. This drew heavily on Summer's 'MacArthur Park Suite'. The song was not a cover but when the first instrumental chorus reaches fifty seconds to one minute fourteen seconds (repeated several times throughout the song) it clearly borrows from the 'MacArthur Park Suite'. The Malaysian dance material was inspired by Summer's work. Whether it was or wasn't intentionally produced that way by the composer S. Atan is hard to say.

In India, the song 'Boom Boom', clearly came with a bass line modelled on 'I Feel Love'. Geeta Dayal's 'Further Thoughts On 10 Ragas To A Disco Beat' (theoriginalsoundtrack.com) discusses the Indian electronic music movement in the Bollywood music productions of the early 1980s, how 'synthesizer tracks' became popular and were 'modelled on 1970s Giorgio Moroder sounds. The song 'Boom Boom', the creation of disco producer Biddu, was sung by Bollywood star Nazia Hassan in 1982. A successful tune, 'Boom Boom' marked them as South Asia's answer to Summer and Moroder. The Summer and Moroder phenomenon had influenced and inspired artists around the globe.

Paul Gambaccini suggests that Summer's songs are so groundbreaking because of the imaginative and creative compositions. That is why Summer's records are so important. 'I Feel Love' and 'Hot Stuff' were both instrumentally revolutionary for disco. As many music fans identified 'I Feel Love' was, according to Gambaccini, the first to take that titanic mechanical sound to no.1 in the UK and the song is groundbreaking. 'Hot Stuff' used hard rock guitar and, with that it leads directly to the inspiration to 'Beat It', where Quincy Jones used rock guitarist Eddie Van Halen on a guitar solo in Michael Jackson's classic song. Gambaccini nevertheless thinks that 'Hot Stuff' was ultimately disposable compared to 'Beat It', the *Billboard* no.1 in 1983.

Summer has also provided compositions for other acts. One of her most high profile was not actually a dance number but a piece of country music. Back in 1979 Donna Summer co-wrote a country song with Bruce Sudano titled 'Starting Over'. Summer, in an interview with Christian John Wikane for *PopMatters*, recalled how 'Starting Over' caught Dolly Parton's attention. Summer explained it started at a party when she sang it; Parton happened to be in the same venue and later heard the song again on TV. Liking what she heard, she requested to record the track herself. Summer immediately agreed and Parton recorded it, making it a no.1 hit in May of 1980. Summer was thrilled with the outcome. 'Starting Over' also entered the *Billboard* Top 40 and *Billboard* Hot Adult Contemporary Tracks at no.35. Writing in *Smart Blonde: Dolly Parton*, (2006) Stephen Miller recounts that the album released in May 1980 titled 'Dolly Dolly Dolly' managed two no.1s including 'an emotional ballad written by disco sensation Donna Summer and her husband' titled 'Starting Over'.

Who would have known that fifteen years later in 1995, country singer Reba McEntire would choose to record the song as the title cut of her album. Thrilled, Summer said in *PopMatters* that this was a good sign as the family had just moved into the area at that time. Summer said it was like the family were supposed to be in Nashville, 'Starting Over'. The no.1 country song also inspired the late John Lennon to write a song bursting with optimism titled '(Just Like) Starting Over'. It was said by Paul de Noyer in *John Lennon: We All Shine On –The Stories Behind Every John Lennon Song 1970–1980* (1997) that apparently Lennon told the BBC that he took the title from a country song – 'Starting Over'. Summer's sentimental tune, recorded by Dolly Parton, tells the story of a middle-aged couple whose thirty years of marriage ends in divorce. Lennon's song was of a long-term relationship whose love was strong but needed to evoke the spirit of its early romance.

Donna Summer's work continues to inspire other acts in the music world. In late 1981 The Real Thing covered 'I Believe In You' and Ann-Frid Lyngstad of ABBA recorded 'To Turn The Stone' for her 1982 solo album 'Something's Going On'. The single 'To Turn The Stone' charted in Belgium and The Netherlands at no.8 and no.52 in Germany. These songs were taken from the legendary unreleased Summer album 'I'm A Rainbow'. In

1982 'All Through The Night' was covered by KC And The Sunshine Band on their 'Painter' album and in 1983 'On The Radio' was covered by country artist Emmylou Harris for her album 'White Shoes'. The track 'To Turn The Stone' was used again, being included on Joe 'Bean' Esposito and Giorgio Moroder's 1983 album 'Solitary Men' and Amii Stewart recorded 'You To Me' and 'Sweet Emotion' for her 'Amii Stewart' album in 1983. The single 'Sunset People' was covered by E.G. Daily on her 'Wild Child' album in 1985 and in the same year, the late Dusty Springfield covered 'Sometimes Like Butterflies', which reached no.83 in the UK charts.

The story behind the selection of this number started when Jenny Cohen was choosing songs for the new Dusty Springfield album. Penny Valentine and Vicki Wickham wrote in their authorized biography of Springfield that Cohen had sent Springfield a lot of demos from America. It was said that she had always had an innate sense of a good song, but Cohen apparently was not very pleased to find out that Springfield had chosen the track 'Sometimes Like Butterflies'.

In *Dancing With Demons: The Authorised Biography Of Dusty Springfield* (2000) Cohen is quoted as saying:

'But Dusty, that was a Donna Summer B-side for Christ's sake!'

Springfield didn't take much notice; she loved the song and insisted on recording the track for the Hippodrome label, releasing it as a single. In *The Complete Dusty Springfield – Revised And Expanded Edition (2007),* Paul Howes writes that some considered it an unwise choice. Springfield had a strong gay following and this was around the time of Summer's fall from grace following her 'remarks' about the gay community. Howes says it was an embarrassing and difficult year for Springfield's career and on top of it all, the single did not get much positive feedback. Fans of both stars can enjoy Springfield's twelve inch version on her 'Heart And Soul' album released in 2002 and the seven inch version featured on her 'Classics And Collectables' in 2004. Listening to the record now, it sounds like very much a 1980s production. However Springfield delivered her favourite song full of emotion, following the style of Summer's B-side, doing justice to the melody created by Summer and Bruce Roberts.

In *Dusty! Queen Of The Postmods* (2009), Annie J. Randall writes:

'Dusty's recording of "Sometimes Like Butterflies", (1985) illustrates aspects of the pop aria's fate – some might say it's complete demise – after the 1960s.'

The book comments that the song 'Sometimes Like Butterflies' is rather simple, lacking the complexity typical of Springfield's work in the 1960s.

In the 1990s, major singers in all categories covered Summer's dance tunes. Countless Summer songs have been selected for covers by established and new young acts. After fourteen years, Summer's 'Love's Unkind', a tale of heartbreak, was given a makeover by Sophie Lawrence. On the 3rd August 1991 music fans listened to her emotional rendition and helped it reach no.21. It spent a total of seven tear-jerking weeks in the UK charts.

In an interview with Rusty Truck for the online magazine annecarlini.com, 'Donna Summer: The Empress Herself', Summer said about 'Love's Unkind' that at that time she recorded 'differently than most people.' Summer records her compositions as an act, giving a character to the song which she targets at a particular market. The UK hit 'Love's Unkind' was 'specifically geared towards young buyers.' When fans listen to the single they know it's a light cheerful composition, 'not a very heavy lyric.' Summer says that 'there are different songs that have different purposes.'

In 1992, the UK group Curve recorded 'I Feel Love' for the *NME*'s fortieth anniversary compilation 'Ruby Trax', which became an instant underground classic. An excellent cover, as good as the original sound, Curve's version brought the classic hit to another dimension. Curve's cover was praised as the best version yet of 'I Feel Love' on the BBC Radio 2 special documentary of *Feelin' Love: The Donna Summer Story* in 2009.

Donna Summer has covered many songs herself, always managing to put her own signature on them. Many people have thought that her cover songs were original recordings. In 1992, Chrissie Hynde recorded 'State Of Independence' for the film *Single White Female*. However 'State Of Independence' was first released as a single in 1981 by Greek duo Jon and Vangelis for their album 'The Friends Of Mr. Cairo'. But it was Donna Summer who made the song a hit, propelling it to an international audience. Given the right song, Summer has always enjoyed remodelling other people's work in her own unique style.

Speaking about Summer's musical career in her heyday, Paul Gambaccini says:

'Every artist experiences their career in terms of what they're doing, not in terms of how people react. Fame is the reaction of other people. To her it would be from that album and that album, the "fusses" are the reactions of other people. She always considers herself as a singer. I don't think she considers herself as an artist. She understands she is the Queen Of Disco, which is why she would be very happy to do "State Of Independence", another historic record and a warm up for "We Are The World" created by Quincy Jones.'

Summer's hit cover, featuring many stars in the choir, inspired Quincy Jones to create the all-star project 'We Are The World'. Take That covered

'Could It Be Magic', reaching no.3 in 1993. Even though it was not an original Summer song, Take That recorded it in an up-tempo style similar to Summer's rather than following the style of the Manilow original. The co-producer of the album 'Take That And Party', Ian Levine, said in *Take That: Now And Then (The Illustrated Story)* written by Martin Roach (2009), that when it was suggested the group record Barry Manilow's 'Could It Be Magic' he only knew of Donna Summer's version, which was huge in America. It is said that Nick Raymonde acknowledged that the young boys desperately needed that 'one absolute dead certain' record to propel their stardom. Ian Levine explained that the first mix of Take That's version 'was directly influenced by the Donna Summer arrangements'. The result was the 'brilliant high energy disco-style version'.

The dance beat, inspired by Donna Summer, took Take That's single higher than their five earlier single releases!

'Could It Be Magic' has also been covered in Malaysia by the legendary singer Datuk Sharifah Aini. Although not a Summer original, Aini performed it in the up-tempo style characterised by Donna Summer's version. The song featured on her 1980 album 'Just For You'.

To date, many musical acts have performed the song in a tempo similar to Summer's although most female singers did not follow her seductive vocal style. Interestingly, the author Peter Shapiro said that Barry Manilow and Take That's singing style and emotion towards the song are much better than Summer's. In his view in *Turn The Beat Around* Summer's vocal couldn't compete with either of these two versions.

Everyone will have their own favourite. Donna Summer fans and, perhaps, other music fans would disagree with Shapiro's view. The original version was a ballad and Barry Manilow naturally captured the emotional side and the 'atmosphere' of the melody. Summer recorded the track in her trademark 'whispering' low vocal style. In contrast, in *Turn The Beat Around* Shapiro agrees that 'State Of Independence' and 'She Works Hard For The Money' suited Summer's singing style.

In 1986 'She Works Hard For The Money' was performed live by Irene Cara in a bar scene from a film called *Busted Up* (1986) based on a true story.

Summer's songs have even been reclaimed by their original author. Summer's 'Dinner With Gershwin' was recorded by its co-producer, Brenda Russell. Russell gave her own version of Summer's 1987 UK hit for her 1990 'Kiss Me With The Wind' album. As well as myriad covers by pop-dance acts, the Californian punk rock band The Mr. T Experience recorded 'I Feel Love' on their album 'Our Bodies Our Selves', released in 1993. In the same year, Finnish psychedelic rock band Kingston Wall recorded 'I Feel Love' for their album titled 'II'. This fantastic cover brings to the song a new dance and rock atmosphere with the drumbeat and the guitar work giving a sensual yet hardcore sound at the same time! The lead singer's vocal fits the part perfectly.

To slow down things a little bit, Summer's sensual ballad 'The Woman In Me' was recorded by Heart in 1993 but unfortunately the single did not make it into the UK single charts. The eminent country singer K.D. Lang covered 'No More Tears (Enough Is Enough)' with Andy Bell from Erasure, which featured in the movie *Coneheads* in 1993. Their version was fresh with Lang and Bell giving it their own signature. In the same year, Whoopi Goldberg covered 'Bad Girls' for the hit film *Sister Act 2: Back In The Habit*. The ballad 'Heaven's Just A Whisper Away' was recorded by Regina Belle in 1993 for her 'Passion' album. Some listeners may prefer the Belle version but fans obviously fancy Summer's touch! In 1994, Kym Mazelle and Jocelyn Brown released a cover of 'No More Tears (Enough Is Enough)', reaching no.13 and spending seven weeks in the UK singles charts.

In 1995 Summer's 'Bad Girls' album tracks seemed to be a popular choice to be covered as supermodel Naomi Campbell covered 'All Through The Night' for her album 'Baby Woman' and Laura Branigan covered 'Dim All The Lights' in 1995 for 'Best Of Branigan'. 'Hot Stuff' was covered by UK producer DJ Miko in 1995, giving the tune a fashionable dance music twist.

The classical violinist Vanessa Mae recorded 'I Feel Love' in 1997, the debut vocal recording for her 'Storm' album. This version presented a fast, high energy dance concept that suited clubbers, in which Mae plays the violin. The single reached no.41 in the UK charts. This opened up a new opportunity, with fans of Mae searching for the original version thereby introducing them to the sound of Donna Summer. However, Mae and other acts that have covered Summer's songs can assume that some existing fans will also purchase their versions. A year later, to celebrate the FA Cup Final, 'Hot Stuff' was covered by Shèna for Arsenal Football Club, with the players as backup vocalists. Some parts of the lyrics were altered. The single climbed to no.9 in the UK chart in 1998.

In 1999, Juliet Roberts reached no.17 in the UK with her cover of 'Bad Girls' (five weeks), while a year later Ru Paul and Lil' Kim recorded the same song for Ms Kim's 'Notorious'. 'Bad Girls' was covered yet again in 2000 by Cheryl Chase for *Rugrats In Paris: The Movie*. The Tom Tom Club covered 'Love To Love You Baby' in 2000 for their album 'The Good, The Bad, And The Funky'. In 2000, Canadian techno group Love Inc. recorded 'I Feel Love' with an updated techno tune on their album 'Into The Night'.

Sheena Easton covered 'Love Is In Control (Finger On The Trigger)' for 'Fabulous' in 2001. This was supposed to be the second single release from the album but was available only as a promo due to the poor performance of Easton's first comeback single. Her first single from 'Fabulous' did not take off in the UK. Martine McCutcheon recorded 'On The Radio', reaching no.7 in the UK charts in February 2001. McCutcheon's version charted higher than Summer's original, which only reached no.32, and enjoyed eight weeks compared to Summer's six. In the same year, No Doubt did a cover of 'Love To Love You Baby' for the *Zoolander* soundtrack. In 2002, American rock guitarist Paul Gilbert recorded 'I Feel Love' for his 'Burning Organ' album. Gilbert was also a guitarist for the heavy metal band Racer X and formerly of the hard rock band Mr. Big.

Summer's classic hits continue to be covered around the world. Finnish electronic music duo Dallas Superstars covered 'I Feel Love' for their 2003 album 'Flash'. In the same year, Blue Man Group (featuring Venus Hum), not a typical musical act but rather a creative organisation that produces theatrical shows and concerts featuring music, comedy and multimedia, covered 'I Feel Love' for 'The Complex' album. Summer's track 'Heaven Knows' was recorded by Faith Evans for the soundtrack of the 2003 film *The Fighting Temptations*.

UK *Pop Idol* contestant Michelle McManus recorded 'On The Radio' as the B-side to her single 'All This Time' in 2004. In the same year 'This Time I Know It's For Real' reached no.14 in the UK music chart sung by Kelly Llorenna, spending four weeks in the charts and in May 2006 the same track was covered by Australian group Young Divas, making the great dance number a hit down-under at no.7 and staying in the chart for fourteen weeks. The covers get even more spicy with The Red Hot Chili Peppers releasing their 2004 version of 'I Feel Love' on 'Live In Hyde Park', their first live double album.

In 2008 Amber and Zelma Davis collaborated on a cover of 'No More Tears (Enough Is Enough)' bringing their own touch to the hit song. A Dutch pop star known by the name EliZe recorded 'Hot Stuff' which was released in September 2008 and appeared in various charts across Europe, with the track reaching no.11 in the Dutch Top 100. British former disco queen Tina Charles recorded 'I Feel Love' for her 2008 digital single release. Charles uses her own style, not imitating the original vocal. Summer's 'love' title theme carries on and in the same year, 'Love To Love You Baby' was covered by the Jad & Den Quintet from France. The cover version opens up the song with a jazzy, ambient, laid-back atmosphere. Kris Allen from

American Idol recorded 'She Works Hard For The Money' for the season eight CD released in 2009.

From a young reality TV star to Hypnogaja, who recorded 'On The Radio' as the B-side to their 2010 'Welcome To The Future' single. The group takes the disco track to another level, stamping it with their signature sound – mournful, sentimental and classily tuneful. Two of the band members, Mark Nubar Donikian and Jason 'ShyBoy' Arnold share the story of how the idea of covering 'On The Radio' came about:

'As a band, we've always gravitated towards melodic music and classic songs. We wanted to cover something that we could flip and make our own – but still convey the beauty and emotion of the original. Donna Summer's music has a universal quality that appeals to so many people it just made sense to try something out.'

The masterminds behind the cover were the lead singer Arnold and the keyboard maestro Donikian. Interestingly, Donikian and Arnold used to perform a cover version of 'On The Radio' in live shows even before Hypnogaja was formed. Sometime in 2009, the two creative minds decided to bring it back into the show and later recorded a studio version as well. The rock band had made an outstanding version of a classic Donna Summer track. In Donikian's own words:

'Honestly, a really great moment for us is always the look of surprise on people's faces when we play our cover of "On The Radio". No one's expecting five scruffy alt. rockers to pull that out. It just shows the universal quality of Donna Summer's songs.'

Hypnogaja's version of 'On The Radio' has been acknowledged by the industry with the lead vocalist winning the award for Best Male Vocal at the 2010 Hollywood Music In Media Awards. In the same year Jennifer Lopez covered 'On The Radio' on her album, 'Love?' but as she had signed to a new label, the dance track was not included.

Apart from being covered by other performers, Summer's songs have also been sampled by other artists. Marc Almond and Bronski Beat, a group with Jimmy Somerville as the lead vocalist, released a duet with an added bridge section titled 'I Feel Love (Medley)' which reached no.3 in the UK charts in April 1985. Almond wrote in his autobiography *Tainted Life* that he found Jimmy Somerville's offer of recording a duet of 'I Feel Love' an 'interesting idea' but he was unsure at first about recording with Somerville's group. Not because of the chosen song or the artist being covered, but as the result of other issues at that time. Almond saw the request as a great concept with its 'pluses and minuses'. Almond notes the irony of covering a song by someone who had allegedly made negative comments about gay people and AIDS, but on a more pragmatic note thought that it would inevitably be a big hit.

Almond admits that Stevo Pearce, a man with many contacts with artists and bands through his management role, eagerly encouraged him to do the record and also suggested that Almond needed a hit single badly! Almond and Somerville, both openly gay, were clearly not concerned with the negative attitude associated with Summer at that time. This contrasts with the approach of Dusty Springfield's management to recording a Summer track. Marc Almond wrote that 'I Feel Love' was one of his favourite records of all time, but perhaps being so captivated with the tune and the beat, he had never actually 'paid attention' to the lyrics before until he started to record the cover version. Even more thrilling for him, the track switches into another of his favourite songs, 'Johnny Remember Me'. The Almond/Bronski Beat cover stayed in the UK charts for ten weeks, just one week less than the original version which was in the chart for eleven weeks in 1977. It was a huge success for the team. Also they featured 'Love To Love You Baby' for the intro and outro of the single.

In the early 1990s, another of Summer's hits, 'Love To Love You Baby', was sampled by Digital Underground for their song 'Freaks Of The Industry' released on the 1990 album 'Sex Packets'. Samantha Fox, a former UK glamour model-turned pop star, sampled and recorded 'Love To Love You Baby' for the track 'More, More, More Love To Love You Baby Medley' for her 1991 'Just One Night' album. Covering Summer's song was perhaps a tribute from Fox. In 2009 she told Kirsty Kane (of the online dance music journal *Beat Port* for 'How Samantha Fox And Marc Mysterio Want To Help Dance Music') that she got her first Summer single 'Love To Love You Baby' at the age of ten. She 'realised' dance music made her feel 'happy, free, and somewhat sexy' and undoubtedly influenced her in her subsequent career as a pop singer.

The popular chant 'toot-toot, beep-beep' from Summer's 'Bad Girls' was sampled by the late hip hop idol Aaliyah for the track, 'Ladies In The House' featuring Missy Elliott and Timbaland on her 'One In A Million' album in 1996.

In 1999, American singer Monifah replayed the elements from 'Bad Girls' for her single, featuring Queen Pen, 'Monifah's Anthem/Bad Girl', the sample giving an interesting funky flavour to the track. Former girl group TLC featured the song 'I'm Good At Being Bad' on their third album, 'Fan Mail', which sampled the chorus of 'Love To Love You Baby'. It is alleged that Summer asked them to remove the sample from the track because now she felt the lyrics were too explicit. All subsequent pressings of the CD do not include the sample. Cassius, the French production duo, sampled '(If

It) Hurts Just A Little' on 'Cassius 1999' which reached no.7 in the UK charts and stayed for four weeks. In the same year, house artist Mousse T sampled the bass line from 'I Feel Love' for his 'Feel Love' remix of Moloko's hit single 'Sing It Back'.

The most outstanding Summer sample to date would be Beyonce's 'Naughty Girl' which sampled 'Love To Love You Baby' on the 2003 'Crazy In Love' album. The up-tempo Arabic-influenced single was perfect for party lovers! The single release was a success in the charts reaching no.3 in the US and no.10 in the UK, not just because the track was by Beyonce, a globally popular artist, but also as a result of the catchy sample. The sample of 'Love To Love You Baby' did not sound as sultry as the original orgasmic turn by the 'First Lady Of Love' Donna Summer. In 2004, J.C. Chasez also sampled 'I Feel Love' for the track 'One Night Stand', featured on his 'Schizophrenic' album.

'Hot Stuff' was partially sampled by The Pussycat Dolls in 2005 for their debut album 'PCD'. It was an interesting project, the verses being slightly altered with the chorus of Donna Summer's 'Hot Stuff' and renamed as 'Hot Stuff (I Want You Back)'.

In 2006 Madonna sampled 'I Feel Love' for her 'Confessions Tour', released on a CD and DVD, and Madonna's album 'Confessions On A Dance Floor' contains a sample of 'I Feel Love' on the track 'Future Lovers'. In *Madonna: An Intimate Biography* (2001), J. Randy Taraborrelli argues that Madonna's music had been composed for all and sundry. The author suggests that before Madonna arrived on the scene, the last act that embraced super-stardom status was Donna Summer. In Taraborrelli's own words:

'Before Madonna, the last singer to meld so effectively dance and pop influences was Donna Summer and her songwriters/producers Giorgio Moroder and Pete Bellotte (and later just Summer and Moroder), whose brand of Europop successfully transcended mere disco. But Summer, however successful, was not armed with Madonna's uncanny musical sense of self and of the market place – instincts integral to creating the hit records that were compiled for "The Immaculate Collection".'

Andrew Morton, in his book *Madonna*, notes that the star used to sing 'Hot Stuff' even before she became a singer. He also claimed that Madonna felt insulted when Summer turned down her request to cover her songs. This rejection coincided with a period of relatively poor chart success for Madonna. Apparently, Summer insisted that she 'would never give her' (Madonna) 'rights to sing her songs'.

No doubt a Madonna cover of a classic Summer disco hit would have been an interesting prospect. Summer's choice of who she allowed, or didn't allow, to cover her work was clearly a matter of very personal choice – and not always clear to onlookers. She did however acknowledge that Madonna was certainly a good example of how to have a successful and long career in the music business. Madonna's sample of 'I Feel Love' on her 'Confessions On A Dance Floor' was immaculate. The album concept was of a modern day disco with continuous music play – a device previously used by Donna Summer on 'Once Upon A Time', on 'Bad Girls' and also 'On The Radio: Greatest Hits Volumes I & II'.

Dance music producer Tim Letteer notes:

'She started the continuous mix and it has become the norm with DJ compilations ... it would be amazing if she did a continuous mix of original tracks.'

Artists will always cover and perform songs from other acts. Over the years, Donna Summer has had her share of successful covers during live performances and many acts have in turn performed her songs live. In 1979, Blondie sang 'I Feel Love' in one of their concerts and later the live version featured on the B-side of their 1995 re-issued single 'Union City Blues'.

In *Mojo* magazine (June 2011) Louis Wilson wrote in an article 'Rock 'N' Roll Confidential: Debbie Harry' that 'I Feel Love' was one of the five songs she included in 'My Tunes Debbie's Delight'.

From punk to New Romantic, another major group that performed a Summer song was Duran Duran. Andy Taylor wrote in *Wild Boy: My Life In Duran Duran* (2008) that they performed 'I Feel Love' during Duran Duran's 1980 debut performance in The Rum Runner, Birmingham, snapping a guitar string in the process. Andy Taylor tells us that on the night, their show was supported by 'all the New Romantic' circle.

In February 1995, the late star Selena performed a medley of the Summer songs 'On The Radio' and 'Last Dance' at her last concert at the Houston Astrodome. Selena's performance was released on the soundtrack for the film *Selena* and the DVD release of *Selena: The Last Concert*. Jamiroquai and Anastacia covered 'Bad Girls' at The Brits 2002 Awards and he then released it as the B-side for his 'Corner Of The Earth' single. Jamiroquai also performed the same song in a concert in Verona the same year.

'I Feel Love' has been covered and sampled by – amongst others – Madonna, The Red Hot Chili Peppers, John Frusciante, Kylie Minogue, Blondie, Basement Jaxx and Finnish progressive rock band Kingston Wall.

Sometime in June 2000, to support her new 'disco' sound, Kylie Minogue did a few promotional club performances. *The Complete Kylie* by Simon Sheridan (2008) wrote that as well as singing her hits, Minogue also sang

'I Feel Love' and two new tracks in the London club G.A.Y. This must have been a huge treat for disco fans. Minogue also sampled the track for her 2002 'Kylie Fever' concert and performed 'Light Years', containing elements of 'I Feel Love', available on DVD. Simon Sheridan critiqued her performance as 'a mind-blowing medley' that 'was utter perfection.' Kylie Minogue was apparently a Donna Summer fan from the start of her career and recorded one of Donna Summer's hit songs for a demo. Sean Smith in his book *Kylie: The Biography* (2006), said that Minogue was so determined 'to be a performer that she paid her own money' to record two demos, one of which was Summer's hit 'Dim All The Lights', which Minogue then presented to the 'Young Talent Time' executives.

Donna Summer has been an icon and an inspiration to everyone from Kylie Minogue to Queen Latifah. Latifah admitted to Donna Summer, in her 1999 TV segment the *Queen Latifah Show*, that she used to perform to Summer's songs during high school auditions. Joss Stone did just the same – early in the soul singer's career, she performed 'On The Radio' in 2001 at the BBC talent show *Star For A Night*, finally winning the contest. Not only have Summer's songs have been performed by other acts, but Donna Summer herself has been copied! In 2001 the award winning UK DJ and dance sensation Sonique transformed herself into Donna Summer, singing 'I Feel Love' in the *Stars In Their Eyes* spin-off *Pop Stars In Their Eyes*, aired on the 6th October that year. Sonique decided to become Summer not only because she was a fan but also because 'I Feel Love' was the first song the DJ ever bought. She told Karen Gillet from the BBC that Summer had amazing stage presence, something that she felt she could relate to herself.

In 2003, 'Hot Stuff' was performed by Roselyn Sanchez for the same TV show, with the star performing the disco-pop-rock anthem with her very own touch – a slow introduction moving to a standard disco beat in the middle and also adding a Latin touch. The version brought a new dimension to the song. In the same evening Whoopi Goldberg, Thelma Houston, Mya, Taylor Dayne and Gloria Gaynor performed 'Last Dance' for the finale of the concert TV special *The Disco Ball*.

Gloria Gaynor said:

'It was great working with other divas. I don't think I was particularly reminded of the disco era when I did it, because I am always doing disco songs and therefore I can never forget the disco era! Still it was great.'

The divas' showmanship was fabulous. The song is a great closing number and was inspirational. Darrell Russ, who recorded and wrote 'Riding Home To Baltimore', remembered the time when he first heard 'Last Dance' broadcasted on the car stereo. The story begins:

'I heard her song "Last Dance" and something surreal happened to me. My mind went off into the stratosphere and beautiful images came to mind ... images of a tropical island and all the beautiful things that come along with such things. I knew this female voice was special ... since that evening ... Donna Summer has been tightly woven into the tapestry of my life. After I got home from NYC, I wanted to write a tribute song to her and got together with a friend to bat ideas around.'

Russell remembered that the first time that he heard Summer was while riding home from Baltimore. Russell and his friend had the hook and title of his song but the bridge was missing. During the final sessions, an idea came and he wrote the words for 'feeling love ... you know I'm feeling love ... feeling love ... yeah I'm feeling love,' inspired by his icon's 'I Feel Love'. He went on to write the lyrics to 'Riding Home From Baltimore'. In his own words:

'You have to listen closely to the lyrics to know it's about Donna. In the line "on a sweet summer night", this is a reference to her music publishing company ... Of course the bridge refers to her classic hit "I Feel Love". However the adlibs at the end are where I reference her directly. "Oh Donna ... don't say good night ... sing one more song ... make everything right ... don't go away ... one more song!" ...'

Many fans would not want their diva to go away and wish for more songs – but if the diva wishes to stop and to go away somehow nobody can stop her! Russ's tribute concept track was recorded and released in 2006 and new upbeat remixes became available in 2009. A European live TV programme, *Symphonic Show*, aired in France in 2006 and featured three stunning popular singers Anggun, Tina Arena and Ginie Line performing 'Hot Stuff'.

Summer's songs continue to be performed on stage in the US, Europe and Asia. In 2007 Kumi Koda, a Japanese singer known for urban and R&B songs, performed 'I Feel Love' with the Blue Man Group at the Summersonic Festival in Japan and on her 2007 tour promoting her album 'Black Cherry'. Four years earlier, a Japanese pop star Yuki Koyanagi sang 'On The Radio' in Japanese, released as a single in 2003. Koyanagi delivered the song in her own style while preserving the original dance tune.

The songs have also been a popular choice in music reality shows. In early 2006, Lucy Benjamin (the UK actor, well known for her role in *Eastenders*), covered 'Last Dance' on *The X Factor: Battle Of The Stars*. In 2008 Alexandra Burke performed 'On The Radio' on the UK talent show *The X Factor*, season five.

In 2007, on *American Idol*, 'She Works Hard For The Money' was performed by Jordin Sparks during season six, also performed by Kris Allen (an acoustic interpretation) in season eight. 'Last Dance' has been performed at least three times on the show, by Ryan Starr, Brenna Gethers and LaKisha Jones. In the final episode of season seven, the top twelve female contestants performed 'Last Dance' with the star herself – Donna Summer!

Most artists feel honoured if their songs are covered and performed by other artists, as Summer certainly did. She expressed her views in an article 'Talking To The Prima Donna' by Johannes Bonke for *Electronic Beats* journal in 2009. The fact that Beyonce Knowles and other acts 'have used pieces of' her music was a 'huge compliment'. To have her work 'carried into another generation' was evidence that new artists appreciated her work. Summer pointed out that the German version of *American Idol* used a lot of her songs and because they 'are not so easy to sing', the programme makers declared that if the contestants 'are going to be able to sing these songs' it would prove that they had a good voice. To hear young hopefuls in auditions singing her melodies in 'a new way' was 'eye-opening' and could help Summer learn new tricks by listening to them performed differently. Summer told A. Scott Galloway in a 2003 interview for the *Sacramento Observer* entitled 'Disco Queen Is Just An Ordinary Girl' that she used to rehearse 'at the same soundstage' as Chaka Khan and that she 'would sneak in and listen' to Chaka when she had the chance.

Pete Bellotte told the BBC during an interview for 'In Tune With Britain's Disco King' for BBC News Online, that he was delighted by the renewed interest in disco by chart recording acts. Bellotte talked about Beyonce having revived Summer's hit 'Love To Love You Baby' on her hit single 'Naughty Girl'.

Many songs have been covered, but only a few acts can cover an old Donna Summer hit well enough to please hardcore fans. However, some of these versions are very interesting, with the original songs elevated to another level by the new interpretations.

According to Paul Gambaccini, this would carry on with sampling and cover versions becoming increasingly used by acts, bands and DJs in the music recording business. In his opinion, the industry is at a low point for original compositions. For instance, hip hop always prides itself on using samples, so at any moment you could hear a record with a sample of 'I Feel Love' or 'State Of Independence'. It is then just a question of whether that record is good or not.

Gloria Gaynor is another contemporary who has had a similar experience. She agrees that Donna Summer was a pioneer who opened the doors for many other disco artists and continues to influence current performers. Summer's music is still popular, with her hits remaining in the public eye and having a contemporary feel as a result of frequent sampling by young acts who love elements of the originals. In Gloria Gaynor's own words:

'Both of us have been inspirational to young artists. I don't say that out of any assessment of my own. I said that because they said that to me. Young artists have come to me ... That's a great honour.'

Young music buyers are introduced to her music often via their favourite acts through sampling. This then leads in some cases to exploration of Summer's back catalogue, thus a new fan is born!

Peter Stengaard, who produced the radio edit of 'I Got Your Love', said that a Summer song has a unique, classic sound and this is one reason that so many international recording acts continue to cover, sample and perform live to her tunes. This sound just isn't made anymore by the industry. Stengaard believes that 'Love To Love You Baby' has to be the most impressive piece of disco music ever.

In an interview for this book, Francissca Peter said she thought it was a blessing that so many acts had recorded Summer's songs, highlighting the admiration and respect they had for her. Peter and many others had grown up with these songs, with acts such as Madonna and Beyonce covering them simply because they loved her music.

Peter Stengaard really enjoyed Beyonce's 'Naughty Girl' with its 'Love To Love You Baby' sample and thought Madonna's 'Future Lovers' tune was excellent, with its great use of 'I Feel Love'. Tricia Walsh Smith, taking time off from filming the *Pineapple Dance Studios* for Sky TV, thinks that artists will cover and sample Summer's songs for decades because her music is timeless and it makes music lovers want to 'leap to their feet and dance, dance and boogie!' In Smith's view, Beyonce's 'Naughty Girl', lost the originality and sensuality of 'Love To Love You Baby', whereas Madonna's 'Future Lovers' kept the sexiness and was true to the queen of disco's original! Tricia Walsh Smith recalls the thrill that Summer's songs brought her:

'In the 1970s I used to go to a club in Mayfair called Gullivers. The DJ would play, "Could It Be Magic", "Love To Love You Baby" and then "MacArthur Park". I boogied like there was no tomorrow! I also blasted the songs from my Mini Cooper as I whizzed round London.'

To capture the essence of Summer's sound is another task. As Summer's vocal is so recognisable, some acts that have covered her have been criticised. Most of the female vocalists covering Summer cannot compare to her 'timbre'.

In Philip Ball's *The Music Instinct: How Music Works And Why We Can't Do Without It*, he says:

'You can say what you like about the beauty of the melodies or the exuberance of the dynamics, but music will leave us indifferent and unmoved if the timbre isn't right. Equally, a change of timbre may transform the meaning.'

Some acts have delivered their Donna Summer cover with good results, with careful attention to the vocal and the musical arrangement. The Malaysian singer Salamiah Hassan insists that Summer's songs will never fade away with covers and samples and current club DJs still playing her hits. Inanna, a UK dance recording act, said in an interview that Donna Summer had recorded many legendary songs which will live on. Mark Nubar Donikian from Hypnogaja says that when an artist writes songs that 'connect' with people, that music tends to be 'enduring'. He continues to say that Donna Summer's music has already proven to be a 'body of work' that will stand the test of time.

In 2011, 'MacArthur Park' and 'Hot Stuff' were covered and performed in *Priscilla, Queen Of The Desert – The Musical*. A review in *Firefox News* from 27th March 2011 tells us:

'Like the movie, the musical uses disco dance hits as the queens' soundtrack but to a greater degree, of course. So, look forward to seeing elaborate numbers performed to hits of ... Donna Summer, ... and other dance-hall legends.'

Donna Summer has inspired fans to write several unauthorised books about her, as well as her authorised appearances in countless publications. For example, there were at least three English and one German publication about Donna Summer at the time of writing.

Images of Donna Summer from Studio 54, on stage and in her 1970s fashion heyday, have been featured in many publications on the subject of fashion and photography. Even her style played an important part in movies based on the 1970s. Summer's hair inspired the *Dream Girls* movie costume designer, Sharen Davis, when styling Sharon Leal for her stage performance as Michelle Morris in *One Night Only* with Beyonce Knowles and Anika Noni Rose. The style can be seen on Summer's album 'The Greatest Hits Of Donna Summer' or her cover for *JET* magazine dated 9th December 1976. Malaysian singer and actor Uji Rashid told me that she loved Summer's style so much that she once styled her hair to match Summer's 1980s hair-do! Rashid's Summer inspired hair-do can be seen on her 1981 album cover for 'Mengapa Berjauhan' translated as 'Why We Are Far Apart'. Sarah Kennedy, in her book 'Vintage Style' (2011), wrote that at the time disco music was at its peak, the pop charts were dominated by disco divas and their exotic fashion styles:

'Donna Summer's sultry x-rated sounds revolutionized dance music with their sexually explicit noises! Donna Summer's splendid look of gleaming skin, huge hair and lips and body to die for made her a disco diva for a generation . . .'

Showing Summer's photo in 1979, Kennedy notes that Summer 'emerged from the scene with extravagant wardrobes'.

Summer's influence continues with 'A Love Trilogy' and 'Four Seasons Of Love' album covers inspiring the 'Lifestyle' section of the jamaicaobsever.com to feature Summer for their 'icon' topic. Their 'Icon Inspiration: Donna Summer' article had them dress up the winner of the Caribbean Model Search fashion model category 2010, Hannah Lettman. The publication (16th July 2011) printed:

'In our final feature on icons with strong fashion identities or who influenced fashion or their genre, we return to the music industry to Donna Summer who ruled the disco world . . . Donna Summer was a HUGE Sex Symbol during those heady disco days.'

The periodical saluted Summer's album covers and her stage performances. They wrote that Summer presented herself with 'garments that were highly provocative, with deep necklines' also 'high slits to flaunt her legs and figure-hugging silhouettes to show off her curves.' The jamaicaobserver.com said:

'We dressed Hannah in swimwear to replicate a couple of the singer's looks. The inspiration piece for the Rock the Cloth garment is a long white dress from the album cover shown. We are still in love with maxis and so this is a great summer dress.'

Donna Summer's fashion style has inspired the *X Factor* judge, Kelly Rowland. In *'Mail Online'* article 'Wigs, Work-outs And A Wonder Wardrobe: How Kelly Rowland Gets Her Fab Factor', Bella Blissett wrote Rowland wants to look 'grown-up and sexy, but intelligent' hence Blissett noted the singer 'channels' fashion icon Donna Summer.

Summer has also been acknowledged by various 'world' artists including Celia Cruz. This time it was slightly different! She recognised Summer's fame and her inspiration to others but noted that it was not so easy for every singer to reach this level of fame. In 'Beats Of The Heart: Popular Music Of The World' (Jeremy Marre and Hannah Charlton) the 'Queen Of Salsa' cited Summer:

'Because so many Latin Americans are on the poverty line, we can't expect to be like Donna Summer in Las Vegas with a full house each night.'

A music icon herself, the late Celia Cruz has achieved twenty three gold albums in her musical career.

In 1996 two of her album sleeve designs featured in *1000 Record Covers* by Michael Ochs in which he compiled some of his favourite album covers from his personal collection. He included 'Bad Girls' and 'She Works Hard For The Money'. In the book's introduction, Ochs explained that the artwork was designed to be as enjoyable to look at as the music was to listen to.

In the spring of 1996, the University Of Massachusetts invited Summer on campus to help the university with a fundraising campaign for scholarship money; Donna Summer was donating her time to raise money for the students. Summer grew up in the nearby Dorchester area and the university worked closely with many of the local schools, including Summer's former school, Jeremiah E. Burke High. It was a wonderful chance for the university to have a star with local history to help them fundraise. One day, Summer received a letter from the Boston University Chancellor's office and in June 1997 she was invited to attend an honorary graduation ceremony. The university had honoured her with a doctorate in fine arts. Even though she had moved on, the star continued to give back to the community with charity work. As a result of this dedication, Massachusetts University decided to honour and acknowledge Donna Summer for her work. At the beginning of the ceremony, the invited guests and graduates had the pleasure of seeing Summer sing the National Anthem.

On the 20th September 2005, 'Love To Love You Baby: A Tribute To Donna Summer' was released. It was a compilation of recordings by other singers who had covered Summer's songs, most of who have been mentioned previously.

BBC Radio 2 celebrated a disco season with an hour-long show dedicated to Donna Summer on 4th July 2009, titled *Feelin' Love: The Donna Summer Story*. It was a comprehensive exploration of her journey to stardom, including interviews with Pete Waterman, Gloria Gaynor and Moby to name but a few. The broadcast surprisingly played short clips of three largely unfamiliar tracks, 'Sally Go 'Round The Roses', 'Lady Of The Night' and 'How I Feel'. A song taken from 'All Systems Go' called 'Voices Cryin' Out', was the theme track. An article on bbc.co.uk titled 'Radio 2's Disco Season – Feelin' Love: The Donna Summer Story' explains:

'The extraordinary thing about Donna's music is just how many musical boundaries it seems to jump over with such ease. Country singers . . . covered her songs; pop artists . . . have sampled Summer's materials; as have electronic dance acts . . . and DJs, remixers and producers like Stuart Price, David Guetta and Moby. Over the decades Donna has moved on from disco music, turning to soul and gospel and she continues to make new albums and tour.'

Tim Letteer said in his 'bio' that:

'My earliest dance music influences came from listening to Donna Summer music. I used to sit for hours analysing Giorgio Moroder's flawless music production while getting lost in Summer's captivating vocals. The music was so ahead of its time, it just blew my mind. Her voice and the brilliant orchestration that accompanied it moves me to this day.'

Stor Dubine, an artist and fan, was inspired to create an unofficial animated video of 'I Got Your Love'. Dubine said he 'fell in love' with the song and as a thank you for all the years that Summer had given fans her songs, and as Internet videos were booming, he decided to do the animation for 'I Got Your Love'. This would also help to raise the profile of Summer's new single and promote her comeback.

Fans loved the video. The concept drew on Donna Summer's style of art, fashion and music. It truly was a tribute to and a thank you to Donna Summer. Dubine was born partially deaf and he used Summer's tunes to learn and understand music and rhythm. The 2005 video was a thrill for many fans. Summer's manager and the star herself were grateful and fascinated with the work. They now have the unofficial DVD of 'I Got Your Love'!

In 2009 Andrew Johnson, a fan and musician, produced a single titled '(I'm In Love With) Donna Summer', an interesting and catchy electronic dance track.

Fans have created tribute websites and discussion forums devoted to Donna Summer. These adoring fans gather information for other fans and provide an important source of information for music lovers. They provide interviews, archives from magazines, newspapers, concert photographs, discography information and allow fans to exchange views about Donna Summer's songs and about the artist herself. Summer's fans also started to exchange and share their Summer collectables. Tribute sites include Endless Summer, a forum page based in Europe and Donna Summer Internet Zone in the US, which began life in 1995. An official site was surely needed and eventually Summer's management decided to endorse the US site in 1996. This site eventually closed but was replaced by a new, official, site in 1999, called Donna Summer: The Official Website, copyright Sweet Summer Night Music. Summer fans were thrilled to find a selection of cassettes, LPs and CDs on sale through the merchandise page. Items for sale included a 'babydoll shirt', 'baseball jersey' and other miscellany such as an autographed *Driven By The Music* poster (from her painting), a key chain, tour book and a tote bag. There have been several sites since, culminating in the current official site donna-summer.com. Endless Summer finally took a bow and closed in 1999. The forum continues, with a link to an unauthorised tribute site.

For Donna Summer's fiftieth birthday in 1998, the creator of donna-tribute.com, Cathy Hawkins, compiled notes from fans from all over the globe and produced a scrapbook called 'Pages From The Heart'.

In September 2009, Hawkins shared the experience:

'The memory book was a lot of fun! I had been chatting online with a number of people about Donna's birthday and we collectively decided that we should do something. Then someone suggested the idea of a memory book to me, and I ran with it. I solicited visitors to the site to send in a page (or two) of their favourite Donna memories – that was the first time I ever invited my readers to "talk to" Donna and it was cool to see the enthusiasm everyone had, and to see what they wrote . . .'

This marvellous tribute consisted of 125 pages compiled from information provided by 70 fans worldwide. I'm one of the fans that participated and my tribute titled 'Tales From The Heart', written on the 12th November 1998, was included in the memory book. It was presented to Donna Summer by Hawkins during her concerts in Atlantic City on 2nd and 3rd January 1999. Donna Summer loved the gift. She sent a thank you note that was posted to Hawkins.

'Rumour Has It' that later on, Summer displayed 'Pages From The Heart' in her office in Nashville.

As written by Donna Summer on 7th January 1999, thanking her fans:

'Dear Cathy & All of My Friends Unknown:

I was so overwhelmed with the "Pages From The Heart" book that you all put together for my 50th birthday. It truly blessed me to see how much you have enjoyed my music through the years. Thank you so much for such a labour of love and hard work putting this together. I will always treasure it. God bless you now and always. Have a very happy and prosperous New Year.

Love, Donna Summer + family'

Donna Summer often refers to her fans as 'friends unknown', a phrase taken from one of the tracks from the 'Mistaken Identity' album. Summer's heartfelt appreciation made fans love her even more. To be successful in the long term, as well as having good songs and personality, it is important to value and appreciate the fans.

The idea behind 'Pages From The Heart' carries on to the present day. Fans posted their love and birthday wishes to Donna Summer on donna-tribute.com and by 2008, fans could leave messages to her and her management team through her Internet sites.

On a personal note, I have paid my own tribute to Summer with an interior design university project in 1995. It was inspired by the idea of an arts and talk show that had Donna Summer as the host. The concept is based on Summer's personality and music. Titled 'TV Set Design – Interpretation', it was published in December 2009 in a former online US lifestyle magazine, *ID-Digest*. The project sketch drawings and design tips were featured in the column 'Laid Back Glamour'. The article was a celebration of Donna Summer's sixty-first birthday.

Summer's songs have touched her fans in many ways and tribute works will no doubt continue to be made for many years to come. It is amazing to see all of the work that had been created by fans (released or otherwise) – fashion design, music video, musical script and publications.

Some serious fans have become avid collectors of all things related to Summer. Eddie Sorell, a dedicated Summer lover, explained that he has been collecting items since the 1970s. The Internet has made the hunt so much easier! 'Denver Dream', 'Virgin Mary' and 'The Hostage' are some rare European singles in his collections. He explains why purchasing the same album again and again simply because the sleeve covers are different makes sense to him:

'. . . and why buy the same songs over and over again? I have asked that question to myself many times . . . The hunt itself is very amusing. I enjoy sitting by the computer and try to find record stores all around the world. Maybe find a release with a different sleeve or a song with a different editing. That's very exciting! I don't think so much about the money it costs me because I enjoy it so much.'

Collectors of Donna Summer items are very keen to get hold of 'DJ only' remixes, supposedly strictly available within the professional DJ circuit. These rare DJ vinyls and compact discs are worth a listen. They include 'Summer Heat', a medley of Donna Summer's hits suitable for club play labelled under 'DMC Mixes II September 1989: Love To Love You Baby Valentine Cut Up' available to DJs through *Remix Culture* title and an up-tempo instrumental mix of Summer's songs called 'Club Life '94' was produced by Hot Tracks productions. Most of these rarities originate from the US.

Ian Shirley, journalist and rare records expert for *Record Collector*, says that many of her records are collector's items, but lack of exposure and public awareness of her current work inevitably affects the value and desirability of previous recordings. Better publicity and commercial success will lead to increased interest in her previous work and will stimulate the market for rarities and oddities. There are numerous ways to find out what's out there, including the usual resources such as record dealers, record shops or even experts within the music business that deal with particular acts. Shirley also points out that the accumulated mass of followers that Summer has gained during a lifetime in the music business is a collector's item in itself!

The *Record Collector Rare Record Price Guide 2012* contains prices for items including 'The Hostage/Let's Work Together Now' (People PED 115), 'Hot Stuff/Journey To The Centre Of Your Heart' (twelve inch red vinyl – Casablanca CANL 151) and 'This Time I Know It's For Real/Whatever Your Heart Desires' (shaped picture disc WEA U 7780P). In 1990, *Record Collector* mentions some rare pressings of Donna Summer songs including 'The Hostage' (promo w/1 sampler ATL 10533), 'Hot Stuff' (twelve inch red vinyl CANL 151), 'Our Love/Lucky' (twelve inch blue vinyl Class X DJ remix), 'The Woman In Me' (twelve inch picture label blue vinyl W 9983CT), 'Pocket Songs' (promo cassette), and 'Words & Music' (3-LP 17/10/82). All worth a search!

Avid collectors will no doubt be keen to get their hands on the 'multi-coloured vinyl' title 'Summer'. Such coloured vinyl discs were produced as early as the 1920s. 'Summer' was produced by CF Productions/Casual Films Records. Tracks include 'Love To Love You Baby' and 'On The Radio', printed in Italy in 1997. It is a beautifully coloured twelve inch disc with shades of pink, a bit of white, a very light blue and black spread onto the vinyl.

In *Extraordinary Records (Colors Magazine)* by Alessandro Benedetti (2009), Giorgio Moroder discusses coloured vinyl discs:

'Lebanon was a major producer of multicoloured vinyl. But many of multi-colors have a defect – they were printed by ghost record labels. These are the infamous bootlegs or pirate records, which often don't have labels. Commercially these records do not even exist because they were not produced officially and are not included in the artist's discography.'

These unofficial or white label records will just add to the thrill of collectors in fulfilling their obsession to own everything.

Frederic Seaman wrote in *John Lennon: Living On Borrowed Time* (1993) that when they discussed music in general, the legendary ex-Beatle told him that he liked Donna Summer's music. According to Donna Summer, in an interview with *Attitude* magazine, John Lennon was a big fan of 'I Feel Love'. When Lennon got hold of the song, he 'locked himself' in a room and played the track continually.

Marc Almond said in *Tainted Life* that 'I Feel Love' had a major influence and inspired many recording acts and the media:

'It bridged the gap between Kraftwerk and David Bowie in the past, and the new nearer-to-home sounds of the Human League's "Being Boiled" and "Reproduction" and Cabaret Voltaire, and it would sweep us all away.'

Summer's sound started a trend for an era. 'Love To Love You Baby' was one of the tracks that rocketed disco from an underground movement to an entire way of life. Disco propelled her career and revolutionised the club scene in 1970s. 'I Feel Love' was the song that brought the high energy, electronic sound to dance culture. Acts that have covered or sampled Summer's songs may not have had the same impact, but their recordings have added new dimensions to her work and introduced it to new audiences.

Donna Summer's tunes are evergreen; as relevant as ever. Her melodies live on in people's collections and in new artists' recordings. Young hopefuls dreaming of stardom learn the hard way about what it takes when they attempt to tackle a Summer song. Practice helps, but talent is something you are born with. Her work has inspired many artists to cover her work or sample it for their own compositions, her back catalogue proving to be a goldmine of ideas and musical innovation. Her many different styles and ability to change her image have no doubt contributed to that rare quality in the music business – longevity. Her continuing popularity has made her a collectable product! Fans from around the world endlessly search out her rare and unusual releases, official or otherwise. They have developed and added to tribute sites and created projects dedicated to their much-loved superstar. Her influence and inspiration will doubtless continue for many years to come.

'Love To Love You Baby', 'On The Radio', 'I Feel Love' – some of the greatest pop songs ever made, will act as inspiration to countless artists in the future.

17

Still Going Strong: A New Departure

In the 1990s, apart from touring in the US, Donna Summer was also working on her semi-autobiographical musical, *Ordinary Girl*. She promoted some of the new material in her concerts between 1997 and 1999. Tracks titled 'My Life' and 'No Ordinary Love Song' were regular tunes. It was thrilling news for die-hard fans. Yet without a new record label it was impossible to see the rise of *Ordinary Girl*.

Summer says in 'Listen To The Music – Catching Up With Donna Summer' by Camp Rehoboth (donna-tribute.com) in April 1998:

'There comes a point when you get tired of doing what everyone else wants you to do. They want you to make a record the way they think it should be made. I want to make the kinds of records now the way I want to make them,' she says. 'I'd rather be doing my own thing than be stuck with a company that doesn't support me. Until I find the relationship that I'm looking for, I don't want to be signed to a label. I have to at least try once to do the record I want to do.'

In 'Fashion Meets Music: Donna Summer' (missomnimedia.com), the star says that in the current showbusiness climate, some record companies don't want to spend time developing an artist. The industry wants to make money first and foremost, so the time and effort needed to nurture new talent is not always a top priority, and second chances are rare.

A talent such as Donna Summer with a good track record of hits and accomplishments is in a different league. Summer may have taken a long time to record an album but this wasn't such a big problem for a label because Summer had a strong following even amongst younger fans.

Despite the delay, Donna Summer fans waited with anticipation for her next release, following her signing with Epic Records owned by Sony Music Entertainment for a multimillion-selling contract. On the 21st June 1999 'VH1 Presents: Live & More Encore!', the first production from Donna Summer's new label, was released. Wayne Isaak, Bruce Gillmer and Lee Chesnut were the executive producers. Because Epic did not have copyright on her songs, this album provided one solution for introducing Donna Summer to the mainstream of music fans.

The live project was recorded on the 4th February 1999 at the Hammerstein Ballroom, Manhattan Center, New York, including selected cuts of Summer's performances. The show was actually a special from *VH1 Divas Live* series that, unlike the standard programme, showcased several well-established singers in the course of one show. VH1 decided to broadcast a full-length Donna Summer concert, a big treat for her followers. It was said that Donna Summer needed to have a show of her own – her status meant she was just too big to share the spotlight. The complete concert performance included some tracks from her upcoming musical *Ordinary Girl* titled 'If There Is Music There' and 'My Life' (edited short version) plus her unreleased tracks 'Don't Wanna Work' and 'Nobody'. The classics 'Someone To Watch Over Me' and 'Riding Through The Storm' were also included. The VH1 team selected other songs according to what they thought the audiences would like to hear. Not surprisingly, VH1 wanted to record 'Love To Love You Baby', but this was declined by the diva although she loves the song. The song 'My Life' is considered to be the highlight of the live album. This track was created by Summer based on her personal experiences and will hopefully be featured in her upcoming musical *Ordinary Girl*. 'My Life' was composed by Summer, Pete Waterman, Paul Berry and Gary Miller.

In a 1999 UK interview (Donna Summer Syndicated Interview' CD promo of Jo Hart PR), Summer said the track was written circa 1992 when she was in London. Summer had called Pete Waterman and said:

'Pete, you got to let me come over, I got an idea for a song. I think it's for the musical, I just have to put it down.'

The two creative teams got together and started writing. After playing around with some ideas, they recorded the song and then Summer flew back to America. Somebody found the tape and it began to get played in clubs. Realising this, Summer worked again on the song, producing a different arrangement because she didn't think the 'My Life' arrangement was ready. Amazingly, somebody else got hold of this new arrangement and yet again Summer did a different arrangement of the song! Summer's idea to perform and record the song for the 'VH1 Presents: Live & More Encore!' was a great gift for fans. Summer also introduced her new collaborator on 'No More Tears (Enough Is Enough)', the foxy Australian singer Tina Arena. The idea came about when by chance Arena came into the studio in New York to say hello to Summer. Arena is a fan and one of the Sony team at that time had an idea for the two to duet on 'No More Tears (Enough Is Enough)' for the VH1 show. However, Summer pointed out that her sister,

Mary Gaines Bernard, normally sang the song with her; it would be hard to replace her sister and sing it on stage with another vocalist. But the idea worked during the rehearsal and it went into the final VH1 TV special. Summer was impressed with Arena describing her as 'kicking' and a 'killer' singer.

Summer's live performances were edited together and called 'Donna Summer Medley'. The package included the live tracks 'On The Radio'/'She Works Hard For The Money'/'Bad Girls'/'Hot Stuff'/'Last Dance' and was only available as a promo. Bizarrely, her vocal level was minimised and only the back-up vocals can be heard!

No live songs have been released as singles from the VH1 project but the album featured two new studio songs, 'I Will Go With You (Con Te Partiro)' and 'Love Is The Healer', proving that Donna Summer had not forgotten her roots in the world of dance music. Not surprisingly, the single 'I Will Go With You (Con Te Partiro)' made it to no.1 in the *Billboard* dance charts in the summer. Although it didn't get much radio play in the US the single made it into the Top100 in the *Billboard* charts, debuting on 24th July 1999 at no.79, stayed in the *Billboard* pop chart for nine weeks. The success of 'I Will Go With You (Con Te Partiro)' continued as it remained in the sales chart for twenty-five weeks. The single spent more time in the chart then any Summer song since 1989's 'This Time I Know It's For Real'.

'I Will Go With You (Con Te Partiro)' is a cover of a famous 1995 song by Andrea Bocelli, later released as a duet in 1997 with Sarah Brightman and sung partly in English, titled 'Time To Say Goodbye'. According to Summer, she sang the song so many times at home that her husband suggested she record it. Following permission from her label, she reworked it as an upbeat track to include in an ultimate dance album. Although it took a while to translate, she celebrated the original composition as a 'wonderful song, great piece of work, a magnificent melody'. Her version of 'I Will Go With You (Con Te Partiro)' was an upbeat tune liked by many listeners. Joel Whitburn, the *Billboard* chart expert, celebrated the song as one of his favourites. Paul Gambaccini enjoyed the track but points out that it is often hard for a song like 'I Will Go With You (Con Te Partiro)' with its lyrics partly in a 'foreign' language, to become a hit in the US. To include 'Con Te Partiro' in the title was not necessarily wise. Still, 'I Will Go With You (Con Te Partiro)' topped the US Club Play chart. The single was released in a wide range of formats and included remixes by Club 69, Rosabel, Trouser Enthusiasts and Skillmasters as well as producer Hex Hector. Was this a cynical moneymaking marketing ploy? Summer has said that multiple versions and remixes may kill the beauty of a composition, but on the other hand, if it brings the song to a wider audience then why not?

In the UK market 'VH1 Presents: Live & More Encore!' barely registered. 'I Will Go With You (Con Te Partiro)' stalled at no.44 on the 30th October 1999 without any big promotion. In Canada it peaked at no.35, whereas in Japan it stayed in the chart for twelve weeks climbing to no.26.

The long-awaited album from Donna Summer peaked at no.43 in the US and stayed in the chart for thirteen weeks. However 'VH1 Presents: Live & More Encore!' failed to climb the UK album chart. It peaked at no.30 in Italy and in Germany it only went to no.75. The album was well received in Spain, achieving Platinum status, with the singles 'I Will Go With You (Con Te Partiro)' and 'Love Is The Healer' making it into the Top 20.

Hex Hector discussed his experience of working with Summer in a 2008 interview for Christian John Wikane's 'She's A Rainbow: A Tribute To Donna Summer' in *PopMatters*. He was thrilled that Epic Records chose him to produce 'I Will Go With You (Con Te Partiro)'. Of all the pop stars he has worked with, 'Donna Summer was the only' recording act he 'was completely star struck with', despite working alongside names such as Madonna, Jennifer Lopez, Jessica Simpson and Ricky Martin. Summer always was and remains his favourite. He was nine or ten years old when he bought 'Love To Love You Baby'. In Hector's own words:

'Once she started, I got goosebumps because it was Donna Summer. She sounded just as powerful as when she was younger. Her voice was so powerful that she had to stand about ten feet away from the mic! As amazing a singer as Donna was, this was probably the hardest vocal I've ever done and the reason for that is, and it's no fault of Donna, translating an opera song onto a dance track is no easy feat. It took a while just to get it right but it was unbelievable!'

Darrell Russ, a singer and a fan, says that her song lifts his spirit when he feels low and the upbeat tempo improves his mood. Russ believes that Summer has a powerful voice that can be most admired when she sings live, a voice that could fill an arena without a microphone! The first time Russ heard his idol's voice in a 1995 concert, it felt like somebody had punched him straight in the chest!

The end high note to 'I Will Go With You (Con Te Partiro)' is a good example. The catchy upbeat track 'What Is It You Want' from 'Mistaken Identity' used a similar formula. In 1999 'I Will Go With You (Con Te Partiro)' was nominated for a Grammy Award for Best Dance Recording.

The other dance track, 'Love Is The Healer', is much more interesting, high energy material. The tune takes Summer into another dimension of New Age hardcore dance beat. Her trademark 'I Feel Love' beat and disco background have influenced and inspired many dance producers. The single featured the 'Eric Kupper's I Feel Healed Mix' and 'Thunderspuss 2000 Club Mix' which sampled the beat from 'I Feel Love'. The twelve inch white label remix of 'Love Is The Healer (Jonathan Peters Vocal Mix)' brought a 1970s flavour to the track.

The greatest hits live performance and the two studio songs provided a great introduction to new listeners who had purchased their first Summer album. The single 'I Will Go With You (Con Te Partiro)' was the first to be released, as a familiar tune is a great way to reconnect her music with a younger crowd. The single might not have been a huge hit in the charts, but club goers knew Summer's cover.

In a review by Steve Kurutz on allmusic.com:

'So much has changed since her late 1970s heyday that on 'VH1 Presents' you can feel Summer gathering up stalwart fans, digging her heels in and getting prepared to fight her way back into the fickle pop consciousness. But if any disco diva has the power to make a comeback, it's Summer and her ballsy voice.'

In 2000, 'VH1 Presents: Live & More Encore!' was awarded the Nashville Music Award Best Rhythm And Blues Album of the year. The live recording 'Someone To Watch Over Me', taken from the album was released for the 'Keeping The Dream Alive' project in 2001.

Following the live project with Epic, it was rumoured that an album titled 'Angel' was supposed to be in the making, but nothing has come of this as of the time of writing. It is said that there were creative differences between Epic and Summer, significant enough for the proposal to be shelved. Some samples of new material called 'Words', 'Valley Of The Moon' and 'Adoni' were posted on the previous site (Donna Summer The Official Website) before it was redesigned. It isn't clear if they were intended for the new album or just part of Summer's ongoing studio work.

After the lack of chart success during the late 1990s, having a big hit now was significant for Summer's future prospects. Further major commitment from the record company management guaranteed more media attention. Pete Waterman says that the fact fans and members of the public love Donna Summer is not as simple as just having a fabulous voice – but it is a major asset. Summer has been blessed with a great voice that has lasted.

When her contract with Epic ended, Summer signed to the Burgundy label. During her career Summer has signed to a few record labels and has worked with other producers, this experience helping her mature as an artist and as a business woman.

Pete Waterman suggests that to sign from one label to another is a positive departure. The artist will also modify their sound and the way they write lyrics. Waterman said in an interview on 10th May 2010:

'... Yes an artist has to move on ... The Beatles changed drastically over their career and they had to as they got older. You can't be making songs about unrequited love like you did when you were eighteen or nineteen when you're forty!'

Age is also a factor influencing a change to a different label. A new label will allow an established star to develop fresh sounds and ideas, as demonstrated when Pete Waterman worked with Summer for the 'Another Place And Time' project. Labels are always keen to sign successful existing acts, tempting them with lucrative offers, but the acts have to be smart in who they choose to work with. A true artist, although interested in success, will want to have the space and opportunity to express their creativity, whereas for the label, the bottom line is commercial success and profit. Gloria Gaynor feels that it's good if a label signs an act for their experience and talent. Donna Summer has been fortunate in that she's well respected by the industry and has loyal followers; this has shown through in her recording achievements over the years. Her projects all have a different sound as she has branched out with different producers and labels, allowing her to express her creativity.

In the US, the A-Z Top 500 Artists from 1955–2005 poll in *Joel Whitburn Presents The Billboard Albums* places Donna Summer at no.137. In the UK, *Hit Singles: Top 20 Charts From 1954 To The Present Day* by Dave McAleer (2007) places Summer at no.32 for All Time Singles Artists In The US with hits from 1975–1989, and at no.72 for Top All Time Singles Artists In The UK with hits from 1976–1996. There are 100 acts in each category.

In 2008, Donna Summer released 'Crayons'; the tracks on the album represent the title track, colourful, with new sounds from reggae, blues, world music and bossa nova/samba. The album was released on a small label called Burgundy Records (Sony BMG SMG).

The new album was marketed as Summer's comeback, but 'Crayons' is not a comeback album. A seventeen-year absence is a very long time to wait for a new studio album but avid fans know, and Summer herself has declared, that she had been in the studio with individual special projects during this time. Summer acknowledged that she had not recorded an album for a very long time. In the article 'Talking To The Prima Donna' for *Electronic Beats*, Summer said she was 'tired of the record company situation'.

As an artist, Summer wished to develop her creativity, but that wish was not 'allowed'. As an artist, Summer didn't want to look back with hits such as 'I Feel Love', 'Bad Girls' and the sounds she had done before. On that note, Summer told the record label to 'forget it'. These hungry lovers of Summer's music had been longing for a brand new full-length album for far too long. But before the completed album was made available, fans could listen to the songs through Summer's website. 'I'm A Fire' was burning in fans' ears; the first new track that provided an introduction to Donna Summer's new and intriguing material.

Not surprisingly, the single remixes of 'I'm A Fire' reached no.1 in the US dance chart. 'I'm A Fire (Solitaire Club Mix)' was an enchanting dance masterpiece. Summer fans knew she was back and meant business! However, this was not the official single release. The special pressing on a two CD set, made available by Perfect Beat, an online retailer, was authorised by Summer's team. When 'I'm A Fire' was marketed, it was their biggest exclusive pressing. The promotional copy was reportedly sold in an online bidding site for much as $500! Summer's first official single was 'Stamp Your Feet', which also reached no.1 in the US dance chart. The next single release, 'Sand On My Feet', peaked in Canada at no.30 and 'It's Only Love' was a no.14 in the US dance chart. In January 2009, 'Fame (The Game)' was released with an official music video, reaching no.1 on *Billboard's* dance chart. The three single releases excluded 'Sand On My Feet' and 'It's Only Love', fully sanctioned from Song/Burgundy and pressed by Perfect Beat – the only authorised reseller for special releases on CD of Summer's three singles. Perfect Beat believed strongly in keeping the great sound quality in an 'actual' CD pressing. From the Perfect Beat album review segment:

'We're so happy we can offer you guys this amazing exclusive ... As the digital age continues to grow, it is times like this you need to support physical CDs if you want to see them continue to get pressed ... otherwise we're all going to be stuck with compressed MP3 music files.'

Even though the singles from 'Crayons' were successful in the dance chart, they failed to register on the US pop chart. 'I'm A Fire' was not released in the UK but 'Stamp Your Feet' was released in the UK and Germany; it failed to enter the UK singles chart but did make it to no.88 in Germany. True blue fans have said that 'Stamp Your Feet' was not the best track to be chosen as the first official single, it was a fast catchy tune but there are other high energy compositions from 'Crayons' that would have made a bigger impact. By now, Summer's singles were being released in digital format.

'Crayons' reached no.17 in the US (six weeks in the chart). This was a major result for Summer in a market in which she had not been successful for several years. Donna Summer's last high-charting album in the US was 'She Works Hard For The Money' at no.9 in 1983. To add to the thrill, 'Crayons' climbed to no.5 in the US R&B/hip hop chart. It was in the chart for fourteen weeks and was also a success in the Digital Albums chart reaching no.17.

Joel Whitburn suggests that 'Crayons' was actually a moderate success in view of her previous chart achievements and the current album charts. Even though it was in the *Billboard* album chart, it dropped out after six weeks. Whitburn, in his opinion, felt that music fans enjoyed it because of the diversity of musical styles.

The album was not promoted in the UK, only reaching no.142 in the charts. Interviews with Summer did feature in the broadsheet papers in the UK but did not contribute to better sales. In reality, not many UK music fans know about its release. Gennaro Castaldo from the HMV Press and PR Department noted that the result for 'Crayons' was disappointing in the UK, especially by Summer's very high standards. Castaldo explained this was because her profile was not really high enough. Summer has been away for so long and shows like *Top Of The Pops*, on which she might have appeared, were no longer broadcasting. Arguably it didn't have strong singles that would have attracted the radio and TV airplay to promote the album and there was no live tour in the UK.

In the case of 'Crayons', Paul Gambaccini says that artists and labels need a crucial focus to sell their product. Usually, an established artist will sell an album over a longer period of time. This creates a lower initial sales figure and the album not climbing to the chart position fans would hope for. Most recording acts reach this point in their musical journey. In the beginning of her musical career, the music buying market rushed to hear the sound of Donna Summer. A new album by an accomplished artist needs to be extremely superior for the public to rush out to purchase it. Gambaccini enjoyed various songs from 'Crayons' and played some tracks on his radio show. He also recognised that listeners would not rush out to buy the album unless they were true fans. The majority of music listeners only purchase an album if they come across it in stores or on websites. Summer's previous recording achievements mean that she will sell through her fantastic back catalogues.

Better publicity would have helped make 'Crayons' more successful in the UK. Her hardcore European fans felt let down, not by the album production but by the marketing department of Summer's record label.

The UK, Europe and Asian release of the album featured an extra track titled 'It's Only Love', bringing Donna Summer back to the 1979 release 'Bad Girls', with the track mimicking the up-tempo sounds of 'Sunset People' and 'Our Love'. With good promotion including regular airplay and a single release, 'It's Only Love' could have brought the one-time Queen Of Disco back into the pop charts, where she belonged. However, not surprisingly, the low profile digital single 'It's Only Love' went unnoticed globally. 'Crayons' was appreciated in Italy with the album reaching no.46. In Germany, where Donna Summer first started her recording career, it reached no.73, in Switzerland no.85 and in Spain no.97.

Fans loved the album; although some did feel that the project could have been more dance-oriented, most will have 'Crayons' in their collection. After waiting for such a long time for a full-length project from their much-loved star, hearing her voice was a wish come true.

Tim Letteer comments:

'It was a nice production. I think the producers tried a little hard at times to sound ... current, but her voice made up for it. Her vocals were perfection.'

A number of fans questioned the too-contemporary tune of 'Mr Music', 'Science Of Love' and 'Fame (The Game)'. An artist is entitled to keep up with the times and adopt new styles whilst keeping their own distinctive style and approach to their music. This will encourage younger fans to explore the music of Donna Summer. Most long-term fans agreed that the production flowed together nicely and Summer herself seemed content with it.

Summer had said the album would be marketed as 'pure Donna Summer'. It's a jukebox full of different styles of music; put in your coin and play whatever suits your mood. The BBC gave a positive review of the album and agreed that Summer had delivered a good performance with all tracks 'given a 2008 sheen', even though it had taken her seventeen years to release an album of originals:

'Summer is keen to prove that she is no disco relic: hers is the world of *American Idol* and the contemporary charts ... it owes more to her golden Casablanca era as opposed to her last recorded work as the 1980s became the 1990s. Although her record company wanted an album of covers, Summer surprised them by her desire to record original material ...'

Thankfully, Summer turned down the suggestion of an album of cover songs, a pop 'American song book'! Fresh new material was vital to re-establish Summer as a modern and productive artist. Many mature and established acts decide to produce albums of standards or covers. Rod Stewart surprised fans with 'The Great American Song Book' in 2002, continuing in the same vein until 2009. Others included Vanessa Williams with 'Everlasting Love' in 2005; Diana Ross with 'I Love You' in 2007 and Barry Manilow with 'The Greatest Songs Of The Seventies' in the same year. Manilow continued the concept, releasing 'The Greatest Songs Of The Eighties' in 2008. Sharleen Spiteri, the former lead vocalist from Texas, recorded her 'Movie Song Book' in 2010.

The concept of the cover album is not new. The idea was routine in the jazz, blues and easy listening market from the very beginning with stars such as Billie Holiday and Frank Sinatra to Diana Krall to Michael Buble making albums of 'standards'. Ella Fitzgerald had released many of the 'American Song Book' albums including 'Ella Fitzgerald Sings The Rodgers And Hart Song Book' (1956), '. . . Sings The George And Ira Gershwin Song Book' (1959) and '. . . Sings The Johnny Mercer Song Book' (1964). Interestingly, Johnny Mercer was the only lyricist that Fitzgerald saluted in her legendry song book projects. These classic recordings remain eternally popular.

Debate continues as to whether cover albums are a sign of declining creativity or a genuine attempt to remodel classic songs that the artist loves and so wants to reinterpret. In the world of jazz, this is not so much of an issue as the jazz classics are timeless. The issue is more relevant in the world of pop and rock; a lazy attempt to cash in on an existing song's success, or genuine artistic endeavour?

Gloria Gaynor believes that a record company may think the experienced star is out of touch with the young generation – or the record labels themselves are out of touch with the 'older' star's recent development.

Acts such as Summer, Manilow and Gloria Gaynor have never left the scene. Some acts are 'stuck' in a particular era but Summer has continually evolved and remained fresh and modern, while Gloria Gaynor has updated her work with the 'I Wish You Love' album. Gaynor noted that one way to develop a career is to take the best from the new generation and use the best from the old, combine the sounds and create something new. Donna Summer is now over sixty – but age is just a number!

In *A Change Is Gonna Come: Music, Race And The Soul Of America,* Craig Werner said that Summer primarily 'learned to sing in church'. The release of the 'novelty' international hit 'Love To Love You Baby' made her a singing sensation. Initially came the classic soft, sexy tones but then Summer later 'demonstrated her powerful voice and hard-edged blues sensibility' in 'Hot Stuff'. In his view, 'Bad Girls' and 'She Works Hard For The Money' were 'very wry comments on her own position as disco diva'.

Summer will no doubt continue to sing standards and 'covers'. She performs the standards during her live shows and in the studio but as yet, the idea of an album entirely made up of covers is not on the horizon. In an interview with Gregg Shapiro for *Windy City Times,* Summer said she would like to record a couple of Joni Mitchell's songs but only if she can bring her own style to them. Summer told the *Sacramento Observer* in 'Disco Queen Is Just An Ordinary Girl' that she was a fan of Joni Mitchell and had all her albums. If Summer ever agreed to the idea and released a covers album or an 'American Song Book' project, it would surely be a hit.

Reviews of her live performances of covers and standards have been positive. As early as the 1970s, an article in *Vibes* magazine said:

'Donna sang "My Man" and an exciting version of "Lady Is A Tramp". Her show-stopping version of "A Song For You" firmly places her in the top female vocalist category as opposed to female disco artist ...'

It also comes down to the creativity of acts and labels. But standards do not always need a facelift, as they are often perfect in their original form. Over-engineering or updating the original sound can sometimes spoil great songs.

Bryan Ferry is famed for his albums of cover songs, made in parallel with his work with Roxy Music and his original solo work. 'Taxi' (1993) was a series of reworked US classics, made over in Ferry's classic style with immense attention to detail and flawless production. 'As Time Goes By' (1999) remained exactly faithful to the original sound of the 1920s, 1930s and 1940s. Jody Watley released 'The Makeover', a series of experimental covers, including reworkings of her own past hits. Creative, full of stunning soulful electronic sound, it was welcomed by music fans. Artists like Ferry and Watley don't simply cover a song; they essentially make it their own.

For the 2008 project, Summer insisted on recording entirely new material to the delight of her fans and proved in the process that she was still 'Hot Stuff'! Summer co-wrote all the songs on the album and shared the credits with many creative forces (Greg Kurstin, Danielle Brisebois, Jonathan Rotem, Evan 'Kidd' Bogart, Meredith Wilson, Ziggy Marley, Toby Gad, Sebastian Arocha Morton, Al Kasha, Lester Mendez, Wayne Hector, Jamie Houston and Fred Kron).

There are many great tunes in 'Crayons': 'Mr. Music' has a trendy New Age feel, 'Crayons', featuring Ziggy Marley, is a fun and catchy reggae-influenced tune. 'The Queen Is Back' shows the star making 'fun' of herself. The song 'Sand On My Feet' has a country feel, 'Drivin' Down Brazil' introduces a Latin beat and 'Bring Down The Reign' portrays Summer behind the public persona. 'Be Myself Again' is a classic Summer ballad, beautiful and sentimental. 'Slide Over Backwards' is a must-hear for all music lovers; a blues-flavoured tune enhanced by Summer's vocal prowess.

Paul Gambaccini asserts that musically Summer flows with the trend but in terms of lyrical content, there is a problem. There has been a lot of change generally from Donna Summer's time. Since she made 'Love To Love You Baby' and 'Hot Stuff', children are becoming sexually aware at a much younger age than in the 1970s. That has a profound effect on pop music that no one talks about. This is the change of subject matter of lyrics. In the 1960s, the public listened to lots of songs that were looking forward to love and romance, full of beautiful compliments and words of commitment. The majority of popular music is bought by teenagers, and the public have to realise that the young buying market now have more sexual awareness. According to the BBC Three TV programme 'How Sex Works: Playing The Field' (16th January 2012), the average sixteen-year-old has lost their virginity. Possibly this has had an effect on the youngsters' lifestyle, including their relationship with music. Continuing with Paul Gambaccini's view, the songs that were talking about looking forward to love are now actually talking about sex in a way which older listeners find offensive because they are not used to the concept. The younger listeners are used to it; it's a part of their lives. Summer could not do that type of lyric. She will not make a record with raunchy lyrics about sexual experiences and practises, even though she wrote 'Love To Love You Baby'. Nowadays this is the exception rather than the rule. So Donna Summer became dated, not because she changed but because human behaviour changed. In Gambaccini's view:

'... pop music never goes back, it goes somewhere else. Songs with horrifying lyrics can be a no.1 song in the US. Unfortunately, young fans now see nothing wrong with productions that come with an 'explicit lyrics' sticker on the cover. However great Donna Summer is and how current her albums are, she will never be that type of act. Therefore the American star will never click with that type of audience.'

Summer may not need to appeal to fans of explicit lyrical content. Indeed if Summer needs to be 'in' with all types of listeners, then perhaps lyrics suitable to her age would win more fans. She still can record graphic lyrics if she wants to but prefers to use suggestion rather than overt description. Her 'Love To Love You Baby' Loverdose advert version says it all! Lyrics such as 'Come here rude boy, boy can you get it up'... 'Is you big enough' by Rihanna in 'Rude Boy' are definitely not for Summer! But Summer has been there and done that! There are many younger singers who do not record or write explicit lyrics but still achieve global fame. Summer targets a classier audience. 'Crayons' is elegantly produced and Summer 'rocks'! The lyrics and rhythm of 'Love To Love You Baby' have evolved into a more subtle and mature sound.

Daryl Easlea applauded the album in his review of 'Crayons' on bbc.co.uk:
'Summer is keen to prove that she is no disco relic ... Although it is far removed from her high-period Giorgio Moroder work, it's much better than even the die-hards could be expecting ... The planet seems to be ready for her. In the US, the album has debuted within the Top 20, and "I'm A Fire" has topped the dance charts. It's good to have her back, sounding quite so contemporary; or, at the very least, like an approximation of what Donna Summer sounding contemporary would sound like.'

In 'Donna Summer: It's Good To Be The Queen' (articles.cnn.com) by K.J. Matthews, Summer explained that she liked to create various sounds and tried not to categorise herself. She liked to think of herself as 'an instrument' that can deliver different tunes. Summer just tried 'to be true'; that is her 'mission'.

'Crayons' had a major impact in the US chart. At no.17 in Billboard Donna Summer became an inspiration and example for other acts. A senior star in the business in a chart dominated by younger names, Donna Summer has more achievements and experience compared to most! It may not be such an important issue for her to gain global chart success at this time in her career but frankly all you need is a Top 20 hit in the US. Summer's 2008 work presented her as an artistic movement. She covered all aspects of her musical journey, from the beginning of her career way back in her early European days. She is an actor after all. *Hair, Godspell,* and *The Me Nobody Knows* taught Summer not only how to sing but how to create music with a story within the songs that she writes and produces.

Mark Nubar Donikian from Hynogaja put it like this:
'In the 1970s, Donna Summer's music represented what was going on in the underground. In many ways, one could say her career was the blueprint that artists like Madonna would later build upon. Donna's music captured what was going on in the clubs and her socially conscious lyrics echoed the changing times in society. The 1980s marked a new side to her artistry – showing how much more diverse she is as a vocalist – and how much of a rock and roller she truly is, especially apparent on the track "Protection", written by ... Bruce Springsteen. Starting in the 1990s and continuing to this day, she's explored a variety of great styles and has toured continually – her catalogue has proved to be classic and enduring.'

Summer's music has evolved over time, her initial success with disco later being repeated with modern dance and electronic music. Summer and her team have been a successful creative force producing a stream of hit songs.

In the 1980s her sound changed to become more pop, New Wave and R&B flavoured. Although her fans continued to buy her records, they also began to explore the new sounds and new acts that were appearing. The 1990s were a smooth yet slow period for Summer's music, during which time she made a few interesting individual recordings. She returned to dance in the 1990s and continued this into the new millennium with a sound that was a mixture of pop and dance.

Summer once said to Elliot Mintz in a 1979 article for *Penthouse* titled 'A Candid Interview With Donna Summer':

'I sang a song, you bought my record, I got the money. That's the bottom line, and that's not cold. I sold a record, but I didn't sell my soul.'

That was over thirty years ago. In *Louis Walsh's Fast Track To Fame,* Walsh's advice about how to achieve success was simple; having a no.1 song, great tunes, endless drive, ambition and the capacity for hard work all lie at the heart of each successful entertainment act. Good promotion is also key to an artist's success. Walsh notes that acknowledging other artists achievements is a good way to improve one's career. It is also vital to respect and connect with die-hard fans after concerts and online. Allowing the fans to feel a connection is a good way to sustain an artist's popularity.

Music historian Michael Ochs said in a TV biography ('Biography', Weller/Grossman Production, A & E Television Network, USA 1995) of Summer produced by Ruben Norte, that Summer is a great song writer and exceptionally talented singer. Ochs believes it's rare to find an act that can deliver any style and Summer proved she can. Ian Shirley from *Record Collector* said that although Donna Summer had been under the radar a lot in recent years, especially in the UK, she still had a very devoted fan base worldwide. Shirley notes that in Summer's case, 'not being a slave to producers' is one key to her success and has helped to sustain her status as a respectable artist.

Paul Gambaccini says:

'Donna was the flagship star of a global movement. At the moment there's really only one pop star and that is Lady Gaga. Gone are the days where you would have The Beatles, Rolling Stones, all the Motown people and Bob Dylan, when you had an extraordinary number of people that were popular all over the world. There's a far greater tendency towards regional repertoire now. But Donna Summer was big news everywhere.'

The great songstress continues her work. Within two years of the release of 'Crayons', Summer delivered a new composition, 'To Paris With Love'. The material was created by Summer and her long-time musician friend Bruce Roberts, with the original version produced by Peter Stengaard. 'To Paris With Love' was also a tribute to Louis Vuitton. Summer told Ray Schweibert in an interview for *Atlantic City Weekly* that she had a long relationship with the luxury brand and was friends with 'several designers for the company'. The company had been kind to her family. *The Examiner* on 27th August 2010 wrote that the song was a fond tribute to the city that Summer loved. Summer and her songs were first welcomed in France in the early days of her recording career. Her idea was to release the song in the south of France but Bruce Roberts had a different agenda, aiming to market 'To Paris With Love' in the summer season globally.

In an article ('Disco Queen Donna Summer Includes New, Old Favorites In Lineup' by Examiner Staff Writer, 27th August 2010) Summer shared her experience of the European approach:

'The advantage of performing in Europe for many years before returning home is that the experience taught me my general outlook on fame. Americans want it right away, but Europeans have a more sober idea of fame. They look at it as a distant thing to achieve.'

On 28th October 2010, billboard.com featured a review of the song; Donna Summer said that when her fans listen to the melody of 'To Paris With Love', they can 'escape into that magic world'. Summer wanted to give her devotees 'something special and exciting' and her way of doing that was to deliver 'the glamour and allure of Paris' to her fans.

The original version has Summer's breathy vocal, reminiscent of her 1970s style, over an attractive electronic melody. The sexy, cool and classic 'chill out' song is the perfect soundtrack to the summer, transporting the listener to Paris where the morning breeze carries the scent of flowers through the warm air. The Wawa Extended, Craig C's Master Blaster and Mandy Club remixes resulted in high energy dance floor material.

A success, 'To Paris With Love' was Summer's 14th no.1 in the *Billboard* dance chart. Reviewed by Gary Trust in *Billboard*:

'Summer Reign: Donna Summer ... "To Paris With Love" rises 3 – 1. The renowned diva's chart-topping sum equals Beyonce's and trails only those of Madonna (40), Janet Jackson (19), Mariah Carey and Kristine W (15 each), dating to the chart's inception as a national ranking Aug. 28, 1976. Summer extends her record for longest span of Dance/Club Play Songs No.1s, having scored her first topper, "Four Seasons Of Love (all cuts)", 34 years ago next week.'

The original single remixes of 'To Paris With Love' were only available in digital format. The single, even though it received great reviews and a no.1 *Billboard* dance chart placing, wasn't noticed by most music fans. Few radio stations had a promotional copy and it went unnoticed around the world. The single was also available as 'To Paris With Love Vol. 2' on digital.

O'Mega Red, who featured Summer in 'Angel', said he is in love with her record 'To Paris With Love'. He commented that Summer's voice is timeless and she still has better vocals than any female singer out there today. A fan of her work, O'Mega Red enjoyed her earlier hits such as 'Love To Love You Baby', 'MacArthur Park', 'Last Dance', 'Bad Girls', 'State Of Independence' and 'She Works Hard For The Money' simply because 'they made her such a phenomenon'.

Summer continues to record. In March 2010, fans were thrilled to see Summer's live performance in Las Vegas at Mandalay Bay. The live album included the concert DVD *Hit Man Returns: Foster & Friends*.

The following email was received by me from one of the team at Warner Brothers Music, US (to spread the album news) on 18th February 2010:

'I work over at WBR with producer David Foster and his upcoming CD/DVD release ... which features Donna Summer. "Hit Man Returns" chronicles one sold out show in Las Vegas at Mandalay Bay with performances by Donna Summer, Earth Wind and Fire, Chaka Khan, Seal, Natalie Cole and more! Donna is featured performing "Last Dance" as well as an incredibly medley with Seal which includes "On The Radio", "Unbreak My Heart" and "Crazy."

The CD/DVD package comes out on March 1st but was wondering if you might be interested in posting this information and a link to our pre order for the product on your Donna Summer facebook page. I'm sure you guys would LOVE this package – Donna is incredible on it as per usual :) I've included some sample copy below. Let me know your thoughts. Thanks for any and all help Nik!'

As expected, she is at her best and fans will especially like the performance of 'Last Dance' on the DVD.

Dedicated fans are continually checking out the music press and Internet for news of her next project or appearance. Club DJs around the globe play her music on the dance floor and remixes of Summer's songs continue to be produced. Her music also gets regular airplay on radio stations everywhere. BBC Radio 2's popular playlist (19 January 2011 – 18 January 2012) included 'Love's Unkind', 'On The Radio' and 'I Feel Love': (to name three). In terms of Summer's music, her UK radio airplay for 2011, compiled by Radio Monitor data, places 'Hot Stuff' as the most popular track, with 14,135 airplays. 'I Feel Love' is at no.2 followed by 'Love's Unkind' whereas 'This Time I Know It's For Real' achieved no.4 and no.5 is 'No More Tears (Enough Is Enough)'. The writer Robert Dimery chose Summer's 'Love To Love You Baby', 'I Feel Love', 'Bad Girls', 'Hot Stuff', 'On The Radio', 'State Of Independence', 'She Works Hard For The Money' and 'Dinner

With Gershwin' to include in his 2010 book *1001 Songs You Must Hear Before You Die*.

Summer continues to write and compose with other musicians; fans can look forward to future solo and collaborative work all stamped with the unmistakable sound of Donna Summer.

18

Into The Future . . .

Her fans have shared the ups and downs of Donna Summer's career. She is a wife, mother and grandmother who remains an iconic presence on the music scene.

The critics that once predicted that Donna Summer would fade quickly when disco came to an end have been proven wrong. Although she no longer dominates mainstream music culture, Donna Summer manages to produce albums that seem to adapt to the newest music trends. Summer is a phenomenon; an international dance diva recognised around the world.

She is also an accomplished artist with successful exhibitions of her work under her belt, her best works including paintings *Jazzman*, *Hard For The Money* and *Faces Of Rio*. She is also a one-time actor having played parts the film *Thank God It's Friday* and the US TV sitcom *Family Matters*.

Donna Summer has received many awards and acknowledgements within the industry. March 18th 1992 had been declared as 'Donna Summer Day' by Los Angeles Mayor, Tom Bradley to celebrate the addition of her name to the 'Hollywood Walk Of Fame'. She was awarded an honorary doctorate in fine arts for work away from her musical territory by the University of Massachusetts, Boston, in honour of her achievements in helping her local community.

The First Lady Of Love also became the first black artist to be heavily promoted on MTV with a high-profile video of 'She Works Hard For The Money' in 1983.

Summer remains the first and only female act to achieve three consecutive no.1 double albums on the *Billboard* album chart with 'Live And More', 'Bad Girls' and 'On The Radio: Greatest Hits Volumes I & II'. Donna Summer was the first female recording star to have three no.1 hits single in one year. The US hits were 'Hot Stuff', 'Bad Girls' and the Barbara Streisand duet 'No More Tears (Enough Is Enough)'. When the category was created in 1997, she was the first artist to be awarded Best Dance Recording at the Grammy Awards for the single 'Carry On '97'.

Donna Summer's work has become collectable. In 1997, she was at no.198

in a poll of the Top 500 Collectable Artists by UK *Record Collector* magazine. Even though she fell to no.433 the following year, Summer managed to climb to no.331 by 1999. In April 2000 she was at no.322. Fanatical collectors spend their money on a duplicate album or single just because the sleeve cover is different, or will purchase a release from each of the countries it was marketed in. This extends to all official press photos and perhaps her artwork, such is the power of her music and personality.

The five-times Grammy Award winner and six-times American Music Awards winner has achieved three Platinum (two of the albums certified double Platinum) and eleven Gold albums, as well as three Platinum and twelve Gold singles in the US. In the UK, Donna Summer achieved nine Gold and three Silver albums and her singles received two Gold and four Silver awards. In Canada, Summer's albums have achieved three Platinum (two of the albums received double Platinum) and five Gold awards and her singles have obtained three Platinum and nine Gold awards. She has had thirteen Top 40 albums in both the US and the UK. Twenty of her singles reached the Top 40 in the US and twenty-nine in the UK. She has had countless more hits across the globe.

Billboard Book Of USA Top 40 Hits by Joel Whitburn lists all the singles that reached no.1 in the *Billboard* Top 40 in 1979. 'Hot Stuff' spent three weeks at no.1, 'Bad Girls' five weeks and 'No More Tears (Enough Is Enough)' two weeks.

In 1996, *The Guinness Book Of British Hit Singles* introduced by Mark Lamarr listed the 20,101 hits that charted in the forty-four years since its beginning in 1952 and based on its own 'sophisticated' points system 'I Feel Love' came in at no.58, an astonishing result! In 1998 'I Feel Love', 'MacArthur Park', 'Hot Stuff' and 'On The Radio' were included in the 1000 best-ever singles, published in the *Enclyclopedia Of Singles* written by Paul Du Noyer, in 1998. In the UK singles chart survey of time spent in the chart in one calendar year, Donna Summer came top in 1979 with a total of forty-six weeks in the chart! In *Billboard* magazine's fiftieth anniversary issue Donna Summer was ranked at no.24 in the Hot 100 Artists of All Time. In 2010, *The Virgin Book Of British Hit Singles Vol. 2* placed Donna Summer at no.44 out of 99 for Top Acts By Weeks On Chart with 299 weeks, a position shared with George Michael.

To many, Summer's songs remain timeless. From her musical theatre background and archetypal songs such as 'Can't Understand', 'Lady Of The Night', 'Love To Love You Baby', 'I Feel Love', 'Bad Girls', 'Dinner With Gershwin', 'The Queen Is Back' and 'To Paris With Love', Donna Summer continues to be a diva respected by the music industry and fans worldwide.

She made 'Could It Be Magic', 'MacArthur Park', 'State Of Independence' and 'I Will Go With You (Con Te Partiro)' her own.

So far, 'I Feel Love' is the Summer track with the most weeks spent in the *Billboard* pop chart. 'She Works Hard For The Money' was the song that spent most time in the charts in the US in the 1980s, and in the 1990s it was 'I Will Go With You (Con Te Partiro)'. For the UK chart, the crown goes to 'Love's Unkind' and 'No More Tears (Enough Is Enough)' from Summer's disco days. 'This Time I Know It's For Real' without a doubt propelled her career in a huge way in the 1980s and 'I Feel Love '95' and 'State Of Independence '96' brought Donna Summer back into vogue in 1990s.

Summer the songstress may be notable for her up-tempo tunes but her ballads 'Winter Melody' and 'The Woman In Me' have had fair success in the pop chart. A brief survey online by me from the tribute Donna Summer Facebook group and during the interview of this project indicated that no.1 'MacArthur Park', no.2 'I Feel Love', no.3 a tie between 'Could It Be Magic' and 'On The Radio' were the fans' favourites. On 30th January 2006, *Slant* magazine placed three of Donna Summer's hits in their 100 Greatest Dance Songs with 'I Feel Love' at no.1, 'Love To Love You Baby' at no.10 and 'MacArthur Park' at no.46.

In 2008, Summer talked to *HBC Nightline Playlist* (for *ABC News*) about her favourite tracks by other artists, including 'I Found The Answer, I Learned To Pray' by Mahalia Jackson, 'I Will Survive' by Gloria Gaynor, 'Take A Piece Of My Heart' by Janis Joplin, 'What's Going On' by Marvin Gaye and 'Hero' by Mariah Carey.

The most obvious marker of her stardom and success are albums sales. In total, Summer's albums generally do better in the US than in the UK. In the US, 'Live And More' (seventy-five weeks in the chart) is the most successful from her disco era. The 'Donna Summer' album (thirty-seven weeks in the chart) was the longest time spent in the chart after her departure from disco. As for the 1990s, the 'VH1 Presents: Live & More Encore!' (thirteen weeks) stole the crown. The UK enjoyed the concept of having songs from various eras in 'I Remember Yesterday' and 'Bad Girls' which spent the longest time in the UK chart in the 1970s (twenty-three weeks). In the 1980s, 'Another Place And Time' (twenty-eight weeks) brought Donna Summer back into the limelight globally! The 1990s was a time to look back on all the hits, with the release of 'The Best Of Donna Summer', which, at nine weeks, was the Summer album that spent most time in the UK charts for that decade.

Publicity and promotion are critical to success. For 'The Journey: The

Very Best Of Donna Summer', the star featured live on a UK TV show celebrating the disco era and took part in a signing session at a record store in London. This helped the album enter the UK Top 10 album chart. When 'Crayons' was marketed, she appeared live on *American Idol* promoting the single 'Stamp Your Feet', a successful marketing strategy that saw the album enter the *Billboard* Top 20 chart.

However, Donna Summer's most successful albums remain her 1970s productions. Her Top 10 most successful releases worldwide include three of her 1980s albums; 'Bad Girls', 'On The Radio: Greatest Hits Volumes I & II', 'I Remember Yesterday', 'Love To Love You Baby', 'Live And More', 'A Love Trilogy', 'The Wanderer', 'Once Upon A Time', 'Donna Summer' and 'She Works Hard For The Money'. When I asked fans to choose their favourite albums in a brief survey carried out for my Donna Summer Facebook Group it was not intentionally for this manuscript. It took place early in the first year of the group's formation in 19th October 2007, to welcome members and get them involved and active in the discussion page (former setting) of Facebook. It was during this endeavour that the research evolved to another level. Results gained from the survey have been included with the interview findings. What a thrill to see her admirers vote the 1970s 'Bad Girls' as their favourite. Summer moved away from disco in the 1980s and it was said by some critics that 'The Wanderer' was a let down! After over thirty years, her fans have proved this wrong by voting the album their favourite from that decade. No surprises that the fans' choices for the 1990s are 'I'm A Rainbow' (marketed in 1996), 'Christmas Spirit' and 'VH1 Presents: Donna Summer Live & More Encore!'

Summer has recorded, contributed and performed live with major acts in her career. She even appeared in Frank Sinatra's video for 'LA Is My Lady'. Summer has worked with, amongst others, Liza Minnelli, Gene Simmons, Kenny Rogers, Joss Stone, Chaka Khan, Gloria Estefan, Seal and the jazz sensation Ella Fitzgerald.

Her most outstanding collaboration to date is undoubtedly 'No More Tears (Enough Is Enough)', a song that has been recorded in three different decades! In 1979 with Barbra Streisand, twenty years later in 1999 it was recorded live with Australian star Tina Arena, then a studio version in 2004 with Westlife.

In the 2007 book compiled by Dave McAleer, *Hit Singles: Top 20 Charts From 1954 To The Present Day*, 'I Feel Love' was at no.36 for the Top 100 Singles 1954–2000.

'The Queen Of Disco' could also be called 'The Queen Of Conceptual' if you look at the numbers of concept albums released by Summer in her heyday ('Once Upon A Time', 'I Remember Yesterday', 'On The Radio: Greatest Hits Volumes I & II'), concepts that will no doubt influence many other acts in the future.

Summer's voice is versatile; her performances and recordings have included a huge variety of music. The slow 'Mimi's Song', a tribute to her daughter, at a high-profile charity concert A Gift Of Song; The Music For UNICEF, 'Reunited' with Kenny Rogers and also Barbra Streisand's hit 'Papa Can You Hear Me' at the 56th Academy Awards show. Summer sang the wonderful 'The Girl From Ipanema' for her 'Live In Brazil' 1993 show. Summer also contributed significantly to the world of R&B. To date, twelve of her albums and eighteen of her singles reached the Top 20 in the *Billboard* R&B chart. Summer has also revisited her earliest musical roots with 'I Believe In Jesus', 'Forgive Me' and a duet with Darwin Hobbs 'When I Look Up'.

Summer began sharing her voice at an early age. She and her siblings entertained friends and others in her child neighbourhood.

Donna Summer wrote about the advice given to her by her mother in her autobiography:

'My mother used to tell me, If you have a gift, you have to share it, and whatever you share will come back to you thirty-, sixty-, even a hundred-fold. We shared our gift of singing with anyone who would listen.'

In Kevin Koffler's article 'Donna Summer Speaks Out On AIDS, Gays And Coming Out Of Exile' she said:

'I learnt that everything that brings you success does not bring you joy. It was a hard lesson to learn, because when I was young, I equated success with happiness. For me, success means work.'

Summer has truly achieved the title *diva*. She arrived on the international scene with a bang and through all the highs and lows of her career, she continued to produce music and adapt to the changes in musical tastes and styles, always maintaining her own strong vision and identity. She embraced religion and had her thoughts misquoted and misinterpreted, leading to some fans turning their backs on her. No star can avoid controversy completely and Donna Summer has had her fair share. The German release of 'The Hostage' was taken off air following the kidnap of a German politician but still achieved success. 'Love To Love You Baby' created a whole new style of music, but was banned by some radio stations because of its content!

At the BBC Radio 1 session (12th November 1994), promoting the 'Endless Summer: Donna Summer's Greatest Hits' compilation Summer, accompanied by her husband Bruce Sudano, talks about Mother Teresa. She is asked who she would make a Saint, and she answers Mother Teresa.

Her brother-in-law (a priest) organised the meeting. She had the privilege to spend a day with the late Mother Teresa in New York at several homeless shelters – they even had lunch together. Summer subsequently described the experience as 'interesting' and 'powerful', discussing the 'humanity' and 'spiritual experience' in a UK interview.

Re-issues of her albums continue on a regular basis and numerous compilations have been released as greatest hit packages. Some of Summer's 1970s hits were re-released in their original twelve inch format, these singles are available for the very first time on CD and, on a visit to a major record store, especially online retail, you are likely to find all her major releases from 1974 to the present day.

In *She Bop: The Definitive History Of Women In Rock, Pop And Soul,* Lucy O'Brien claims that Donna Summer played a crucial part in the music movement with her disco songs; she was the first to popularise the twelve inch single format in the 1970s.

Summer refused to sing 'Love To Love You Baby' in the 1980s, but now she is happy to do so. The song's seductive sound was described in *She Bop: The Definitive History Of Women In Rock, Pop And Soul* as:

'. . . the surreal, sensual sound of a woman's orgasm locked . . . into a hypnotic synthesized beat . . . set a completely new tone for female pop.'

Summer's work acts as a continuing inspiration to other artists. The iconic 'I Feel Love' is one song that has continually evolved and inspired other artists. In the Get Happy section of *1000 Songs To Change Your Life* (Time Out Guides), Peter Shapiro establishes that the most important Euro-disco records were 'Love To Love You Baby' and 'I Feel Love'.

'Once Upon A Time' LaDonna Adrian Gaines flew away to say hello to 'Virgin Mary' and returned home as 'Donna Summer', waving to all her 'Friends Unknown' as she said 'Love To Love You Baby' and was crowned 'The Queen Of Disco'. The one-time Crow now has over forty years of experience within the entertainment world!

The success of Summer's future releases is unpredictable. So many factors are involved – the artist, the management, the marketing and the record label – THE TEAM! To her dedicated followers, just having the chance to listen to her new compositions is enough. But to see the work recognised by the critics and public at large brings an extra level of satisfaction and a sense of pride in their icon.

Various media figures and fans may think Donna Summer is underrated as a singer but the fact is that she has achieved far more than most other stars within the business and in her very own way. Donna Summer is indeed a 'fire', and she has swept through the world of popular music.

Having conducted extensive research for this endeavour it is clear to me that Donna Summer is held in high regard by the industry. Understandably her success in the 1970s has somewhat overshadowed her subsequent work in the 1980s and 1990s, periods when she produced some outstanding work. As previously discussed, Summer's profile in the music world became pretty low key from the mid nineties. This was perhaps the result of a combination of a desire to take a break from the business and have a 'normal' life, but also possibly because her vision of where she thought she should be as an artist did not coincide with that of the record company. Whatever the reasons, Summer's artistic journey will continue to electrify music fans. She has evolved her talent to keep pace with an ever-changing musical landscape and she continues to move forward positively. Her music and lyrics are enriched by her long experience in the world of the musical artist. Her rich and varied musical history, the people she has met and worked with and the highs and lows of an amazing career all combine to ensure that Summer continues to mature as an artist.

Her first solo performance of the gospel song 'I Found The Answer, I Learned To Pray' brought joy to the Parker Hill Avenue household and the church audiences. Summer's journey had begun and her ambition to become a singer came true beyond her wildest dreams.

Her 'Melody Of Love' will continue to light up people's lives.

The song 'My Life' says it all:

'. . . I used to dream of going far . . . Dreams come true, for those that dream . . .'

Dr. Donna Summer, or may I say Mrs. Sudano, thank you.

Evolution.

The Thrill Goes On!

UK Singles Chart (Longest Weeks)

Note: Chart number besides the year is the highest position held.

1)	This Time I Know It's For Real	14 weeks	1989 no.3
2)	Love's Unkind	13 weeks	1977 no.3
	No More Tears (Enough Is Enough)	13 weeks	1979 no.3
3)	Unconditional Love	12 weeks	1983 no.14
4)	I Feel Love	11 weeks	1977 no.1
	Love Is In Control (Finger On The Trigger)	11 weeks	1982 no.18
	State Of Independence	11 weeks	1982 no.14
	Dinner With Gershwin	11 weeks	1987 no.13
5)	Down, Deep Inside (Theme from *The Deep*)	10 weeks	1977 no.5
	MacArthur Park	10 weeks	1978 no.5
	Hot Stuff	10 weeks	1979 no.11
	Bad Girls	10 weeks	1979 no.14
	I Feel Love '82	10 weeks	1982 no.21
6)	Love To Love You Baby	09 weeks	1976 no.4
	I Love You	09 weeks	1977 no.10
	Dim All The Lights	09 weeks	1979 no.29
	I Don't Wanna Get Hurt	09 weeks	1989 no.7
7)	Rumour Has It	08 weeks	1978 no.19
	Last Dance	08 weeks	1978 no.51
	Heaven Knows	08 weeks	1978 no.34
	She Works Hard For The Money	08 weeks	1983 no.25
8)	Could It Be Magic	07 weeks	1976 no.40
	I Remember Yesterday	07 weeks	1977 no.14
	Back In Love Again	07 weeks	1977 no.29
9)	Winter Melody	06 weeks	1977 no.27
	On The Radio	06 weeks	1980 no.32
	The Wanderer	06 weeks	1980 no.48
	Love's About To Change My Heart	06 weeks	1989 no.20

10) Sunset People	05 weeks	1980 no.46
I Feel Love '95	05 weeks	1995 no.8
State Of Independence '96	05 weeks	1996 no.13

US Singles Chart (Longest Weeks)

Note: Chart number besides the year is the highest position held.

1) I Feel Love	23 weeks	1977 no.6
2) Hot Stuff	21 weeks	1979 no.1
Last Dance	21 weeks	1978 no.3
Dim All The Lights	21 weeks	1979 no.2
She Works Hard For The Money	21 weeks	1983 no.3
3) Bad Girls	20 weeks	1979 no.1
The Wanderer	20 weeks	1980 no.3
MacArthur Park	20 weeks	1978 no.1
4) Heaven Knows	19 weeks	1979 no.4
5) Love To Love You Baby	18 weeks	1975 no.2
Love Is In Control (Finger On The Trigger)	18 weeks	1982 no.10
6) On The Radio	17 weeks	1979 no.5
This Time I Know It's For Real	17 weeks	1989 no.7
5) The Woman In Me	16 weeks	1982 no.33
6) No More Tears (Enough Is Enough))	15 weeks	1979 no.1
7) There Goes My Baby	14 weeks	1984 no.21
8) Cold Love	12 weeks	1980 no.33
9) I Love You	11 weeks	1977 no.37
Walk Away	11 weeks	1980 no.36
Who Do Think You're Foolin'	11 weeks	1981 no.40
Dinner With Gershwin	11 weeks	1987 no.48
9) Winter Melody	10 weeks	1976 no.43
State Of Independence	10 weeks	1982 no.41
10) Rumour Has It	09 weeks	1978 no.53
I Will Go With You (Con Te Partiro)	09 weeks	1999 no.79

UK Albums Chart (Longest Weeks)

Note: Chart number besides the year is the highest position held.

1) Another Place And Time	28 weeks	1989 no.17
2) I Remember Yesterday	23 weeks	1977 no.3
Bad Girls	23 weeks	1979 no.23
3) On The Radio: Greatest Hits Volumes I & II	22 weeks	1979 no.24
4) The Greatest Hits Of Donna Summer	18 weeks	1977 no.4
5) Live And More	16 weeks	1978 no.16
Donna Summer	16 weeks	1982 no.13
6) Once Upon A Time	12 weeks	1977 no.24
7) A Love Trilogy	10 weeks	1976 no.41
8) Love To Love You Baby	09 weeks	1975 no.16
The Best Of Donna Summer	09 weeks	1990 no.24
9) The Journey: The Very Best Of Donna Summer	06 weeks	2004 no.6
10) She Works Hard For The Money	05 weeks	1983 no.28

US Albums Chart (Longest Weeks)

Note: Chart number besides the year is the highest position held.

1) Live And More	75 weeks	1978 no.1
2) Once Upon A Time	58 weeks	1977 no.26
3) Bad Girls	49 weeks	1979 no.1
4) I Remember Yesterday	40 weeks	1977 no.18
5) On The Radio: Greatest Hits Volumes I & II	39 weeks	1979 no.1
6) Donna Summer	37 weeks	1982 no.20
7) She Works Hard For The Money	32 weeks	1983 no.9
8) Love To Love You Baby	30 weeks	1975 no.11
9) Four Seasons Of Love	29 weeks	1976 no.29
10) A Love Trilogy	27 weeks	1976 no.21

Fans' Favourite Songs – Brief Online And Interview Survey

1)	MacArthur Park	1978
2)	I Feel Love	1977
3)	Could It Be Magic	1976
	On The Radio	1979
4)	Love To Love You Baby	1975
5)	Try Me, I Know We Can Make It	1976
	Hot Stuff	1979
	Bad Girls	1979
	This Time I Know It's For Real	1989
6)	Last Dance	1978
7)	Love's Unkind	1977
	No More Tears (Enough Is Enough)	1979
	Dinner With Gershwin	1987
8)	Now I Need You	1977
	State Of Independence	1982
	She Works Hard For The Money	1983
	I Will Go With You (Con Te Partiro)	1999
9)	Spring Affair	1976
	Summer Fever	1976
	I Remember Yesterday	1977
	Take Me	1977
	Rumour Has It	1977
	On My Honour	1979
	Lucky	1979
	Sunset People	1979
	Dim All The Lights	1979
	I'm Free	1984
	The Power Of One	2000
	All Systems Go	1987
	Love On And On (original recording)	1998
	The Queen Is Back	2008

Fans' Favourite Albums –
Brief Online And Interview Survey

1)	Bad Girls	1979
2)	Live And More	1978
3)	Four Seasons Of Love	1976
	Once Upon A Time	1977
	The Wanderer	1980
4)	Donna Summer	1982
	Cats Without Claws	1984
5)	A Love Trilogy	1976
	I Remember Yesterday	1977
	On The Radio: Greatest Hits Volumes I & 11	1979
	Another Place And Time	1989
	Crayons	2008
6)	I'm A Rainbow	1981 (1996)
	All Systems Go	1987
	Christmas Spirit	1994
	VH1 Presents: Live & More Encore!	1999
7)	She Works Hard For The Money	1983
	Mistaken Identity	1991
8)	Love To Love You Baby	1975

BBC Radio 2 Airplay 2011

Donna Summer Airplay Report BBC Radio 2
Wed 19th Jan 2011 - Wed 18th Jan 2012

1) Love's Unkind
2) On The Radio
3) I Feel Love
4) No More Tears (Enough Is Enough)
5) Last Dance
6) State Of Independence
7) This Time I Know It's For Real
8) Heaven Knows
9) Hot Stuff
10) MacArthur Park
11) Love To Love You Baby
12) I Remember Yesterday
13) Love's About To Change My Heart
14) The Woman In Me
15) Bad Girls
16) Could It Be Magic
17) Winter Melody
18) Dinner With Gershwin

Complete UK Radio Airplay 2011

Donna Summer Airplay Saturday 01 January – Saturday 31 December 2011
Radio Monitor Data

Artist	Title	Plays
	All Titles	**37,270**
Donna Summer	Hot Stuff	14,135
Donna Summer	Love's Unkind	4,699
Donna Summer	I Feel Love	4,167
Donna Summer	This Time I Know It's For Real	4,409
Donna Summer & Barbra Streisand	No More Tears (Enough Is Enough)	1,533
Donna Summer	On The Radio	1,879
Donna Summer	State Of Independence	861
Donna Summer	Last Dance	106
Donna Summer	Heaven Knows	26
Donna Summer	MacArthur Park	867
Donna Summer	I Remember Yesterday	618
Donna Summer	Bad Girls	1,824
Donna Summer	She Works Hard For The Money	622
Donna Summer	Love's About To Change My Heart	45
Donna Summer	Could It Be Magic	46
Donna Summer	Winter Melody	209
Donna Summer	Love To Love You Baby	169
Donna Summer	Dinner With Gershwin	623
Donna Summer	The Woman In Me	2
Donna Summer	Love Is In Control (Finger On The Trigger)	145
Donna Summer	I Don't Wanna Get Hurt	186
Donna Summer	Down Deep Inside	55
Donna Summer	Back In Love Again	8
Donna Summer	Dim All The Lights	14
Donna Summer	Unconditional Love	9
Donna Summer	The Wanderer	13
Donna Summer	Working The Midnight Shift	–

Discography: Global Release

A) Studio Recordings

1974 Lady Of The Night
1975 Love To Love You Baby
1976 A Love Trilogy
1976 Four Seasons Of Love
1977 I Remember Yesterday
1977 Once Upon A Time
1979 Bad Girls
1980 The Wanderer
1981 I'm A Rainbow (Unreleased)
1982 Donna Summer
1983 She Works Hard For The Money
1984 Cats Without Claws
1987 All Systems Go
1989 Another Place And Time
1991 Mistaken Identity
1994 Christmas Spirit
1996 I'm A Rainbow
1999 Christmas Spirit
2003 Bad Girls Deluxe Edition
2005 20th Century Masters – The Christmas Collections:
        The Best Of Donna Summer
2008 Crayons

B) Live Recording

1978 Live And More
1983 A Blue Live Lady
1999 VH1 Presents: Donna Summer Live & More Encore!
2008 Live From New York

C) Compilations With New Studio Or New Remix Tracks

1979 On The Radio: Greatest Hits Volumes I & 11
1993 The Donna Summer Anthology
1994 Endless Summer: Donna Summer's Greatest Hits
1995 Greatest Hits
2000 Remixed And Early Greats
2003 The Journey: The Very Best Of Donna Summer
          (Limited Edition Bonus CD)
2004 The Journey: The Very Best Of Donna Summer
          (Limited Edition Bonus CD)
2005 Gold

D) Single Special Projects

1971 Sally Go 'Round The Roses (as Donna Gaines)
1972 If You Walkin' Alone (as Donna Gaines)
1974 Denver Dream
1975 Virgin Mary
1982 I Feel Love '82 Patrick Cowley Remix
1995 I Feel Love '95
1996 State Of Independence 1996
1997 Carry On '97 (Donna Summer & Giorgio Moroder)
1998 Carry On '98 (Donna Summer & Giorgio Moroder)
2003 I Got Your Love
2010 To Paris With Love

E) Soundtracks With New Studio Tracks

1968 *Haare*
1971 *The Me Nobody Knows*
1971 *Ich Bin Ich*
1972 *Godspell*
1977 *The Deep*
1978 *Thank God It's Friday*
1980 *Foxes*
1982 *Fast Time At Ridgemont High*
1983 *Flashdance*
1996 *Let It Be Me* (Unreleased)
1996 *Daylight*
2000 *Naturally Native*
2000 *Pokemon The Movie 2000: The Power Of One*

F) Various Artist Special Projects With New Tracks Or New Remixed Tracks

1973   The Veith Marvos Red Point Orchestra
1978   A Gift Of Song: Music For UNICEF
1982   Disco Round 2
1989   Spirit Of The Forest
1993   Tribute To Edith Piaf
1994   Grammy's Greatest Moments; Vol. 1
1994   Earthrise: The Rainforest Album
1996   One Voice
1996   Mouse House; Disney's Dance Mixes
1998   Disney's Greatest Pop Hits; A Decade Of Radio Singles
1999   Sing Me To Sleep Mommy
1999   The Today Show Presents: The Best Of Summer Concerts Series
1999   Child Of The Promise
2000   Another Rosie Christmas
2000   The Mercy Project
2001   Keeping The Dream Alive
2004   Discomania
2005   So Amazing: An All-Star Tribute To Luther Vandross
2005   Songs From The Neighbourhood
2005   Night Of The Proms
2011   Hit Man Returns; David Foster & Friends

G) Guest Recordings

1976   Tom Winter: Troublemaker
1977   Brooklyn Dreams: Brooklyn Dreams
1977   Paul Jabara: Shout Out
1978   Gene Simmons: Gene Simmons
1979   Paul Jabara: The Third Album
1980   Brooklyn Dreams: I Won't Let Go
1981   Bruce Sudano: Fugitive Kind
1983   Musical Youth: Different Style
1992   Giorgio Moroder: Forever Dancing
1994   Liza Minnelli: Gently
1998   Peter Thomas: Moon Flowers & Mini-Skirts
2000   Darwin Hobbs: Vertical
2007   Dave Koz: At The Movies
2012   O'Mega Red: Angel

H) Compilations

1977	Star Collection
1977	Greatest Hits
1977	Disco Queen
1978	The Best Of
1977	The Greatest Hits Of Donna Summer
1977	Star Gold
1978	Lo Mejor De Donna Summer Vol. 1
1978	Lo Mejor De Donna Summer Vol. 2
1979	On The Radio Greatest Hits Vol. I
1979	On The Radio Greatest Hits Vol. II
1980	Walk Away; The Best Of 1977–1980 Collectors Edition
1984	The Box
1985	The Summer Collection
1987	The Dance Collection; A Compilation Of 12-inch Singles
1989	12-inchers
1991	The Best Of Donna Summer
1991	The Complete Hits Collection
1991	Donna Summer; Best
1991	The Dance Collection
1993	This Time I Know It's For Real 16 Classic Tracks
1994	Donna Summer Retrospective
1994	The Complete Donna Summer
1997	Master Series
1998	Donna Summer Greatest Hits
1999	Millennium Edition
1999	The Universal Masters Collection Classic
2001	Greatest Hits 2001
2003	The Millennium Collection: The Best of Donna Summer
2003	Les Legendes Du Disco: Donna Summer & Diana Ross
2003	The Ultimate Collection
2003	20th Century Masters; The Millenium Collection
2004	The Journey: The Very Best Of Donna Summer
2005	The Universal Masters Collection
2005	Chronicles
2006	20th Century Masters: The Best Of Donna Summer
2007	20th Century Masters: The Best Of Donna Summer
2009	Classic
2009	Best Selection

I) Videography

1979   A Hot Summer Night
1985   A Hot Summer Night With Donna Summer
1994   Endless Summer: The Donna Summer's Greatest Hits
1999   VH1 Presents: Donna Summer Live & More Encore!
2000   Manhattan Centre
2004   20th Century Masters: The Best Of Donna Summer
       The DVD Collection
2004   Donna Summer Live At Manhattan Centre
2005   She Works Hard For The Money
2005   Eternal Summer
2006   Donna Summer
2007   In Concert
2008   Disco Queen
2009   Live From New York

Bibliography

Books

Almond, Marc, (1999), *Tainted Life: The Autobiography*. London: Macmillan Publishers Ltd.

Ball, Philip, (2010), *The Music Instinct*. London: The Bodley Head.

Benedetti, Alessandro; Moroder, Giorgio, (2009), *Extraordinary Records*. UK: Taschen.

Betts, Graham, (2004), *Complete UK Hit Albums 1956–2005*. UK: Collins.

Black, Johnny; Brend, Mark; Heatley, Michael; Jerome, Thomas; Morrish, John; Rooksby, Rikky; Simons, David, (2006), *Albums: The Stories Behind 50 Years Of Great Recordings*. UK: Backbeat Books.

Black, Johnny; Brend, Mark, (2006), *Singles: Six Decades Of Hot Hits And Classic Cuts*. UK: Outline Press Ltd.

Collin, Robert, (1993), *Het Belgisch Hitboek 1954–1993 40 Jaar Hits In*. Vlaanderen: Colofon.

Crampton, Luke; Ress, Dafydd, (2010), *MTV Pop And Rock World Records 2011*. UK: Carlton.

Echols, Alice, (2010), *Hot Stuff: Disco And The Remaking Of American Culture*. New York: W.W. Norton & Company, Inc.

Eddy, Chuck, (1997), *The Accidental Evolution Of Rock 'n' Roll*. New York: Da Capo Press.

Elborough, Travis, (2009), *The Long-Player Goodbye: The Album From Vinyl To IPod And Back Again, London, UK*. Sceptre.

Frith, Simon; Straw, Will; Street, John, (2001), *The Cambridge Companion To Pop And Rock*. UK: Cambridge University Press.

Gambaccini, Paul; Rice, Tim; Rice, Jo, (1988), *The Guinness Book Of British Hit Albums: Third Edition*. London: Guiness Publishing Ltd.

Gregory, Hugh, (1991), Soul Music A-Z. New York: Sterling Publishing Co. Inc./ (1998), *A Century Of Pop*. UK: Hamlyn.

Hardy, Phil; Laing, Dave; Bernard, Stephen; Perretta, Don, (1987), *Encyclopedia Of Rock*. Spain: Macdonald Orbis.

Harris, Larry, (2009), *And Party Every Day: The Inside Story Of Casablanca Records*. US: Backbeat Books.

Haskin, Jim; Stifle, J. M, (1983), *Donna Summer: An Unauthorised Biography*. Boston: An Atlantic Monthly Press Book.

Howard, Josiah, (2002), *Donna Summer: Her Life And Music*. US: Tiny Ripple Books.

Howes, Paul, (2007), *The Complete Dusty Springfield: Revised And Expanded Edition*. London: Reynolds And Hearn Ltd.

Johnstone, Nick, (1999), *Melody Maker History Of 20th Century Music*. UK: Bloomsbury.

Lamarr, Mark, (1996), The Guiness Book Of British Hit Singles. 11th Edition: Guiness Publishing Ltd. United Kingdom.

Larkin, Colin, (1993), *The Guinness Who's Who Of Fifties Music*, (1993), *The Guinness Who's Who Of Country Music*, (1993), *The Guiness Who's Who Of Soul Music*, (1995), *The Guinness Who's Who Of Blues*, (Second Edition). UK: Guinness Publishing Ltd./(2000), *The Virgin Encyclopedia Of Nineties Music*. UK: Virgin Publishing Ltd./(2002), *The Virgin Encyclopedia Of Seventies Music*, (Third Edition). UK: Muze UK Ltd. / (2007), *The Virgin Encyclopedia Of Popular Music*, (Fifth Edition). UK: Omnibus Press.

Lwin, Nanda, (1996), *The Canadian Singles Chart Book 1975–1996*. Canada: MDC Music Data Canada.

Marre, Jeremy; Charlton, Hannah, (1985) *Beats Of The Heart: Popular Music Of The World*. London: Pluto Press.

McAleer, Dave, (2007), *Hit Singles: Top 20 Charts From 1954 To The Present Day*, (Sixth Edition). UK: Carlton Brooks Ltd.

Miller, Chuck, (2001), *American Records*. US: Krause Publications/(2001), *Warman's American Records 1950–2000: Identification And Price Guide*. US: Krause Publications.

Miller, Stephen, (2006), *Smart Blonde: Dolly Parton*. UK: Omnibus Press.

Moon, Tom, (2008), *1000 Records To Hear Before You Die: A Listener's Life List*. New York: Workman Publishing.

Morton, Andrew, (2001), *Madonna*. UK: Michael O'Mara Books Ltd.

Noyer, Paul Du, (1995), *The Virgin Story Of Rock 'n' Roll*. UK: Carlton Books Ltd./(1998), *Encyclopedia Of Singles*. UK: Dempsey Parr Books/(2006), *We All Shine On: The Stories Behind Every John Lennon Song 1970–1980*. UK: Carlton Books.

O'Brien, Lucy, (1995), *She Bop: The Definitive History Of Women In Rock, Pop And Soul*. UK: Penguin Books.

OCC, (2010), *The Virgin Book Of British Hit Singles Vol.2*. UK: Virgin Books.

Ochs, Michael, (1996), *1000 Record Covers*. Italy: Benedikt Tashen Verlag Gmbh.

O'Dair, Barbra, (1997), *The Rolling Stone Book Of Women In Rock: Trouble Girls.* New York: Random House.

Randall, Annie J, (2009), *Dusty: Queen Of The Postmods.* US: Oxford University Press USA.

Record Collector, (2010), *Record Collector Rare Record Price Guide 2012*, Eleventh Revised Edition. UK: Diamond Publishing.

Roach, Martin, (2008), *The Virgin Book Of British Hit Singles.* UK: Virgin Books/(2006, 2009), *Take That Now And Then: The Unofficial Illustrated Story.* UK: Harper Collins Publishers.

Routledge, (2005), *International Who's Who In Popular Music*, Seventh Edition. London: Routledge.

Sanjek, Russell, (1988), *American Popular Music And Its Business – The First Four Hundred Years 1900–1984 Vol III.* US: Oxford University Press.

Savage, Jon; Kureishi, Hanif (1995), *The Faber Book Of Pop.* London, Boston: Faber And Faber.

Scapolo, Dean, (1997), *New Zealand Music Charts 1966–1996 Singles.* New Zealand: IPL Books.

Seaman, Frederic, (1991), *John Lennon: Living On Borrowed Time – A Personal Memoir.* UK: Xanadu.

Shapiro, Peter, (2005), *Turn The Beat Around: The Secret History Of Disco.* London: Faber And Faber Limited, (2006) *The Rough Guide To Soul And R&B.* London: Rough Guides Ltd.

Sheppard, David, (2008), *On Some Faraway Beach: The Life And Times Of Brian Eno.* UK: Orion Books.

Shepherd, John; Horn, David; Laing, Dave; Oliver, Paul; Wicke, Peter, (2003), *Continuum Encyclopedia Of Popular Music Of The World: Vol. I.* UK: Continuum.

Shepherd, John; Horn, David; Laing, Dave, (2005), *Continuum Encyclopedia Of Popular Music Of The World: Vol. VII.* Europe: Continuum.

Sheridan, Simon, (2008), *The Complete Kylie.* UK: MPG Books Ltd.

Slooten, Johan Van, (1998), *Hit Dossier 1939–1998*, Seventh Edition. Becht: Haarlem.

Smith, Joe; Fink, Mitchell, (1989), *Off The Record: An Oral History Of Popular Music.* UK: Sidgwick & Jackson.

Smith, Sean, (2006), *Kylie: The Biography.* UK: Pocket Books.

Summer, Donna; Eliot, Marc, (2003), *Ordinary Girl: The Journey.* New York: Villard Books, Random House Publishing.

Taraborrelli, J. Randy, (2001), *Madonna: An Intimate Biography.* UK: Sidgwick & Jackson/(2007), *Diana Ross: An Unauthorised Biography.* London: Sidgwick & Jackson.

241

Taylor, Andy, (2008), *Wild Boy: My Life In Duran Duran*. UK: Orian Books.

Taylor, Paul, (1985), *Popular Music Since 1955: A Critical Guide To The Literature*. UK: Mansell Publishing Limited.

Time Out, (2008), *1000 Songs To Change Your Life*. London: Time Out Group Ltd.

Valentine, Penny; Wickham, Vicki, (2000), *Dancing With Demons: The Authorised Biography Of Dusty Springfield*. London: Hodder And Stoughton.

Vail, Ken, (1996), *Lady Day's Diary: The Life Of Billie Holiday 1937–1959*. UK: Castle Communications Plc.

Walsh, Louis, (2007), *Louis Walsh's Fast Track To Fame*. London: Bantam Press.

Warwick, Niel; Kutner, Jon; Brown, Tony, (2004), *The Complete Book Of The British Charts: Singles And Albums*, Third Edition. UK: Omnibus Press.

Wendt, Wille, (1993), *Topplistan – The Official Swedish Single And Album Charts 1975–1993*. Stockholm: Premium Publishing.

Werner, Craig, (2000), *A Change Is Gonna Come: Music, Race And The Soul Of America*. UK: Canongate Books Ltd.

Whitburn, Joel, (1990), *Billboard Hot 100 Charts: The Seventies*. US: Winsconsin/ (1991), *Billboard Hot 100 Charts: The Eighties*. US: Winsconsin/(2000), *Billboard Hot 100 Charts The Nineties*. US: Winsconsin/(1992), *The Billboard Book Of USA Top 40 Hits*, Fifth Edition. New York: Guinness Publications/(2006), *Joel Whitburn Presents Billboard Albums*, Sixth Edition. US: Winsconsin/(2006), *The Billboard Hot 100 Annual*, Seventh Edition. US: Winsconsin/(2007), *Joel Whitburn's Billboard Top Pop Singles 1955–2006*. US: Record Research.

Zero, Johnny, (2008), *An Essential Guide To Music In The 1970s*. UK: Parkbench Publications.

Journals/Periodicals/Newspapers/Internet

Adams, Ace, Inside The Record World Mini-Reviews, *Daily News*, (7 October 1977).

Album Artist 89 Donna Summer, Music, tsort.info

Argyropulo, Demitri, The Munich Machine; Disco Fever, *The History Of Rock*, (1984), issue 106, Volume 9, pp 2118–2120.

Bad Girls Deluxe Edition, *Blues & Soul*, (September 2003).

Baker, K.C. Surviving Depression, *People*, (9 June 2008).

Barbour, Matthew, Health: 24 Hours To Beat Depression, *The Sun*, (4 November 2010).

Behrens, Andy, Disco Demolation: Bell-Bottoms Be Gone! Espn, espnchicago.com, (12 July 2009).

Bell, Andy, Biography – The Early Days, www.andybell.com.

Blissett, Bella, Wigs, Work-outs And A Wonder Wardrobe: How Kelly Rowland Gets Her Fab Factor, MailOnline, (5 November 2011).

Bishop, Tom, In Tune With Britain's Disco King, *BBC News*, (29 September 2004).

Bond, Jennie, The Full Monarchy, BBC online, (13 November 1998).

Bonke, Johannes, Talking To The Prima Donna, *Electronic Beats*, (15 September 2009).

Bradley, Lloyd; Brown, Geoff; Chuck, Stevie; Elliott, Paul; Hutcheon, David; Male, Andrew; Savage, Jon; Trunk, Jonny; Waring, Charles; Wilson, Lois, Soul 70, *Mojo*, (September 2010), Issue 202.

Britt, Bruce, *Los Angeles Daily News* (October 1987).

Bronson, Fred, Endless Summer, *Billboard* (3rd September 1994).

Burnett, Richard, The Queen Is Back, (X)Press, ottawaxpress.ca, (10 December 2008).

Buskin, Richard, Giorgio Moroder: Electric Dreams, Sound On Sound, soundonsound.com, (March 1998).

Buskin, Richard, Donna Summer 'I Feel Love' Classic Tracks, Sound On Sound, soundonsound.com, (October 2009).

Buskin, Richard, Giorgio Moroder: Electric Dreams With Donna Summer, *Sound On Sound*, (March 1998).

Buston, Paul, Donna Summer: What's She Like? *Attitude*, (December 1994), pp 18–21.

Button, Simon, *The Sunday Express*, (13 June 2004).

Cane, Clay, The Queen Is Back, *Pride Source*, (21 August 2008).

Cardenas, Georgina, She Works Hard For The Love Of It, *Miami Music*, (May 1997).

Casablanca, Spring Into Summer: A Casablanca Record And Filmworks Production, *Billboard*, (21 May 1977).

Chang, Kee, Fashion, *Anthem Magazine*, (15 April 2009).

Cocks, Jay, Gaudy Reign Of The Disco Queen Still Tops In The Clubs, Donna Summer Wants A Wider Audience, *Time Magazine*, (4 December 1978).

Coon, Caroline, Donna Summer: Futuristic Space Drama And Old World Romance, *Melody Maker*, (9 July 1977).

Cridland, Nicole, Union Flash Mob Rallies Outside Prahran MP's Office, *Stonnington Leader*, (25 July 2011).

Dan, Bean, Juan Atkins Interview, bleep43.com, (4 October 2009).

Dayal, Geeta, Further Thoughts On '10 Ragas To A Disco Beat', Geeta Dayal, *theoriginalsoundtrack.com* (6 April 2010).

Dene, Lewis, Import Pressure, *Blues & Soul*, (17 Mar. 1998), No 761, pp 33–36.

Donna Summer Bad Girls Deluxe Edition, *Billboard*, (16 August 2003).

Easlea, Daryl, Donna Summer; Crayons, BBC Review, (13 June 2008).

Ellen, Barbara, Slipped Disco – Donna Summer May Have Slowed Her Pace, But The Beat Goes On, unknown newspaper, (26 March 1996).

Flick, Larry, A Benefit For The Gay Men's Health Crisis (GMHC) Carnegie Hall New York, *Billboard*, (16 March 1998).

Galloway, Scott, Disco Queen Is Just An Ordinary Girl, *Sacramento Observer*, (30 October 2003).

Gammell, Caroline, George Formby Lyrics Censored By The BBC, *The Telegraph*, (17 December 2007).

Gillet, Karen, Sonique: The Interview, BBC, (November 2003).

Gilmore, Mike, Is There Life After Disco? *Rolling Stone*, (23 March 1978).

Gollner, Adam Leith, Hero Donna Summer, The Disco Queen With The Religious Gift Thanks God, So Do We, *V Magazine*, (2006).

Grant, Kevin, Donna Summer News – Edition 2, Donna Summer Internet Zone, (26 May 1996), What Is The Donna Summer Internet Zone? Some History – Edition 4, Donna Summer Internet Zone, (20 July 1996).

Graustark, Barbara, The Long Hot Summer, *Newsweek*, (2 April 1979).

Grusvenor Jr, Charles R, Music From Commercials Of The Seventies, inthe70s.com, (1995–2010), Songs From The Eighties That Have Been In Commercials, Products Beginning With D, inthe80s.com, (1995–2010), Music From Commercials Of The 90s, inthe90s.com, (2000–2010).

Hawkins, Cathy, The Totally Unauthorized Donna Summer Tribute Site, (1997–2011), The Fans Have Spoken!!!! donna-tribute.com (1998).

Heroajex, Top 20 Greatest Love Songs, listverse.com,(22 September 2008).

Hilburn, Robert, Disco Derby Boots Some Long Shots Home, *Los Angeles Times*, (28 August, 1977)/Disco Diva Summer Proves Hot As Ever, *Los Angeles Times*, (7 August 1995).

Hill, Dave, Burning Up The Dance Floor With Donna Summer, Disco Fever, *The History Of Rock*, (1984), Issue 106, Volume 9, pp 2110–2112.

Hockney, Karen, Boogie Night: Diva Donna Summer Celebrates 70s In Style, UK TV Magazine (19 June 2004).

Holden, Stephen, Donna Summer's Hot-To-Trot 'Bad Girls', *Rolling Stone*, (12 July 1979).

Hoskyns, Barney, From Sex Goddess To Bad Girl To American Superwoman, *NME*, (18 December 1982), pp 22–23.

Huey, Steve, Donna Summer Biography, allmusic.com (2008).

Hunter, James, Bad Girls Deluxe Edition, *Rolling Stone*, (21 August 2003).

Kagan, Shel, Rock & Roll At The Summit: Superstars Of Rock Give A Concert For UNICEF, Circus Magazine, (13 February 1979), Cher, Donna, Village People – Disco Crossovers Make Good, *Circus Magazine*, (26 June 1979).

Kane, Kirsty, How Samatnha Fox And Marc Mysterio Want To Help Dance Music, beatport.com, (25 September 2009).

Kelly, Ray, Entertaiment News, Donna Summer Wins Big At Mohegan Sun Concert, masslive.com, (9 July 2008).

Keeps, David A, Pop View Disco's Born-Again Bad Girl, *New York Times*, (3 March 1996).

Kimberley, C, *South Africa Chart Book: Singles 1976–1989*, (May 1997).

Kimberley, C, *Zimbabwe Albums Chart Book July 1973–Dec 1998*, (December 1998)/*Zimbabwe Singles Chart Book Updated Version*, (November 2000).

Kinser, Jeremy, You Should Be Dancing, advocate.com, (19 July 2011).

Kurutz, Steve, VH1 Presents Live And More Encore! Reviews, *All Music Guide*, (1999).

Koffler, Kevin, Not The Last Dance; Donna Speaks Out On Aids, Gays And Coming Out Of Exile, *Advocate*, (4 July 1989).

Lacava, Jude, Phoenix Symphony Goes Back To The Days Of Disco, myfox-phoenix.com, (16 October 2010).

Larsen, Peter, Entertainment, Donna Summer Delights With Disco And More, *The Orange County Register*, (23 August 2008).

Lauderdale, Fort, Donna Summer Exclusive Interview. Bringing Her Summer Tour To Hard Rock Live On August 18, Contributor Report, allvoices.com, (29 July 2010).

Letteer, Tim, Producer/Remixer/DJ Tim Letteer Aka Trl – Bio, timletteer.com.

Leigh, Spencer, Unfit For Auntie's Airwaves: The Artists Censored By The BBC, *The Independent On Sunday*, (14 December 2007).

Lopresti, Theresa, Celebrity Feature, *Diamond Hard Music & Entertainment*, (July 1996).

Lorez, Jeff, Flower Power ! Jody Watley, *Blues & Soul*, (17 March 1998), No. 761, pp. 31–32.

Marlow, Wil, 'Disco's In Our DNA' Says Donna, icwales.co.uk (14 June 2004).

Marshall, Ben, Single Review: Donna Summer And Giorgia Moroder Carry On (Almighty). *The Guardian*, (27 June 1998).

Marsh, Dave, The Wanderer: A Rock & Roll Road Map Of Donna Summer's Soul, *Rolling Stone*, (19 March 1981).

Mattera, Adam, Donna Summer, *Attitude*, (August 2004), No 124, pp 36–39.

Matthews, K.J, Donna Summer: It's Good To Be The Queen, CNN International, (2008).

Mclean, Craig, Donna Summer: Too Hot To Handle, *The Telegraph*, (13 June 2008).

Mintz, Elliot, A Candid Interview With Donna Summer, *Penthouse*, (July 1979), pp 86–92.

Nathan, David, Donna Dinner Is Served, *Blues & Soul*, (13 October 1987), No 494, pp 10–12.

Novak, Ralph, All Systems Go: Donna Summer, *People Magazine* (26 October 1987).

Ollison, Rashid D, Sun Pop Music Critic Bad Girls Deluxe Edition, *The Sun*, (13 August 2003).

Pacheco, Patrick, The Sensuous Diva Of Sex Rock, *After Dark*, (April 1977).

Palmer, Robert, The Pop Life; Donna Summer Seen On Two Pop Music Videos, *The New York Times*, (26 September 1984).

Paoletta, Michael, Singer Summer Charting New 'Journey', *Billboard*, (25 October 2003).

Petridis, Alexis, Leaders Of The Banned, *The Guardian*, guardian.co.uk, (12 April 2002).

Rehoboth, Camp, Letters From Camp Rehoboth: Listen To The Music Catching Up With Donna Summer, (10 April 1998, donna-tribute.com/articles/98/camp.html).

Revoir, Paul, Revealed: The Less Than Shocking Classics The BBC Banned, dailymail.co.uk, (17 December 2007).

Rosen, Craig, On Nashville, Christmas, Barbra: An Image-Breaking Q & A, *Billboard*, (3 September 1994), pp 22–24.

Ruggieri, Melissa, Former Disco Queen Embarking On Yearlong Greatest-Hit Tour, *Music Times*, (27 February 1996).

Sanders, Charles L, Donna Summer Singer Talks About Her Love, Her Child, That Rumor, *Ebony*, (October 1977).

Savage, Jon, The 70 Best Soul Albums Of '70s! Soul 70, *Mojo*, (September 2010).

Scheck, Frank, Radio City Music Hall, New York, *Radio City*, (6 March 1996).

Shapiro, Gregg, Summer All Year Long: An Interview With Donna Summer, *Windy City Times*, (26 November 2003).

Slomowicz, DJ Ron, Moby Interview, about.com, (2011).

Smith, Graham K, Serman Chanted Evening, *Record Mirror*, (15 October 1983), pp 24–25.

Smith, Richard, Wrongly Punished, *Gay Times*, (November 1999).

Song Artist 74 Donna Summer, Music, tsort.info

Sprague, David, Divas 2000: A Tribute To Diana Ross, *Variety*, (17 April 2000).

Springer, Jacqueline, Review Of Donna Summer's Greatest Hits, *People*, (19 December 1979)/Summer Heat, *Blues & Soul*, (12 December 1994), No 677, pp 26–27.

Stanley, Bob, The Music The BBC Banned, *The Sunday Times*, (6 August 2008).

Steinhardt, Simon, Disco Demolition Night, *Swindle*, (Issue 09).

Strauss, Neil, A Disco Queen Parades Her Greatest Hits, The New York Times, (Radio City Music Hall Performance), *Pop Review*, (6 March 1996).

Summer, Donna, Latest News, donnasummer.com, (2009–2011).

Summer, Donna, Sisterspeak: Let's Embrace Our Heritage Of Many Cultures, *Ebony*, (2 September 2008).

Townsend, John, Bella Donna: An Interview With Donna Summer, *Lavender*, (June 2005).

Trunk, Rusty, Donna Summer: The Empress Herself, annecarlini.com, (2004).

Trust, Gary, Weekly Chart Notes: Elton John, Taylor Swift, Shakira, *Billboard*, (28 October 2010).

Turker, Ken, Donna Summer; I Remember Yesterday, *Rolling Stone*, (11 August 1977).

Twomey, John, Pilditch, David, Gun PC 'Used Song Titles' In His Evidence At Mark Saunders Inquest, *Daily Express*, (2 November 2010).

Ward III, Aubrey, The Review: *Priscilla, Queen Of The Desert – The Musical* (2011), *Firefox News*, (27 March 2011).

Warnken, Brent, Donna Summer Tickets – Queen Of Disco, articles natch.com.

Weinert, Ellie, Summer In Munich, *Billboard*, (3 September 1994).

Wikane, Christian John, The Queen And Her Crayons: An Interview With Donna Summer, popmatters.com, (20 May 2008)/She's A Rainbow: A Tribute To Donna Summer, popmatters.com, (19 May 2008).

Wilmont, Howard, From Being The Queen Of Disco, To Being Shunned By Queens Everywhere, Donna Summer Has Nevertheless Spent Three Decades Blowing Away The Competition. Howard Wilmont Met The Definitive Disco Diva, *Boyz*, (October 1999).

Wilson, Lois, Rock 'n' Roll Confidential: Debbie Harry, *Mojo*, (June 2011).

Windeler, Robert, It's That Record You Turn Off When The Kids Are Listening: Donna Summer's 'Love To Love You Baby', *People Weekly*, (1 March 1976), Vol. 5, No 8.

Wynn, Ron, Cats Without Claws, Overview, allmusic.com.

Yampert, Rick De, *The Tennessean,* www.donna-tribute.com/articles/98/ tenn.html, (10 July 1998).

Without Credit

Biography Of Donna Summer, The Internet Movie Database, Imdb.Com. Show Business & TV, Time, (29 December 1975), Vol 106, No 26.

Donna Summer, *Cash Box,* (2 July 1977).

Who In The World: Summer's Time Is Here, *Record World,* (13 August 1977).

Soul Star Of The Month: Donna Summer, *Song Hits,* (December 1978).

The Queen Of Disco Is Softening Her Act, But She'd Still Love To Love You, Baby, *People Magazine,* (4 December 1978).

Billboard Spotlight Review, *Billboard,* (5 May 1979).

No Girl Was As Bad As Donna, *People Magazine,* (19 December 1979).

Disco May Die, But Long Live It's Queen, Donna Summer, Who's Hot Stuff Now In Rock, Film And TV, *People Magazine,* (4 February 1980).

Donna Summer Annouces New Album, US Tour, *Contemporary Christian Music,* (June 1981).

Radio Interview Notes: The Hot Ones, Donna Summer Forever, True Sandrocks Site, (March 1983).

Donna's Back At Her Best, *TeleSkop,* (February 17th-23rd 1990).

Record Collector's Special Pressings Price Guide: Stupids To Summer, *Record Collector,* (May 1990), No 129.

Donna Summer: A Retrospective, *Blues & Soul,* (1994), No 656.

Donna Has Not Gone Country, *Parade,* (10 March 1996).

Giorgio Moroder Interviews, Giorgio Moroder At Future Music (1996), italfree.com, (1996).

Family Matters 'Pound Foolish', The Internet Movie Database, imdb.com, (1997).

Carnegie Hall: Meet The Artist, *Stagebill,* (March 1998).

Madonna. Bands Of '98. Goldie. Simple Minds, *Q,* (March 1998), No 138.

The Real 70s Disco Inferno! *Q,* (April 1998), No 139.

Top 500 Artists, *Record Collector,* (May 1998), No 225.

Disco: It Will Survive, *The Independent Magazine,* (10 April 1999), pp 23–29.

Diva Debacle, First For Music News, *NME,* (4 October 1999).

Donna Summer Challenged To Renounce Homophobia, outrage.org.uk (20 September 1999).

'Banned' Frankie Tops Chart, Entertainment, bbcnews.co.uk, (6 October 2000).

Donna Summer Forever True – Album Review, sandrocs.kit.net, (2002).

Sing If You're Glad To Be Gay, bothways.com, (2003).

50 Best Duets Ever, Rock And Jazz Music, *The Telegraph*, (8 November 2003).

BBC News Channel, BBC, (5 January 2004).

Mojo, http://www.donna-tribute.com/articles/04/mojo.htm,(January 2004).

Titi Mahalia Jackson, Wikipedia, wikipedia.org, (3 April 2004).

The Sound Of Summer, BBC News, (17 June 2004).

We Love Telly! The Big Chat, *Daily Mirror*, (19 June 2004).

Here Comes Summer Again, *The Telegraph*, (24 June 2004).

Disco Demolition! whitesoxinteractive.com, (July 2004).

The Independent Review, *The Independent,* http://www.donna-tribute.com/articles/04/independent.htm, (1 June 2004).

Sold On Song Top 100, BBC Radio 2, BBC Home, bbc.co.uk, (April 2005).

Reflection From A Lifetime, Review: Donna Summer The Ultimate Collection, tunedintomusic.wordpress.com, (12 June 2007).

Banning Songs Not A Rare Occurrence For The BBC, nzherald.co.nz, (19 December 2007).

Summer's Holiday, *The Age*, (8 June 2008).

Donna Summer: I'm a Fire Remix EP Limited Edition, Closer Look Notes, perfectbeat.com (2008).

Donna Summer Fame (The Game) CD1 Remix EP Limited Edition, Closer Look Notes, perfectbeat.com (2008).

Jade Ewen: It's My Time – UK 2009 Eurovision Song Contest: Oslo 2010, BBC (2009).

Radio 2's Disco Season, *Feelin' Love: The Donna Summer Story*, BBC Radio 2, (4 July 2009).

Donna Summer Fan Has Speakers Confiscated, *The Telegraph* (12 August 2009).

Fashion Meets Music: Donna Summer, missomnimedia.com, (28 September 2009).

Sex Has Physiological And Psyhological Effects That Can Increase Life Span, immortalhumans.com, (11 January 2010).

Complete Razzie History 1980–2010, The Razzies: Home Of The Golden Raspberry Award Foundation, razzies.com.

Golden Raspberry Award For Worst Original Song, Wikipedia, wikipedia.org, (28 February 2011).

Sidney Poitier, Wikipedia, wikipedia.org, (22 April 2011).

James Brown's Sex Machine Is Top Of The Dance Floor Tunes, walesonline.co.uk, (25 July 2011).

Donna Summer: The Queen Of Disco Music (December 31, 1948–Present), discomusic.com.

Karyn White Biography, The Essential Karyn White Fansite, urban music.tripod.com.

Icon Inspiration: Donna Summer, Lifestyle, jamaicaobserver.com (16 July 2011).

Disco Queen Donna Summer Includes New, Old Favorites In Lineup, Entertainment, The Examiner (27 August 2010).

Press/Research Material

Once Upon A Time, Casablanca Records, (1977).

Donna Summer Performance Reviews From *Vibes, Variety, Chicago Defender, Billboard, Casablanca Records*, (1977).

Thank God It's Friday, Columbia Pictures, (1978).

I'm A Rainbow Official Information, Donna Summer Management, (4 June 1996).

Summer Tour Has A New Look! Donna Summer Management, (4 June 1996).

Donna's Dance Single Comeback, Donna Summer Management, (4 June 1996).

Donna Is Working On Writing A Broadway Play About Her Life, Donna Summer Management, (30 May 1996).

VH1 Presents: Donna Summer Live & More ... Encore! Epic Records, (1999).

Disco Demolition Promoter Apologizes, The Associated Press, ljworld.com, (13 July 2001).

Canadian Recording Industry Association, Donna Summer, CRIA (9 February 2011).

The British Recorded Music Industry, Certified Awards Search, Donna Summer, BPI, (27 April 2011).

Recording Industry Association of America, RIAA'S Gold & Platinum Programme, Donna Summer, searchabledatabase, (27 April 2011).

Airplay Report BBC Radio 2 (Wednesday 19th January – Wednesday 18th January 2012).

Airplay 2011 Donna Summer Data Report, Absolute Radio (2012).

Donna Summer Airplay Data Saturday 1st January – Saturday 31st December 2011 From Radio Monitor (Compared With 23rd April 2012).

Broadcast

Soul Train, Season Episode 31, Series Episode 176, US, (20th March 1976)

American Band Stand, US, (11 July 1976).

Soul Train, US, December 25th 1976, season episode 19, series episode 203 (1976).

American Band Stand, US, (27 May 1978).

Spotlight Special, ABC Watermark, US, (21 October 1984).

Jacobs Stege – Jacob Dahlin Interviews Donna Summer, Sweden, (1987).

Talk Live, ABC TV, US, (1991).

Surgery, Capital Radio, UK, (3 November 1994).

BBC Radio 1, UK, (12 November 1994).

BBC Radio 1, UK, (18 November 1994).

BBC 3 TV, UK, How Sex Works: Playing The Field, (16th January 2012).

Biography, Weller/Grossman Production, A & E Television Network, US (1995).

Behind The Music, VH1, US, (10 June 1999).

Oprah Winfrey, US, (8 July 1999).

BBC Radio 2, interviewed by Jonathan Ross, UK, (3 October 1999).

Jo Hart PR, Donna Summer Syndicated Interview, United Kingdom, (1999).

The Queen Latifah Show, US, (25 November 1999).

BBC2 *When Disco Ruled The World*, UK, (6 March 2002).

BBC1 *Breakfast Show*, UK, (17 June 2004).

Travis Smiley Shows, US, (19 May 2008).

Feelin' Love: The Donna Summer Story, BBC Radio 2, UK, (4 July 2009).

On Point With Tom Ashbrook, Donna Summer Trying To Be Free, US, (9 April 2010).

Legends: Herb Alpert – Tijuana Brass And Other Delights, BBC4 TV (17 September 2010).

TV Adverts' Greatest Hits, More 4 TV, UK, (25 June 2011).

Index

256